Television and Society

Television and Society

Nicholas Abercrombie

Polity Press

First published in 1996 by Polity Press in association with Blackwell Publishers Ltd.
Reprinted 1997

2 4 6 8 10 9 7 5 3

Editorial office:
Polity Press
65 Bridge Street
Cambridge CB2 1UR, UK

Marketing and production:
Blackwell Publishers Ltd
108 Cowley Road
Oxford OX4 1JF, UK

Published in the USA by
Blackwell Publishers Inc.
Commerce Place
350 Main Street
Malden, MA 02148, USA

ISBN 0–7456–1435–3
ISBN 0–7456–1436–1 (pbk)

A CIP catalogue record for this book is available from the British Library and the Library of Congress.

Typeset in 10½ on 12pt Plantin
by Wearset, Boldon, Tyne and Wear
Printed in Great Britain by TJ International Ltd, Padstow, Cornwall

This book is printed on acid-free paper.

*For
Bren*

Contents

Figures

Tables

Boxes

Acknowledgements

A number of friends have contributed to this book. Brian Longhurst and I have, over more years than we want to remember, together mulled over issues in the sociological analysis of culture. In addition he and Celia Lury patiently read early drafts of this book and made many ingenious and helpful comments. Dede Boden kindly read and commented on the final draft and Norman Fairclough made available some of his unpublished materials on the discourse of television. As always, the staff of Polity Press, Julia Harsant, Sue Leigh, Fiona Sewell and John Thompson were extremely patient and formidably efficient. My thanks, too, to the anonymous Polity reader who read the manuscript and to Chris Stephens who drew the cartoons. Lastly, I want to record my long-standing debt to the supportive intellectual atmosphere of the Sociology Department in the University of Lancaster, whose staff and students have made it such a stimulating place to work, and to the many other members of staff in the university who have given a central place to interdisciplinary work in the social sciences and humanities.

Television is a domestic medium and we typically learn about it in households. Rob and Joe have introduced me to realms of popular culture that I never knew existed and, in doing so, have taught me new ways of watching and thinking about television.

My greatest debt is to Bren, who has not only applied her publisher's pen to the manuscript, and saved me from many mistakes, but spent hours educating me about television. To her I dedicate this book in love and friendship.

The author and publishers wish to thank the following for permission to use copyright material. Blackwell Publishers for tables

7.2, 7.4 and 7.5 from T Liebes and E Katz, *The Export of Meaning*, 1993, pp. 91, 105, 128; British Film Institute for fig. 6.1 from D Morley, *The Nationwide Audience*, 1980, p.136; Cassell Academic for fig. 4.1 from A Miles, *Home Informatics*, 1988, Pinter Publishers, fig. 3.1, p.38; and table 4.2 from R Negrine and S Papathanassopoulos, *The Internationalization of Television*, Pinter Publishers, table 7.1, 1990; A S C Ehrenberg for table 6.6 from G Goodhardt, A Ehrenberg and M Collins, *The Television Audience: Patterns of Viewing*, 1987, Gower Publishing Ltd, table 9.6, p.104; Greenwood Publishing Group, Inc for table 5.1 from M. Intintoli, *Taking Soaps Seriously*, 1985, Praeger Publishers, table 6.1, p. 123; *The Guardian* for box 3 from Stephen Bates and Andrew Culf, 'PM backs Aitken in attack on BBC', *The Guardian*, 28.3.95; The Controller of HMSO for table 6.1 from *Social Trends 1992*, table 10.5 p.177; Hodder Headline for table 4.1 from A Sreberny-Mohammadi, 'The Global and the Local in International Communications' from J Curran and M Gurevitch, eds, *Mass Media and Society*, Hodder & Stoughton/New English Library, 1991; Routledge for table 3.1 from R Wallis and S Baran, *The Known World of Broadcast News*, 1980, table 3.2. p.58; table 4.4 from J Tunstall, *Television Producers*, 1993, table 1.2, p.20; table 7.1 from J Lull, *Inside Family Viewing*, 1990, fig. 2.1, p.36; and fig. 2.3 from John Fiske, *Television Culture*, Methuen & Co, 1987, pp. 135–6; Sage Publications Ltd for tables 6.3, 6.4 & 6.5 from P Barwise and A Ehrenberg, *Television and its Audience*, 1988, tables 3.1, 3.2 & 5.2, pp. 26, 28, 52; and table 3.1 from R Collins, N Garnham and G Locksley, *The Economics of Television*, 1988.

Every effort has been made to trace all the copyright holders, but if any have been inadvertently overlooked the publishers will be pleased to make the necessary arrangement at the first opportunity.

1

The Importance of Television

Television and the Information Society

It is often argued that there is a profound divide between the modern and pre-modern worlds, a divide so great and affecting so many aspects of life that the worlds are mutually unrecognizable. One feature of this divide is claimed to be that modern everyday life is thoroughly invested with *images* and with *information*; or as Featherstone (1991) puts it, with 'the rapid flow of signs and images which saturate the fabric of everyday life in contemporary society' (p. 67). The result is that modern everyday life is richly symbolic, even if people are largely unaware of it, with images and information coming from a large number of sources, including advertising, fashion, style in household goods, television, newspapers, books, and so on. J. Thompson (1990) puts it thus:

> Today we live in a world in which the extended circulation of symbolic forms plays a fundamental and ever-increasing role. In all societies the production and exchange of symbolic forms – of linguistic expressions, gestures, actions, works of art and so on – is, and has always been, a pervasive feature of social life. But with the advent of modern societies, propelled by the development of capitalism in early modern Europe, the nature and extent of the circulation of symbolic forms took on a new and qualitatively different appearance. Technical means were developed which, in conjunction with institutions oriented towards capital accumulation, enabled symbolic forms to be produced, reproduced and circulated on a hitherto unprecedented scale . . . These developments in what is commonly called mass communications received a further impetus from

advances in the electrical codification and transmission of symbolic forms, advances which have given us the varieties of electronic tele-communication characteristic of the twentieth century. (p. 1)

An important source of images and information is the modern media of mass communication. Our everyday lives are so interwoven with the media that we are scarcely aware of them. So, newspapers, magazines, books, radio, advertising, tape and CD players, television and video are constant features of the daily round. Drawing attention to a parallel, related development, other writers (see Miles, 1988) refer to an 'information revolution' in which every household will have access to an ever-increasing flow of information and entertainment through devices of ever-increasing sophistication. To the media of mass communication mentioned above can be added the telephone and the use of fibre optic cable, communication by satellite, and the more extensive use of computers. Major innovations are expected as telephony, computing, and satellite transmissions are brought together in providing an information-rich environment.

Of course, one has to be aware that, despite these claims that technological changes of various kinds have ushered in a new age of media saturation and are about to add yet further to the provision of entertainment and information (Collins, 1990), changes of this kind rarely happen quite as quickly as the prophets promise. Furthermore, even if the devices for the supply of images are there, it is by no means clear that people actually make use of them. For example, as I shall show later in this book, many people have only the haziest idea how their videorecorders work and most households do not use many of the facilities, such as freeze-frame and indexing, that their machines provide. Perhaps even more important is the fact, pointed out by Golding and Murdock (1991), that, since it costs a good deal of money to participate in the information and entertainment revolution, many poorer citizens will be excluded.

Despite these doubts about the information revolution, it is clear that television is central to the processes of media saturation. Indeed, television is central to modern society altogether. Some 97 per cent of households in Britain own at least one television set and 53 per cent own two or more, that figure rising to 65 per cent for families with children. Sixty-eight per cent have a videorecorder while 7 per cent own two or more. At the moment about 14 per cent of households can receive satellite transmissions. People also commit a substantial amount of *time* to watching the television set or sets. Between 1980 and 1990, the average daily hours of viewing varied over the year between 4.9 and 5.3 hours per household and between 3.0 and 3.8 hours for each individual (Sharot, 1994). That is obviously a very substantial commitment indeed. Television watching occupies more time than all other leisure pursuits combined and ranks with working and sleeping as time-consuming activities, although, as we shall see, it is by no means clear what people are actually doing while the set is on.

All this implies that television reaches a very large number of people. Individual programmes and films can be seen by almost half the total population and *Coronation Street* regularly attracts audiences of 18 million. This implies that television is an important – perhaps the most important – source of common experience for the British people, who are otherwise divided by class, ethnicity, gender, region, personal tastes and a host of other factors. As a result, conversation about television programmes is a routine and taken-for-granted aspect of everyday social interaction. At work, in the home, in the street, in the bus or in the pub, people talk about the characters in soap opera, marvel at the latest natural history programme, and discuss the issues raised in news broadcasts or documentaries. In recognition of the importance of television in everyday life, television programmes and the doings of television personalities occupy a substantial proportion of daily newspaper coverage. Politicians realize the importance of appearing on television and presenting a good television image. When the Labour Party were debating who should be their next leader following the death of John Smith, one of the potential candidates, Robin Cook, was apparently ruled out because he would not look good on television.

These phenomena are not, of course, confined to Britain. Television is a central institution in all advanced industrialized countries and is rapidly becoming so in the developing world, as chapters 4 and 6 will show. As an American study of television argued (Allen, 1992):

What people do with television is a topic worth thinking about and studying because television enters into the everyday lives of so many different people in so many different places in so many different ways. Today, around the world, 3.5 billion hours will be devoted to watching television. But nowhere is television such an integral part of everyday life as in the United States. Ninety-two million homes in the U.S. have at least one TV set (98 per cent of the population). Nearly 70 per cent of those homes have more than one set. More American homes are equipped with television sets than telephones. Those sets are on in the average household for more than seven hours every day. Between seven and eleven p.m., Americans of every demographic, social, and economic group are spending most of their time in a place where a television set is playing. (p. 1)

Attitudes to television

Despite the popularity of television, or, more likely, because of it, many people express some contempt for the medium or alarm at its possible effects. Although less prominent than in the 1950s when television was becoming established, attitudes of contempt still persist. Many ordinary viewers, indeed, frequently express guilt at their television watching, worrying that they are addicted, that programmes are trivial, that they should be doing something more active, or that the unreality of television takes them away from the pleasures of the real world, feelings which are illustrated in the cartoon in Figure 1.1. Such attitudes derive in some measure from 'high cultural' preconceptions that active pursuits, like reading a

Figure 1.1 Television and the real world

book, are inherently better than apparently passive television watching. As Goodwin (1990) notes, many authorities, even those within television organizations, appear to believe that visual material is inherently inferior to print.

More seriously, beliefs that television is positively harmful are widely held, both by 'ordinary' viewers and by influential people. Such notions of harm can take many different forms. For example, Postman (1986) argues that television has trivialized and effectively destroyed the public discourse that underpins politics, education, and all activities in the public sphere. Holding strongly the notion that the medium in which ideas are expressed crucially influences the content of those ideas, he compares the medium of print with that of television. From its beginning until well into the nineteenth century, the United States was dominated by the printed word and a tradition of political debate and oratory firmly rooted in print. In Postman's view, print reflects and encourages particular habits of mind: 'The printed page revealed the world, line by line, page by page, to be a serious, coherent place, capable of management by reason, and of improvement by logical and relevant criticism' (p. 63). Above all, print had an inextricable relationship to all forms of *public* expression.

Television, on the other hand, is seen as destroying rational habits of mind because it is essentially a medium of entertainment and makes all that appears on it into entertainment. Postman seeks to show 'that television's conversations promote incoherence and triviality; that the phrase "serious television" is a contradiction in terms; and that television speaks in only one persistent voice – the voice of entertainment . . . Television, in other words, is transforming our culture into one vast arena for show business' (p. 81). Such a transformation is incompatible, in Postman's view, with a discourse in which public affairs can be conducted rationally. For example, news broadcasts are a surreal form of communication of important events in which the newsreaders give just as much emphasis to trivial events as to serious ones. In addition, the television news is routinely interrupted by commercials, which make the whole thing seem banal.

Another popularly expressed view about television's alleged harmful effects concerns violence. It is often claimed that violence on television causes viewers, or some viewers at any rate, to become violent in real life. This is thought to be particularly true of some vulnerable sections of the audience, especially children. As Gunter and McAleer (1990) describe this phenomenon:

it is not uncommon to read stories in the press about individuals committing a violent crime, the idea for which arose from something seen on television. We are told that television can provide examples of bad behaviour which young viewers especially may copy, or that seeing well-known television characters using violence to solve their problems provides some justification for young viewers to emulate their heroes. (p. ii)

The Prince of Wales confirmed these views in a speech on the opening of the Museum of the Moving Image in London in 1988, which was reported in the *Daily Mail*:

He said: 'A museum of this kind draws our attention to the past – the kind of standards which used to exist throughout the film-making profession.'
    And, he argued, it was not difficult to draw comparisons and to ask a few basic questions.
    'For instance, do we have to tolerate an incessant menu of utterly gratuitous violence on both cinema and television – especially television – and most particularly videos?
    'Those of us with children are very concerned by the appalling lack of restraint shown by those who make such films and videos, and who define their so-called art by insisting on the absolute necessity of portraying real life.
    'They say that all you have to do if you don't like it is to switch the television off. And if, as parents, you complain that a diet of freely-available and insensate violence is likely to influence the way some people behave and relate to others, then you are told there is absolutely no proof that violence on TV has any effect on people's behaviour.
    'But that, as we all know, is palpable nonsense.'
    The Prince, who wrote the speech himself, labelled this an attempt by 'so-called experts' to confuse people – to make them feel they didn't know what they were talking about and that what they were seeing with their own eyes was an illusion. (quoted in Buckingham, 1993a, p. 3)

Such attitudes to television do seem to depend on particular premises about how television is produced and how audiences are affected. For example, Postman's book, discussed above, makes strong claims about the impact of television on American society. It is, however, largely a book about the *content* of television programmes, in that he claims that the medium, intended primarily for entertainment, therefore necessarily trivializes any issue of importance. There is relatively little about the organizations and people that produce television of this kind. Investigation of producers might help to explain why television takes the form it does and might provide some basis for assessing whether it could take a different form. Above all, there is no account of actual audience behaviour. Rather, it is *assumed* that the audience will behave in a particular way in response to texts organized in particular ways. Similarly, in the debate about the effect of television violence on children, the assumption is made that children are passive viewers who are directly affected by what they see. As Buckingham (1993a) puts it, 'Children's relationship with television is typically regarded as a one-way process of cause-and-effect, in which children themselves are seen merely as powerless victims' (p. vii). Viewers, including children, might well contest such an assumption, if applied to themselves. The passive viewer is always someone else. *We* are rational and able to make judgements about television's offerings, or – even better – to turn the set off.

Organization of this book: Text, Producer and Audience

This book is a textbook. The assumption upon which it is organized is prompted by the discussion in the previous section, namely, that any full analysis of the role of television in society has to pay attention to three interrelated aspects. First, there has to be investigation of the form and content of television programmes or television *texts*. This investigation occupies chapters 2 and 3. Second, texts clearly do not produce themselves and there is therefore a need to study *producers* and the means by which television is produced, by looking both at the television industry as a whole and at the organizations that produce programmes. Discussion of this issue is provided in chapters 4 and 5. Finally, television programmes are ultimately produced for *audiences*, whose interpretations and reactions are clearly critical to an understanding of television's effects. An evaluation of any theory of the relationship between television and society has to take all three of these aspects into account as well as assessing their interactions.

A textbook on television has to cope with the rapidly changing nature of its subject matter. Most of the studies on which this book is based take as their object of study programmes which have long gone off the schedules. I have tried to provide more recent examples where this is possible, but even these will date very quickly. Ultimately, the only solution is for readers to try to apply the general or abstract points made in this book to their own television watching.

2

Television as Text

I begin with the treatment of television as text. On the face of it, it is strange to refer to television programmes as 'texts'. We are, after all, familiar with the use of the word to refer to books, or other literary output, that is written and read, but not perhaps to visual material. As Fiske and Hartley (1978) point out, much literature comes down to us from societies whose organization was very different. Television, on the other hand, is very much the product of the modern industrial age. More fundamental still, the conventions of television belong not to the written word but to speech. There are other differences, as Fiske and Hartley also point out:

> The written word (and particularly the printed word) works through and so promotes consistency, narrative development from cause to effect, universality and abstraction, clarity, and a single tone of voice. Television, on the other hand, is ephemeral, episodic, specific, concrete and dramatic in mode. Its meanings are arrived at by contrasts and by the juxtaposition of seemingly contradictory signs and its 'logic' is oral and visual. (p. 15)

In a sense, however, the comparison may be apt and the use of term 'text' appropriate. Television programmes are a *little* like books, precisely because they are made to be 'read', taken in, and interpreted by an *audience*. The act of creation of a television programme is not unlike that of a book, and television audiences will bring to their viewing some of the skills, expectations and attitudes that they employ in the appreciation of books, and derive from them many of the pleasures of reading, including, for example, following the progress of a story. It is not surprising, therefore, that many of the ideas and methods of analysis used in literary criticism have found a home in the study of television – as they have in most areas of cultural analysis.

Television and film

More interesting than any comparison between books and television is that between film and television, media which are at least initially similar. They are both media that combine sound and image, they are used primarily for entertainment and information, and they both use the conventions of narrative fiction. An examination of their differences, however, shows up some of the distinctive features of television texts.

Ellis (1982) suggests that there are four principal areas of difference between film and television. First, film is primarily designed to be a *public* event and its characteristic mode is the single performance complete in itself. Television, by contrast, has as its major means of presentation a progression of segments often arranged as a series or serial, watched relatively casually in *private* or domestic circumstances. These conditions of production and reception give television some of its particular features. It is an essentially domestic medium and television programmes by and large assume a family audience. In addition, the televisual style is everyday and conversational; its way of addressing its audience is consistent with the position of the television set in the home; it is almost as if it were simply another participant in a family conversation (see the section below, 'The domestic style of television', for an elaboration of this point). Second, the technology of cinema permits a much higher quality of both image and sound than is possible in television. Film has a photographic quality that gives a particularly intense experience to the audience, which makes identification with what is going on in the film possible. The result is that film demands, and receives, *sustained* attention while, for television, the audience can be fairly inattentive at times. As Ellis puts it, the typical way of watching the television is the glance not the gaze. Looking intensively at the television set – gazing at it – is often thought to be somewhat inappropriate to the medium. Third, film and television have different forms of narration – different ways of organizing their material as story. Cinema narrative typically starts with a disordered state of some kind and then moves through a series of ups and downs to a resolution of that disorder and a restoration of equilibrium. With television, there is no such resolution, no such closure. Television presents itself as a set of repeated segments which do not form a unity. The series or serial is again a typical instance of this. Each episode may be complete in itself, but there is rarely any sense of resolution across the series itself; continuity is provided, not by narrative, but by character or location. Fourth, film and television have different views of their spectators. Film assumes a spectator who awaits narrative resolution in a state of pleasurable anxiety. In a sense, the spectator is given control in the same way that the reader of a book is given control. Television, however, functions much more on behalf of the viewer. It functions as an eye with which the viewer can see the world. The result is, in Ellis's words, that the viewer delegates 'his or her own look to the institution of TV' (p. 170).

Three further points of contrast between film and television might be added to Ellis's list. First, there is the role of individuals as artists in film and television production. Ellis suggests that stars are an exclusively cinematic feature, or at least are not to be found in television. The reason is that they represent the extraordinary and the exceptional. Television, on the other hand, is an ordinary, domestic, everyday medium. The result is that, while one may have television personalities, there are no television stars. Similarly, film is often associated, not only with stars, but with a *particular* director or producer, who, in this respect, functions rather like the author of a book – and is treated as such. Television programmes, by contrast, on the whole, are collectively produced and are not defined by the particular artistic inclinations of individuals (Allen, 1992). Second, as Flitterman-Lewis (1992) points out, television offers an essentially fragmented view by comparison with film. This can work at a number of levels including the apparently simple level of camera-work. For example, in soap opera there is typically a very great variety of shot set-ups. 'Even though action takes place in a limited number of locations . . ., scenes are marked by a constant diversity of camera angles and distances within a single space. Camera distance is further complicated by a continually moving (or zooming) camera that often rests only momentarily on a conversation before moving again. For this reason, there is a perpetual "fracturing" of the televisual space' (p. 228). Third, there is a certain level of directness and immediacy about television, often referred to as its directness of address, which is further discussed in the section below on 'The domestic style of television'. This immediacy is enhanced by the fact that much television takes the form of live transmission, of news, current affairs or sports, for example.

The account of the differences between film and television offered by Ellis and others does tend to exaggerate the differences between the two media, an account perhaps partly promoted by a prejudice against television or in favour of film. Much of the rest of this book takes issue with some of the alleged points of difference. However, the contrast does show up some of the distinctive features of television texts and it is to a more detailed consideration of these that I now turn.

Television Flow

Daily television consists of a number of different types of programme. Any evening's viewing will consist of news, documentary, soap opera, police shows, situation comedy, all rubbing shoulders in an apparently chaotic way, as figure 2.1 shows.

These may appear as a set of discrete programmes each of which has its own rules of composition and which viewers choose to watch having consulted a programme schedule, in much the same way as they choose a book to read or go to the cinema to see a film. R. Williams (1974) points out that this misrepresents the television experience, for what is really offered is a *sequence* of events. Furthermore, for him, there has been a decisive shift from sequence as *programming* to sequence as *flow*. It may appear that discrete programmes are important – they are still timed and the timings are published – but actually the experience is not of discrete events. It is instead a continuous flow which is indicated in saying that we are watching television not watching a specific programme. The list below illustrates this flow by showing the actual programmes watched by one family (mine) in the evening whose programme schedule is given in figure 2.1.

7.00	Wish You Were Here	ITV
7.30	Coronation Street	ITV
8.00	Brookside	C4
8.30	University Challenge	BBC2

9.00	Modern Times	BBC2
10.00	ITN News	ITV
10.30	Newsnight	BBC2

Williams was brought to this view of television flow by the experience of watching American television for the first time in the late 1960s, an experience now common throughout the world in the 1990s:

> One night in Miami, still dazed from a week on an Atlantic liner, I began watching a film and at first had some difficulty in adjusting to a much greater frequency of commercial 'breaks'. Yet this was a minor problem compared to what eventually happened. Two other films, which were due to be shown on the same channel on other nights, began to be inserted as trailers. A crime in San Francisco (the subject of the original film) began to operate in an extraordinary counterpoint not only with the deodorant and cereal commercials but with a romance in Paris and the eruption of a prehistoric monster who laid waste New York . . . Here was something quite different, since the transitions from film to commercial and from film A to films B and C were in effect unmarked. There is in any case enough similarity between certain kinds of films, and between several kinds of film and 'situation' commercials which often consciously imitate them, to make a sequence of this kind a very difficult experience to interpret. I can still not be sure what I took from that whole flow. I believe I registered some incidents as happening in the wrong film, and some characters in the commercials as involved in the film episodes, in what came to seem – for all the occasional bizarre disparities – a single irresponsible flow of images and feelings. (pp. 91–2)

For Williams, one particular development symbolizes this change. While in the early days of broadcasting there were intervals between programme units, latterly these intervals have been filled in by advertisements, announcements, or trailers for future programmes. Viewers are then surrounded – for Williams perhaps drowned is a better word – by a continuous flow of images, sound and feelings, which can now last all day and through the night.

It is tempting to deduce from these observations the conclusion that the television flow is random or chaotic. For Williams, however, that is not the case. There are actually two structuring principles that work in different ways. Underlying the apparently chaotic flow is a disguised attempt at planning, for television networks put a great deal of effort into constructing schedules which attempt to keep the viewer watching one channel. This process is described in

1 BBC1

5.35pm Neighbours
The kids' band needs new talent.
Partners are picked for the ball, but has
Debbie had the last dance?
Helen Daniels...............................ANNE HADDY
Doug Willis..............................TERENCE DONOVAN
Pam Willis.................................SUE JONES
Gaby Willis...............................RACHEL BLAKELY
Lou Carpenter.............................TOM OLIVER
Rick Alessi...............................DAN FALZON
Julie Martin..............................JULIE MULLINS
Philip Martin.............................IAN RAWLINGS
Hannah Martin.............................REBECCA RITTERS
Debbie Martin.............................MARNIE REECE-WILMORE
Mark Gottlieb.............................BRUCE SAMAZAN
Annalise Hartman.........................KIMBERLEY DAVIES
Danni Stark...............................ELIZA SZONERT
Brett Stark...............................BRETT BLEWITT
Cody Willis...............................PETA BRADY
Andrew "Makka" MacKenzie..................JOHN MORRIS
Drew Grover...............................CHRISTOPHER KIRBY
Sam Kratz................................RICHARD GRIEVE
Dave Gottlieb.............................IVAR KANTS
Anne Teschendorff.........................LOIS COLLINDER
Packo.....................................VERITY MCINTYRE
Stonefish................................ANTHONY ENGLEMAN
Shown at 1.30pm. Stereo Subtitled....619844

6.00 Six O'Clock News
With Anna Ford and Jill Dando.
Subtitled
Weather Michael Fish 283

6.30 Regional news magazine
See Monday for details 863

7.00 This Is Your Life
Michael Aspel springs more surprises
and reunions on unsuspecting guests
when he presents them with the
famous red book.
Director Brian Klein; Producer Malcolm Morris
Stereo Subtitled 7660

7.30 Here and Now
Another edition of the current affairs
magazine programme that travels all
over the country, responding to the
news that matters, giving a new angle
on the big stories and speaking to the
people whose lives are affected by the
politicians and decision-makers.
Editor Paul Woolwich 937

8.00 Hearts of Gold
Esther Rantzen is joined by her two
co-presenters, Carol Smillie and
Mickey Hutton, for the series that gives
the Hearts of Gold Award to unsung
heroes and heroines from all over the
UK who have shown outstanding
bravery and dedication. This week, the
story of the 3-year-old who dragged his
sister from a burning car; a champion
fundraiser whose achievements have
provided life-saving hospital
equipment for children; a reward for
three men who saved the life of a
drowning man; and recognition for the
founder of a cancer charity.
Director Stuart McDonald; Series producer Nick
Vaughan-Barratt Stereo Subtitled 933554
NOMINATIONS: viewers with nominations for the
Hearts of Gold Award should write to: Hearts of Gold,
BBCtv, London W12 7TS.

8.50 Points of View
Anne Robinson with viewers' opinions
on BBC television programmes.
Write with your comments to Points of
View, BBCtv, London W12 7RJ. Or
telephone/fax on 081-576 4560. The
e-mail address is: pov@bbcnc.org.uk
Producer Bernard Newnham
Stereo Subtitled 684991

9.00 Nine O'Clock News
With Michael Buerk. Subtitled
Regional News
Weather Michael Fish 5047

**9.30pm Secrets of a serviceman:
Stephen Mackye (Mark Drewry) has
information that could hit the headlines**

9.30 Harry
An eight-part series about a Darlington
news agency, starring **Michael Elphick**
4: A soldier with a secret can be a
dangerous business, especially when
the establishment conspires to cover it
up. When Harry finally uncovers the
shocking truth, will he be allowed to tell
it? Meanwhile, Snappy and Jonathan
stake out an ageing rock star who
returns from the dead.
Harry Salter...............................MICHAEL ELPHICK
Snappy....................................IAN BARTHOLOMEW
Alice.....................................JULIE GRAHAM
Jonathan..................................TOM HOLLANDER
Cheryl....................................ALPHONSIA EMMANUEL
Tommy.....................................OZZIE YUE
Stephen Mackye............................MARK DREWRY
Dee Mackye................................AMANDA DREWRY
Don Webster...............................KEVIN WILLIAMS
Josey.....................................AMANDA HOWARD
Mrs Webster...............................HOPE JOHNSTONE
Sandra....................................MAGGIE MCCARTHY
Episode written by Robin Mukherjea
Producer Joy Spink; Director Sid Roberson
Stereo Subtitled 133134

10.20 Comic Relief Special
Michelle's Story
CHOICE Robbie Coltrane introduces
a tale of drug abuse and
recovery. In this frank and
emotional video diary, Michelle
Kenny describes her attempts to make
a break with her past with help from a
Comic Relief-funded project.
See today's choices.
Producer Tony Steyger Subtitled 450573

11.00 The Stand Up Show
Comedy, tonight from Sean Meo, the
Umbilical Brothers, Will Durst, and Noel
James. Introduced by Barry Cryer.
Director Mark Mylod; Producer Claudia Lloyd
Stereo 5172

11.30 Heartbreakers
CHOICE Romantic comedy starring
Peter Coyote, Nick Mancuso
Two close friends – Blue, a
struggling artist, and Eli, a
successful businessman – are both
experiencing mid-life relationship and
career crises. Then Eli falls in love with
Liliane, a French art gallery assistant
who is really attracted to Blue.
Blue......................................PETER COYOTE
Eli.......................................NICK MANCUSO
Liliane...................................CAROLE LAURE
King......................................MAX GAIL
Cyd.......................................KATHRYN HARROLD
Candy.....................................CAROL WAYNE
Terry Ray.................................JAMES LAURENSON
Libby.....................................JAMIE ROSE
Director Bobby Roth (1984)................741028
◆ FILM REVIEWS pages 42–46
1.05-1.10am Weather

2 BBC2

5.40pm One Lump or Two?
Tea on the Move. Glynn Christian visits
one of the last remaining tea gardens
and discovers how a Frenchman has
turned a traditional British custom into
a thriving business. He also takes a ride
on the Orient Express to sample its
famous afternoon tea. 686641

**6.00 Star Trek: the Next
Generation**
Starring **Patrick Stewart**
The Masterpiece Society. When
Jean-Luc Picard contacts a colony on
what was thought to be an uninhabited
planet to warn them of impending
disaster, he is informed that to
evacuate its people would destroy their
genetically-engineered Utopian
society. In an attempt to find a
solution, a team beams down to the
planet – but the arrival of the colony's
first visitors leads to some unforeseen
complications.
Captain Jean-Luc Picard...................PATRICK STEWART
Commander William Riker...................JONATHAN FRAKES
Lt Commander Data........................BRENT SPINER
Dr Beverly Crusher.......................GATES MCFADDEN
Lt Commander Geordi La Forge.............LEVAR BURTON
Counsellor Deanna Troi....................MARINA SIRTIS
Lt Worf...................................MICHAEL DORN
Aaron Conor..............................JOHN SNYDER
Hannah Bates..............................DEY YOUNG
Marcus Benbeck...........................RON CANADA
Ensign....................................SHEILA FRANKLIN
Stereo Subtitled 513028

**6.45 Natural Born
Footballers**
Striker Denis Law is regarded as one of
the greatest Scottish footballers ever.
A dominant player of the 60s and 70s,
and one of Manchester United's
favourite sons, Law achieved the
ultimate accolade of European
Footballer of the Year in 1964. He also
won two championship medals and a
cup winner's medal during his time at
Old Trafford.
Series producer Michael Wadding
Revised rpt Stereo Subtitled 109283

7.00 Churchill
CHOICE A second showing of the
four-part television biography
of Britain's wartime leader,
Renegade and Turncoat. The first
episode tells the story of Churchill's
early life and political career up to
1940, when he became Prime
Minister. Presented by Martin Gilbert.
See today's choices.
Director Marisa Appugliese; Series producer Jeremy
Bennett Rpt Subtitled 6641

8.00 Magic Animals
CHOICE Last in the series exploring
the real and symbolic lives of
four animals.
The Snake. No creature elicits a
more contradictory response than the
snake. Its alien appearance is feared,
yet it has coiled itself around almost
every culture and religion. Narrated by
Miranda Richardson.
See today's choices.
Written and directed by Ann Hawker; Series
producer Mark Harrison Stereo Subtitled ...4950

8.30 University Challenge
The first semi-final, between the two
highest-scoring teams in the series so
far – the University of Aberdeen, who
beat the Open University in the
quarter-finals, and Trinity College,
Cambridge, who defeated St Andrews.
Jeremy Paxman asks the questions.
Director Jenny Dodd; Producer Kieran Roberts
Stereo Subtitled 7347

**9.00pm Choosing to die: terminally ill
patient Cees van Wendel de Joode elected
to end his suffering by lethal injection**

9.00 Modern Times
Death on Request
CHOICE The first television portrayal
of a mercy killing. Made in
Holland, where euthanasia is
permitted, it tells the story of a
62-year-old patient with an incurable
illness, his wife, and the doctor who
agrees to administer the fatal injection.
Tonight's *Late Show* at 11.15pm
explores some of the issues raised by
the programme. **See today's choices.**
Producer Maarten Nederhorst; Series editor
Stephen Lambert Subtitled 2825
◆ See This Week: page 4

10.00 Room 101
Another chance to see Bob
Monkhouse outlining his pet hates to
Nick Hancock for consignment to the
flames of *Room 101.* They include Cilla
Black's singing voice, the French, and
The Golden Shot, a quiz show that
Monkhouse himself presented.
Producer Liesa Evans; Series producer Dan
Patterson Rpt Stereo Subtitled 40757
Followed by **Conundrum**

10.30 Newsnight
With Peter Snow. Subtitled 786628

11.15 The Late Show
A special debate on euthanasia,
following this evening's programme
in the *Modern Times* series.
Contributors include the producer of
Death on Request, Maarten
Nederhorst, the doctor featured in the
programme, Dr Wilfred van Oijen,
veteran pro-euthanasia campaigner
Ludovic Kennedy, and Professor
Ronald Dworkin. The discussion is
chaired by Michael Ignatieff.
Producer Nigel Leigh Stereo 657844

11.55 Weatherview

12.00 Open University
12.00 Environment: Forest Futures
An expedition to one of the last areas of
tropical rainforest on the Malaysian
mainland. 8640697
12.50-1.15am The Record
Today's debates in Parliament, with
Robert Orchard. Stereo 3774210
2.00 Nightschool TV
Teaching Today – Modern Foreign
Languages Two programmes on the
classroom, from the point of view of the
teacher and the learner. 32061
4.00-4.15am BBC Select
Benefits Agency Today Interesting
developments in Wales. 13243158

Figure 2.1 An evening's viewing
Source: *Radio Times*, 11–17 March 1995, © *Radio Times*

ITV GRANADA

5.40pm Early Evening News
With John Suchet. *Subtitled*
Weather Siân Lloyd 680467

6.00 Home and Away
Shown at 1.25pm *Subtitled* 160134

6.25 Regional news magazine
For details see Monday *Subtitled* 861202

7.00 Wish You Were Here .. ?
In tonight's programme, Judith
Chalmers explores the Ile de France;
former *EastEnders* star Mike Reid and
his wife Shirley visit the USA's top golf
resorts in Carolina; and Anna Walker
journeys to Llandudno as it celebrates
its 150th anniversary.
Series producer Douglas Hammond; Repeated on Friday at 2.50pm Stereo Subtitled 9028

7.30 Coronation Street
Why are the police making an arrest
and how is Rodney planning to liven up
the Rovers?
Gail Platt.....................................HELEN WORTH
Martin Platt....................................SEAN WILSON
Audrey Roberts..............................SUE NICHOLLS
Alma Baldwin...............................AMANDA BARRIE
Steve McDonald............................SIMON GREGSON
Sean Skinner.............................TERENCE HILLYER
Mike Baldwin................................JOHNNY BRIGGS
Betty Turpin...................................BETTY DRIVER
Des Barnes..............................PHILIP MIDDLEMISS
Mavis Wilton................................THELMA BARLOW
Derek Wilton.................................PETER BALDWIN
Jack Duckworth...........................WILLIAM TARMEY
Liz McDonald..........................BEVERLEY CALLARD
Don Brennan..............................GEOFF HINSLIFF
Alf Roberts...................................BRYAN MOSLEY
Nick Platt................................WARREN JACKSON
Rodney Bostock.............................COLIN PROCKTER
Reg Holdsworth...............................KEN MORLEY
Episode written by Mark Wadlow; Producer Sue Pritchard; Director Michael Kerrigan Subtitled 115

8.00 Arachnophobia

Comedy horror starring
Jeff Daniels.
In the small Californian town of
Canaima, Dr Ross Jennings has to
overcome his arachnophobia when a
host of killer Venezuelan spiders brings
terror to the local community.
Dr Ross Jennings..........................JEFF DANIELS
Molly Jennings......................HARLEY JANE KOZAK
Delbert McClintock...........................JOHN GOODMAN
Dr James Atherton...........................JULIAN SANDS
Sheriff Parsons............................STUART PANKIN
Chris Collins............................BRIAN McNAMARA
Jerry Manley..................................MARK L TAYLOR
Dr Sam Metcalf............................HENRY JONES
Henry Beechwood.............................PETER JASON
Director Frank Marshall (1990) Subtitled 3931
◆ FILM REVIEWS pages 42-46

10.00 News at Ten
With Trevor McDonald. *Subtitled*
Weather Siân Lloyd 37283
10.30 Regional News; Weather 706554

10.35 Being There
All the President's Men. Mark Yates
from Birkenhead started out as a
nightclub bouncer. Today he trains
former KGB officers to become
bodyguards. This film follows him on his
most recent trip to the former Soviet
Union, giving a rare insight into the
methods used in the training of men
who will end up protecting presidents.
Director William Daws
Producer David Clapham 244283

11.05 Champions League Highlights
The quarter-final, second-leg matches
in the most prestigious competition in
club football. The featured match is
Benfica v AC Milan, plus highlights of
Paris St-Germain v Barcelona.

RadioTimes 11-17 MARCH 1995

**7.30pm Home truths: Martin (Sean
Wilson) offers cold comfort to
distraught wife Gail (Helen Worth)**

Gothenburg v Bayern Munich and Ajax
v Hajduk Split. Commentary by Alan
Parry and John Helm. Introduced by
Bob Wilson with Jack Charlton.
Director David Wood; Series producer
Mike Inman 315931

**12.10am The Disaster
Chronicles**
High Rise Fires. The story of one of the
worst hotel fires in US history at the
MGM Grand Hotel in Las Vegas,
Nevada, in 1980. *Rpt Stereo* 4392622

12.40 Alien Nation
The Game. A series of Newcomer
deaths remind George of a gruesome
game played on a slave ship, similar to
Russian roulette. *Stereo* 1964158

1.35 Hollywood Report
More up-to-the-minute news about the
latest films. *Stereo* 2021061

2.05 The Beat
The latest singles, albums and film
reviews. Presented by Gary Crowley.
Repeated tomorrow 1.15am Stereo 6723516

3.00 The Album Show
Including a spotlight on Celine Dion.
Repeated tomorrow 2.15am Stereo 9467326

4.05 Shift
Showcase for new directors. 2036784

4.55 The Time ... the Place
Shown at 10.00am *Stereo* 7553239

**5.30-6.00am
Morning News** 84546
News reports throughout the night

BBC1/ITV/S4C VARIATIONS
Regions may show different programme episodes
BBC1 WALES 6.30-7.00pm Wales Today
BORDER 6.40pm as Granada **6.00** Regional
news **6.30** Home and Away **7.00** as Granada
10.40 Champions League Highlights **11.40**
Bodies of Evidence **12.40am** as Granada
CENTRAL 5.40pm as Granada **10.40** as
Border **11.40** Central Sports Special **12.40am**
as Granada **4.05** Jobfinder **5.20** Asian Eye **5.30**
as Granada
HTV 5.40pm as Granada **6.30** Regional news
7.00 as Granada **10.40** as Border **11.40**
MacGyver **12.40am** as Granada
YORKSHIRE 5.40pm as Granada **5.55**
Regional news **6.30** Cross Wits **7.00** as
Granada **10.40** as Border **11.40** Film: Cherry
2000 **1.25am** Hollywood Report **1.55**
Videofashion **2.26** The Album Show **3.25** Noisy
Mothers **4.20** Jobfinder **5.30** as Granada
S4C 5.30pm Countdown **6.00** Newyddion 6
6.15 Heno **7.00** Pobol y Cwm **7.30** 'Nol Am
Noson **8.00** Amser Rhyfel **8.30** Newyddion
9.00 Tydi Coleg Yn Grêt **9.30** Rap **10.00**
Brookside **10.30** E R **11.25** Dispatches
12.05am Racing **12.40** The Golden Girls
1.10-1.40am Ellen

CHANNEL 4

5.50pm Terrytoons
More cartoon calamity. 870009

6.00 All American Girl
Yung at Heart. After a trip to the
shops, Margaret returns home
empty-handed. Grandma receives
a proposal of marriage from the
man of her dreams.
Stereo Subtitled 221

6.30 Boy Meets World
Me and Mr Joad. After reading a
book about mistreated farm
workers, Cory fights for his rights
as a student. With Ben Savage.
Stereo Subtitled 573

7.00 Channel 4 News
Presented by Jon Snow and Cathy
Smith. *Subtitled*
Followed by Weather 720776

7.50 The Slot
Viewers offer their opinions on
events making the news. ...788134

8.00 Brookside
The growing hostility between
Jacqui and Beth erupts on the
street, Barry's got a proposal to
consider and there's concern as
more residents fall mysteriously ill.
Eddie Banks.......................PAUL BROUGHTON
Rosie Banks........................SUSAN TWIST
Carl Banks.....................STEPHEN DONALD
Jimmy Corkhill.................DEAN SULLIVAN
Jackie Corkhill.....................SUE JENKINS
Barry Grant.........................PAUL USHER
Ron Dixon............................VINCE EARL
Jacqui Dixon...........ALEXANDRA FLETCHER
Mike Dixon..........................PAUL BYATT
Max Farnham...................STEVEN PINDER
Patricia Farnham........GABRIELLE GLAISTER
Jean Crosbie....................MARCIA ASHTON
Mick Johnson....................LOUIS EMERICK
Gemma Johnson..............ANNA FRIEL
Mandy Jordache...........SANDRA MAITLAND
Beth Jordache.......................ANNA FRIEL
Rachel Jordache.........TIFFANY CHAPMAN
Katie Rogers........................DIANE BURKE
Sinbad.............................MICHAEL STARKE
George Manners................BRIAN MURPHY
Emma Piper...........................PAULA BELL
Garry Salter....................STEPHEN DWYER
*This week's episodes written by Joe
Ainsworth; Producer Mal Young; Director
Jeremy Summers Stereo Subtitled* .6318

**8.30 The Real Holiday
Show**
The fourth of six programmes
looking at the reality of a wide
range of holidays, as seen by the
holidaymakers themselves. This
week, two gay friends have a
weekend away in Amsterdam; a
married couple fly off to their
friends' casino in Biloxi, near New
Orleans; and 10-year-old James
Davis enjoys a family holiday in
Corfu. Introduced by Gaby Roslin.
*Executive producer David MacMahon; Series
editor Jonathon Holmes*
Stereo Subtitled 5825

9.00 Dispatches
Another edition of the
award-winning current affairs
programme.
Repeated tomorrow at 12.35am
Subtitled 940370

9.45 Out of Order
Sarah Kent, art critic of London
listings magazine *Time Out*, and
Giles Auty, art critic of *The
Spectator*, clash in the jammed lift
over the vexing question: is
modern art rubbish?
Subtitled 222554

**8.30pm Gaby Roslin presents a
selection of more real films from
more real holidaymakers**

10.00 E R
Continuing the drama series,
scripted by Michael Crichton, set
in the emergency ward of a
Chicago hospital.
Benton and Langworthy compete
for a fellowship, while Ross and
Hathaway find their mutual
attraction is escalating.
Dr Susan Lewis...........SHERRY STRINGFIELD
Dr Peter Benton..................ERIQ LA SALLE
Dr Langworthy...................TYRA FERRELL
Dr Douglas Ross............GEORGE CLOONEY
Carol Hathaway.........JULIANNA MARGULIES
Chloe.......................KATHLEEN WILHOITE
Jennifer.....................CHRISTINE HARNOS
Dr John Taglieri.............RICK ROSSOVICH
Stereo Subtitled 4680
◆ Dr Mark Porter: page 33

11.00 Racing
A comprehensive review of the
day's action from the Cheltenham
Festival. The main talking point is
Viking Flagship's bid for a second
successive triumph in the Queen
Mother Champion Chase.
Stereo 3202

11.30 Moviewatch
Film news and reviews.
Shown last Friday *Stereo* 346486

12.05am The White Room
Stevie Wonder features in this
new, studio-based music show
introduced by Mark Radcliffe.
Shown on Saturday *Stereo* 2841239

1.05 The Django Legacy
A documentary on the legendary
jazz guitarist Django Reinhardt and
his gypsy tradition which lives on
and influences musicians today.
Rpt 8177852

**2.10-3.50am The Loves
of Carmen**

Melodrama starring
Rita Hayworth
Glenn Ford.
In 19th century Seville, an army
officer falls for a passionate gypsy
and becomes embroiled in
jealousy and murder.
Carmen Garcia................RITA HAYWORTH
Don José............................GLENN FORD
Andres.........................RON RANDELL
Garcia..............................VICTOR JORY
Dancaire..........................LUTHER ADLER
Colonel.........................ARNOLD MOSS
Remendado...................JOSEPH BULOFF
Pablo........................BERNARD NEDELL
Lucas........................JOHN BARAGREY
Director Charles Vidor (1948) 897142
◆ FILM REVIEWS pages 42-46

more detail in chapter 5. Second, and even less apparent, there is a certain unity given to the flow of programmes by the values of the culture and by what Williams calls the *structure of feeling*.

A number of authors have pointed out that the word 'flow' as applied to television has unfortunate implications (Ellis, 1982; Fiske, 1987). It suggests a smooth and uninterrupted process continuing throughout a period of viewing. Ellis argues that, although many of the ideas incorporated in Williams's notion of flow are correct, television is actually a sequence of *segments* which gives a discontinuous and fragmented experience. This segmentation is intrinsic to television and is manifested at many different levels. Advertisements segment other programmes, and are themselves sometimes presented as segments, and there are frequent trailers for other programmes which punctuate continuity. Increasingly, factual programmes are presented in magazine format, effectively with one short item following another instead of as a continuous treatment of a single topic in depth. The news comes as a succession of discrete items unrelated to each other. As Lewis (1986) points out, this can confuse the audience. Most news programmes have a short introductory section to each item which is actually intended to refocus the attention of the audience, which is still absorbed by the previous item. Audience members, cannot as a rule, refocus that quickly and material in the introduction may be lost to them. Most television drama is actually composed of segments, a tendency enhanced by the characteristically fragmented camera-work of television noted in the last section. So Williams's flow actually takes place across groups of segments.

One of the most extreme examples of flow and segmentation is the MTV channel in the United States, which shows music videos continuously for twenty-four hours a day. The extract in box 1 from a study of MTV by Kaplan argues that the channel is *both* segmented *and* continuous, producing a particular kind of 'decentred' viewer; that is, a viewer whose experience is fragmented and is not organized around a single, concentrated element, a centre. Kaplan suggests that, although extreme, MTV is actually characteristic of the television experience and that this indicates the way that television is becoming increasingly postmodernist (but see Goodwin, 1993, for a critique). This issue is taken up again later in this chapter.

Box 1 The segmentation of MTV

MTV's programming strategies embody the extremes of what is inherent in the televisual apparatus. The channel hypnotizes more than others because it consists of a series of extremely short (four minutes or less) texts that maintain us in an excited state of expectation. The 'coming up next' mechanism that is the staple of all serials is an intrinsic aspect of the minute-by-minute MTV watching. We are trapped by the constant hope that the next video will finally satisfy and, lured by the seductive promise of immediate plenitude, we keep endlessly consuming the short texts. MTV thus carries to an extreme a phenomenon that characterizes most of television. The 'decentering' experience of viewing produced by the constant alternation of texts is exacerbated on MTV because its *longest* text is the four-minute video.

Later on in the book, I will be extending this discussion so as to clarify precisely the nature of the televisual 'imaginary' as against the filmic one. I will be arguing that MTV reproduces a kind of decenteredness, often called 'postmodernist', that increasingly reflects young people's condition in the advanced stage of highly developed, technological capitalism evident in America. As an apparatus developed only in recent decades, TV may be seen as at once preparing for and embodying a postmodern consciousness. MTV arguably addresses the desires, fantasies, and anxieties of young people growing up in a world in which all traditional categories are being blurred and all institutions questioned – a characteristic of postmodernism.

Source: Kaplan (1987), pp. 4–5.

The Domestic Style of Television

In the contrast between film and television, probably the most important characteristic is that the latter is a *domestic* medium. A number of features are related to the simple fact that the bulk of TV reception takes place in private homes. Some of these I have already discussed – the way in which segmentation is produced by the inability of the audience to give full attention in a domestic setting; the conversational and immediate style of presentation; the way that programming is often taken up with family concerns. In this section I look in a little more detail at some of these, and they will be taken up again in chapter 7.

In the first place, although it may seem obvious, television is an integral part of everyday life. As Silverstone says: 'Watching television and discussing television and reading about television takes place on an hourly basis, the result of focused or unfocused, conscious or unconscious attention' (1994, p. 3). It is so much part of everyday life that we take it entirely for granted. It forms part of the daily household routine and helps to mark out the passage of time.

Second, television texts are very much concerned, though not exclusively, with the family, home, and domestic life. Almost all situation comedy and soap opera, for example, is organized around the domestic setting. Furthermore, both types of text also often assume that a particular type of family occupies that setting, one that comprises parents and children. Ellis argues that even the news assumes a family spectator, as evidenced in remarks in commenting on the effects of the budget like 'the effect on the *average* family is . . .'

Third, the style of television is often that of a conversation with the viewer. A large number of programmes take the form of a 'direct address' to the viewer. As Scannell (1991) says:

> Radio and television are live media. Like the telephone, the talk they produce exists in real time: the moment of speaking and the moment of hearing are the same. In the early years of both radio and television all transmissions were live. In both cases, the development of technologies for recording talk came later, and although today many programmes are prerecorded, they are recorded in such a way as to preserve the effect of liveness . . . As such this talk is intentionally communicative. The people speaking in the studio or other contexts do not appear to be either talking to themselves or locked in private discourse from which viewers and listeners are excluded. (p. 1)

Announcers, weathermen and women, newsreaders, talk show hosts and many others face the camera directly and are therefore giving the illusion of having an intimate, direct, domestic conversation with the person watching. As Kozloff (1992) says of the American television news anchorman, Dan Rather: 'Such a strong impression is given of direct, interpersonal exchange that when Rather says, "Good night", I, for one, am likely to answer back to the screen, "Good night, Dan" ' (p. 81). This sense of direct address is reinforced by the conversational language employed by television. Much television actually *is* conversation. Soap opera and situation comedy largely consist of conversation between people often in private, domestic spaces. Other sorts of television consist of *simulated* conversation in which the participants pretend to be having the kind of conversation (in the public setting of television) that viewers might have round the kitchen table. Programmes like *Newsnight* and *The Late Show* are examples. The result here is that the language of much television is *colloquial* – the language of everyday life (Fairclough, 1994).

Fairclough argues that one of the effects of this conversationalized style of television is that the barriers between the public and private spheres are being broken down. At one time the public sphere, the institutions of public life, of politics, of the state, of work, of the mass media, all utilized relatively formal language in the way that they addressed their publics. These institutions are, however, being invaded by the language of the private sphere, the conversational style that belongs to the domestic arena. The media play an important part in this process. As Fairclough (1995) says:

> I want to suggest that the discourse practice . . . is a significant part of a shift in social practice which involves, in the terms of Habermas (1989), a 'structural transformation of the public sphere' of politics. One aspect of this transformation is a restructuring of the relationship between the traditional sphere of politics, the media as a domain of entertainment, and private life. Public life, including important elements in the political process such as conferences, elections, and the proceedings of Parliament, has become increasingly open to media coverage. However, there is a contradiction and a gap between the public nature of media production and media sources, and the private nature of media reception, which is embedded within home and family life. The gap has been bridged . . . by a progressive (if not always even) accommodation of public practices and discourses towards the private conditions of reception. One aspect of this movement has been a 'domestication' (Cardiff) or 'conversationalization' (Fairclough) of mediated public discourse. (p. 72)

Narrative

Novels, films and television all tell stories. These stories are structured and the concept of *narrative* is of major importance in understanding that structure. Narratives are sequences of events, settings and characters arranged in a logical order through time, the sequence being driven by cause and effect. The importance of narrative in the telling of stories is therefore to impose a non-random order on the story, to make it, as Fiske (1987) says, 'sensible'.

In this sense television appears to be a narrative medium. Soap operas, situation comedies, cop shows all obviously have a narrative structure. So also do commercial advertisements which in thirty seconds manage to tell a story narratively. Increasingly advertisements are being used to tell a story over a number of episodes. The now famous Gold Blend series told the story over a fairly long period of the romance of two neighbours whose relationship started with the borrowing of a jar of Gold Blend instant coffee. Documentaries may also take a narrative form, borrowing the format of a story. There are, however, forms of television which do not seem to be narrative, and I return to these later.

There are a number of different, but complementary, ways of understanding narrative in general. One can argue that, however apparently diverse are the stories recorded in novels, films or television programmes, there are actually comparatively few narrative structures or forms that underpin that diversity. This has been put at its simplest by Todorov (1977), who suggests that narratives begin with a state of equilibrium or harmony, chart the disruption of that equilibrium by an act of nature or of a villain, and record, in an act of narrative closure, the restoration of harmony, often by the activities of a hero. A more complex and very influential account has been offered by Propp (1968). He analysed a large number of Russian folk tales and found a common narrative structure in each of them, consisting of thirty-two narrative functions which he arranged in six sections. The list below reproduces this structure.

● *Preparation*
  1 A member of a family leaves home.
  2 A prohibition or rule is imposed on the hero.
  3 This prohibition/rule is broken.
  4 The villain makes an attempt at reconnaissance.
  5 The villain learns something about his victim.
  6 The villain tries to deceive the victim to get possession of him or his belongings.
  7 The victim unknowingly helps the villain by being deceived or influenced by the villain.

● *Complication*
  8   The villain harms a member of the family.
  8a A member of the family lacks or desires something.
  9   This lack or misfortune is made known; the hero is given a

request or command, and he goes or is sent on a mission/
quest.
10 The seeker (often the hero) plans action against the villain.

● *Transference*
11 The hero leaves home.
12 The hero is tested, attacked, interrogated, and, as a result,
receives either a magical agent or a helper.
13 The hero reacts to the actions of the future donor.
14 The hero uses the magical agent.
15 The hero is transferred to the general location of the object of
his mission/quest.

● *Struggle*
16 The hero and villain join in direct combat.
17 The hero is branded.
18 The villain is defeated.
19 The initial misfortune or lack is set right.

● *Return*
20 The hero returns.
21 The hero is pursued.
22 The hero is rescued from pursuit.
23 The hero arrives home or elsewhere and is not recognized.
24 A false hero makes false claims.
25 A difficult task is set for the hero.
26 The task is accomplished.

● *Recognition*
27 The hero is recognized.
28 The false hero/villain is exposed.
29 The false hero is transformed.
30 The villain is punished.
31 The hero is married and crowned. (Fiske, 1987, pp. 135–6)

Propp called these elements 'functions' because what they do is
more important than what they are and the function can be performed by a variety of different agents. The analysis of character follows a similar logic. It is not so much what kind of person
characters are that matters, but rather what role they play in the
narrative – what their sphere of action is. It is therefore perfectly
possible for the same character to play different roles during the
course of the narrative or for a number of individuals to discharge
the function of a particular character, the villain for instance.

Another formal analysis of narratives is provided by Lévi-Strauss (1968), who was an anthropologist primarily interested in giving an account of the structure of myths in simple societies. Lévi-Strauss argues that all myths in a society can be analysed as a set of binary oppositions, sets of opposed qualities, like good and bad. These binary oppositions are not always directly apparent in any myth, but the story nevertheless revolves around them. In turn, the oppositions symbolize or represent real contradictions or issues that are crucial to the life of that society. For example, an aboriginal tribe in Australia has a myth which involves a snake which comes out of a lake, floods the land, and swallows two sisters. This opposition between the snake and the sisters symbolizes the opposition in the real lives of the society between the wet season and the dry season. The snake represents the rain and the male, fertilizing element, while the sisters represent the dry season and the female, fertilized element. Lévi-Strauss holds that the audience understand, if unconsciously, the connection between the oppositions in the myth and those in their lives. But the fact that the myth resolves the opposition between snake and sisters symbolically resolves the opposition between wet and dry seasons. In general, then, myths reconcile *symbolically* the contradictions that *actually* occur in society, allowing members of that society to live with their difficulties.

Lévi-Strauss is providing a very general account of myth, and a number of writers have attempted to apply his analysis to contemporary popular culture, arguing that stories that appear in film or television are mythic in that they resolve at the level of the story contradictions that appear in the everyday lives of the audience. Eco (1966), for example, argues that James Bond stories can be analysed in terms of a set of binary oppositions like that between chance and planning, while Wright (1975) performs a similar task for the Western.

An alternative way of seeing the operation of narrative is not to try to discover patterns of events and characters but instead to describe the processes by which the text conveys *meaning* through the narrative (see Corner, 1991c). Barthes (1975) offers an influential account of these processes in terms of a set of *codes*. Barthes identifies five such codes (see Fiske, 1987). The symbolic code represents the basic binary oppositions that are characteristic of a culture, between male and female or good and evil, for example. Second, the semic code refers to the way that common cultural stereotypes, the mother-in-law for example, are made into characters in the narrative so that the reader or viewer knows what a character represents. Third, the referential code is the means by which the text refers to wider cultural concerns in society. Fourth, the proairetic code relates the actions within the text to those that the reader or viewer knows from other texts. Lastly, and most important, the hermeneutic code controls the way in which the enigmas that initiate a narrative are resolved – the narrative is closed. Typically it involves three elements (Fiske, 1987; Lewis, 1991). It begins with an enigma, a mystery, a set of questions which capture the audience's attention. The second stage consists of a period of suspense during which the enigma remains unresolved but the narrative carries on, almost elaborating the lack of resolution. In the third and last stage, the narrative is brought to a conclusion by a solution to the mystery, an answer to the enigma.

Todorov, Propp, Lévi-Strauss and Barthes all articulate theories which claim considerable generality of scope in suggesting that narratives are to do with very fundamental ways in which societies see themselves. They are not simply stories; they deal with basic conflicts, events and relationships that characterize human societies. In this sense, narratives of all kinds, including TV narratives, have a *mythic* quality. Fiske and Hartley (1978) capture some of this sense in their notion of bardic television. As they say: 'It seems, then, that television functions as a social ritual, overriding individual distinctions, in which our culture engages in order to communicate with its collective self' (p. 85).

It is possible to criticize these theories of narrative for their abstract and formal quality. They are also founded in literary studies and may therefore be difficult to translate to television. Indeed, although much of television is clearly narrative, it is obvious that the form that the narrative takes is distinctively different from that found in novels, say. The critical differences stem from television flow. Television consists not of a single narrative complete in itself but of a flow of narratives, some of which may be far from complete.

One obvious way in which television narratives differ from, say, film narratives is that they are interrupted by commercial breaks, announcements, and trailers for future programmes. Television producers have adapted to this by organizing programmes around the breaks. Breaks may therefore come at convenient moments in the narrative to emphasize a high point or to signal a shift in time. At the same time, commercials may be screened whose content has some relation to the programme they interrupt. Indeed, in recent years narrative disruption has been piled on narrative disruption as advertisers now break commercials into a number of parts which are interrupted by the programme. Two complete narratives are thus intertwined as they simultaneously progress. The advertisers' message is only complete when the whole programme has been watched. Advertisers are therefore borrowing the narrative conventions of television in more ways than one. Not only are single advertisements narratives but an advertisement in several parts mimics the structure of television narratives and borrows from them the suspense that may actually be engendered by interruption.

The most important distinctive feature of television narrative, however, is the widespread, almost dominant use of the series or continuing serial format. *Series* are those shows in which the characters and settings are used over and over again but in which each episode is a complete story in itself. Examples from British television are *Cracker* and *Peak Practice*. American examples are *Roseanne* and *M*A*S*H*. *Continuing serials*, by contrast, use the same characters and settings but no episode is ever a complete story; the narrative is never closed. Soap operas are the obvious examples here.

As Kozloff (1992) points out, the series format has several consequences for television narratives. Besides the fact that there is no narrative closure in the series form (as Ellis has noted), the series implies the form of the dilemma rather than that of resolution and closure – the viewer is not placed in suspense because he or she knows that the central characters will return next week. In addition, although some series may succeed in developing characters from episode to episode, there is more usually little sense of history or of progress through time so that characters refer back to events in the past of the series. In most series, the characters live in the present only. Serials also face particular narrative problems. They cannot count on viewers seeing every episode and consequently much of the narrative involves repetition from week to week to enable less faithful viewers to catch up. Secondly, because many of the narrative mechanisms noted above are missing or muted (lack of enigma, for example), the serial has to resort to other devices to ensure a measure of audience suspense. In soap opera, for example, simply the desire to see what is going to happen to the characters is enough to make sure that viewers come back to future episodes. Sometimes, some more direct device may be used. Cliffhangers, where the narrative is suspended at a crisis point at the end of an episode, are one such device, more common in American soap opera than British, which can, however, occasionally provide a mini-cliffhanger before commercial breaks.

As Feuer puts it (1986), television replaces the linear form of film narrative with a serial form, whether it is a series or a continuing serial, and a major effect is the diversion of interest from events to character. And the serial form is becoming ever more common in television. Even stories, *Lonesome Dove* or *The Singing Detective* for example, which might have been previously presented as a single drama are now played out over several weeks or even months in a number of episodes, which do, however, come to a conclusion. The serial form has clear economic advantages for television production. Actors, sets and locations can be more intensively used, and acting and writing talent, which are in comparatively short supply, can be spread more thinly.

One last distinctive feature of television narratives deserves mention. They are increasingly becoming less discrete and separate, and are blending with each other. One aspect of this I have already noted in the way advertisements and programmes become intertwined both in subject matter and in narrative form. In addition, television is more *intertextual*, that is, one text makes references to others. For example, an actor playing a character from one situation comedy will appear in a promotion for another. In general television increasingly refers to itself; a great deal of television comedy, for example, depends on a detailed knowledge on the part of the viewer of what goes on in television in general.

So far I have argued that television is narrative but that it adopts a particular form of narrative. At the same time, it is clear that only certain types of television – drama in particular – take this form in an obvious way. It is difficult, for example, to imagine sports presentations, talk shows or game shows fitting in easily to any of the narrative schemes so far discussed. It is true that these forms of television may have *some* narrative features – the use of enigma, the cliffhanger and the restoration of equilibrium, for instance – but they do not do so in any thoroughgoing way. The news, however, is a more awkward example, and to illustrate the difficulty I turn to a study of the narrative structure of the news by Lewis (1991).

Lewis argues that the structure of the news is quite unlike that of, say, soap opera, not because it deals with information, but because the two have very different styles of story telling. In the case of the news this style derives from the newspaper. The typical style of the newspaper report is to begin with the main points and then to fill in the detail. The assumption is that the busy reader may not read the whole of the story and may only want to catch the main points.

Television news takes a similar form, beginning with the 'main points', usually presented by the news anchor, and then proceeding to a more detailed report, usually compiled by one or two reporters or correspondents. The TV reporter will sometimes make a small gesture toward more traditional forms of narrative by 'wrapping up' the story with some concluding remarks. Like newspapers, the space devoted to stories bears very little relation to their complexity or the amount of information required to understand them. The more newsworthy the story, the more details will be presented. (p. 130)

This form has very few of the narrative conventions that I have described. There is no enigma that is resolved at the end and no causal sequence. Instead the resolution, the punch line, is presented *first*, followed by a set of details presented often in no particular order. As Lewis remarks, the news has the structure of a shopping list. A few news stories, usually to do with events overseas, do have a traditional narrative that draws audiences into the story. They begin with an enigma and proceed to a resolution by a series of linked steps. Interestingly, Lewis finds that news stories with a narrative structure of this kind are more easily remembered and understood than are the majority of stories which lack it.

Realism

Television seems to be describing the world as it is. This is most obvious with news and current affairs programmes. These clearly make a claim to be telling the truth; they are describing the world as it really is. This claim is enhanced by the feeling that television is operating in the present, unlike any other medium. Not only is it describing reality, it is giving us the events as they happen. As Feuer (1983) puts it, television has the quality of 'liveness'. Contemporary satellite technology has enhanced these qualities, with often dramatic and bizarre results. For example, during the Gulf War, there were television reports of American bombing of Baghdad which described missiles as they passed the reporter's hotel window.

Realism, however, is not only a characteristic of factual programming. Perhaps more importantly, fictional output can be described in this way. Television drama of all kinds usually tries very hard to give the *feel* of reality. An historical drama, *The Buccaneers* for example, creates a period setting in loving detail and, even if the speech may be modern, a great deal of care goes into trying to persuade the audience that it is actually present in the Victorian period. Similarly, soap operas like *EastEnders* aim to be realistic. Trouble is taken to make the characters and sets authentic so that the illusion is created that these are real people in a real east London setting.

Although this attempt at creating reality may seem to be an obvious feature of television, the concept of realism itself is very difficult to define (Lovell, 1980). Abercrombie et al. (1992) argue that there are three features that distinguish realist texts. First, realism offers a 'window on the world'. In the case of television, there is no mediation between the viewer and what he or she is watching. It is as if the television set were a sheet of clear glass which offered the viewer an uninterrupted vision of what lay beyond. Television is, or *seems* to be, like direct sight. Second, realism employs a narrative which has rationally ordered connections between events and characters. Realist cultural forms, certainly those involving fictional presentations at any rate, consist of a caused, logical flow of events, often structured into a beginning, a middle and a closed conclusion (see previous section). Events and characters, therefore, do not have a random or arbitrary nature, but are organized by rational principles. In these respects, realist forms may be contrasted with those texts that are essentially 'spectacular'. The pleasure of texts that involve 'spectacle' lies in the images themselves; it is a visual, not a narrative pleasure. It is important to note that static images can also be narrative. Many photographs and paintings often have a 'before' and 'after' outside the specific moment captured in the frame. They are episodes in a story and imply the rest of the narrative; the meaning of the picture is given by its place in an implied narrative. Non-realist forms do not imply such a narrative. They do not so much tell a story as invite contemplation.

The third aspect of realism is the concealment of the production process. Most television is realist in this sense in that the audience is not made aware, during the programmes themselves, that there is a process of production lying behind the programmes. The illusion of transparency is preserved. It is as if there were no author. The form conspires to convince us that we are not viewing something that has been constructed in a particular fashion by a determinate producer or producers. This concealment of the production process, this hiding of the author's hand, is best seen when the occasional television programme does not follow the convention. When in the 1995 series of *A Bit of Fry and Laurie* the camera moves from filming the set to following one of the characters out of the set and into the studio with its plain brick walls, other cameras, and a maze of cables and other equipment, the audience feels a shock as the illusion of realism is disrupted.

However powerful its effects, realism is only a *convention*. Television may appear to be a window on the world but it is not really transparent. What it offers is essentially a *construction* of the world, a version of reality. This is not a conspiracy to mislead the audience. It is simply that there is no way in which any description of reality can be the only, pure and correct one, just as people will give very different descriptions of what they see out of their kitchen window. As soon as television producers start to film, they are necessarily selecting and interpreting; they *must* do so in order to present a coherent programme of whatever kind. As a result, of course, all sorts of thing can be excluded by realist conventions. For example, Jordan (1981) argues that:

> *Coronation Street* conventionally excludes everything which cannot be seen to be physically present . . . This means, in effect, that most social explanations, and all openly political ones, are omitted. The differing situations, the troubles or successes, of the various characters are explained largely in terms of their (innate) psychological make-up, occasionally attributed to luck. (p. 29)

The critical question raised by the convention of realism is then: is there a *systematic* exclusion of particular features of the world from television? A number of writers argue that there is and the effect on audiences is particularly powerful because the realist convention does *seem* to be a correct description of the world. Television presents one reality and audiences are persuaded to accept it as the only reality. MacCabe (1981a, 1981b) argues for this position. He suggests that a variety of points of view may be articulated in a television text, but one reality is still preferred; there is a dominant point of view, that of the narrator, which is presented as the natural, transparent one. There is therefore a *hierarchy of discourses* or points of view in which one discourse controls the others.

It might be replied, however, that MacCabe's is too simplified a view (McArthur, 1981). Jordan (1981), for example, argues that there is not a single realism in television, but rather a number of realisms. She therefore describes *Coronation Street* as a version of realism which she calls soap opera realism. This is a combination of the social realism of films of the 1960s with the realism of soap opera. The former demands that:

> life be presented in the form of a narrative of personal events, each with a beginning, a middle and an end, important to the central characters con-

cerned but affecting others in only minor ways; that though these events are ostensibly about *social* problems they should have as one of their central concerns the settling of people in life; that the resolution of these events should always be in terms of the effect of personal interventions; that characters should be either working-class or of the classes immediately visible to the working classes (shopkeepers, say . . .) and should be credibly accounted for in terms of the 'ordinariness' of their homes, families, friends; that the locale should be urban and provincial (preferably in the industrial north); that the settings should be commonplace and recognisable (the pub, the street, the factory, the home and more particularly the kitchen); that the time should be 'the present'; that the style should be such as to suggest an unmediated, unprejudiced and complete view of reality; to give, in summary, the impression that the reader, or viewer, has spent some time at the expense of the characters depicted. (p. 28)

The latter, on the other hand, requires that:

though events must carry their own minor conclusions they must not be seen as finally resolving; that there should be an intertwining of plots so deployed as to imply a multiplicity of experience whilst effectively covering only a narrow range of directly 'personal' events; that these personal events should be largely domestic; that there should be substantial roles for women; that all roles should involve a serious degree of stereotyping; that the most plausible setting, in view of these later requirements, would be the home; and that the long-term passage of fictional time should mirror fairly accurately the actual passage of time. (p. 28)

Although this form of realism does exclude certain features, as I pointed out before, it also does allow alternative realities to emerge. Furthermore, as Jordan notes, the pleasure of a soap opera like *Coronation Street* may partly lie in the perception by the audience that it *is* a construction. The programme, in other words, breaks with the third feature of the definition of realism put forward at the beginning of this section. It may, indeed, be doing this quite deliberately in a number of ways. For example, some of the characters are caricatures rather than realist depictions. Reg Holdsworth in *Coronation Street* is a good example. Again, the programme uses the self-conscious linking technique of shifting to a scene involving characters who have been the subject of a conversation in the previous scene. As Jordan argues:

My argument then is that *Coronation Street*, though deploying the devices of the Soap Opera Realism upon which it is based, far from attempting to hide the artifice of these devices (other than by the generic imperative to hide) rather asks us to take pleasure in its artistry, much as a stage magician will not show us how his tricks are done yet never claims . . . that he has *actually* sawn a woman in half. (p. 39)

Jordan's view of *Coronation Street* suggests that there can be a substantial dislocation of realism's effects. Such dislocation may, of course, be even more noticeable in other sorts of programme which set out to *play* with reality (*The Singing Detective*, for example).

Television as Ideology

One of the arguments reviewed in the previous two sections is that, however natural realism and narrative appear to be, they are no more than *conventions*. Because they are conventions and therefore necessarily partial, and because of their apparent naturalness, they can mislead audiences. For example, Todorov argues that particular narrative structures support the social order. In his view, narratives, since they involve a restoration of equilibrium, will work against the forces of disorder and favour the status quo in society. Realist television fictions can present one version of reality while persuading that it is the *only* version. These misleading or deceiving television conventions are often summed up by means of the concept of ideology. As Fiske (1987) puts it:

> Realism, in this view, is a reactionary mode of representation that promotes and naturalizes the dominant ideology. It works by making everything appear 'realistic' and 'realisticness' is the process by which ideology is made to appear the product of reality or nature, and not of a specific society and its culture . . . The conventions of realism have developed in order to disguise the constructedness of the 'reality' it offers, and therefore of the arbitrariness of the ideology that is mapped onto it. Grounding ideology in reality is a way of making it appear unchallengeable and unchangeable, and thus is a reactionary political strategy. (p. 36)

Ideology is one of the most controversial notions in sociology, everything from its meaning through its explanation to its very existence being the subject of extensive debate, and this controversy and lack of agreement extend to the application of the concept in television studies. It is my intention not to go into this debate at any great length (see, for example, Larrain, 1979; J. Thompson, 1984; K. Thompson, 1986; Eagleton, 1991) but only to try to relate some of the basic ideas to television texts. Ideology may be provisionally defined in terms of sets of ideas, beliefs, attitudes, language, 'structures of feeling' and rituals. As Kellner (1987) puts it:

I propose that we view ideology as a synthesis of concepts, images, theories, stories, and myths that can take rational systematic form . . . or imagistic, symbolic, and mythical form (in religion, the culture industries, etc.). Ideology is often conveyed through images (of country and race, class and clan, virginity and chastity, salvation and redemption, individuality and solidarity). The combination of rational theory with images and slogans makes ideology compelling and powerful. (p. 472)

Furthermore, ideologies have particular *effects* of supporting the existing distributions of power, authority, wealth and income and of ensuring conformity. As J. Thompson (1984) says: 'To study ideology, I propose, is to study the ways in which meaning (or signification) serves to sustain relations of domination' (p. 4). Much the same notion of effect is used by Kellner (1982) more specifically for television:

Today television is the dominant producer of cultural symbolism. Its imagery is prescriptive as well as descriptive, and not only pictures what is happening in society, but also shows how one adjusts to the social order. Further, it demonstrates the pain and punishment suffered by not adjusting. The endless repetition of the same images produces a television world where the conventional is the norm and conformity the rule. (p. 474)

How does ideology work in texts, especially television texts? The central issue here is how television helps us to give a *particular meaning* to events, or people, or issues. The meanings of the signalmen's strike, of the behaviour of the police in *The Bill*, or of Ricky, Natalie and Bianca in *EastEnders*, as they appear on television, are not objectively given; they are not the only meanings possible. Yet one set of meanings is given prominence in the course of the programme and others are subordinate or even absent altogether. As Hall (1982) puts it more generally:

Because meaning was not given but produced, it followed that different kinds of meaning could be ascribed to the same events. Thus, in order for one meaning to be regularly produced, it had to win a kind of credibility, legitimacy or taken-for-grantedness for itself. That involved marginalizing, down-grading, or de-legitimating alternative constructions. Indeed, there were certain kinds of explanation which, given the power of and credibility acquired by the preferred range of meanings, were literally unthinkable or unsayable. (p. 67)

Television, then, defines our world in particular ways. Hall (1980) encapsulates the idea in his notion of *preferred reading* or *preferred meaning*. Of all the possible ways of constructing an event, television prefers one. Further, this preferred reading is one that fits in with the most powerful, dominant ways of looking at the world that obtain in television, the rest of the media, and society generally. As Hall says: 'The domains of "preferred meanings" have the whole social order embedded in them as a set of meanings, practices and beliefs: the everyday knowledge of social structures, of "how things work for all practical purposes in this culture", the rank order of power and interest and the structure of legitimations, limits and sanctions' (p. 134). It is then a further move to say that these dominant conceptions of the world are such as to support the current distributions of power (see J. Thompson, 1990). This point is taken up more directly in the analysis of news programmes in the next chapter.

So far, I have tried to present an account of television texts as ideological in the sense that they favour one, the dominant, way of looking at the world. This still leaves the question of how they achieve that effect, what the mechanisms are that organize the text around the preferred reading (Hall, 1982; O'Shaughnessy, 1990). First, one might point to the *naturalizing* effect television has. As has already been said, television presents itself as a 'window on the world', a picture of what the world is really like. This impression is further reinforced by its visual character, which convinces us that we are looking directly at the world with our own eyes. However, of course, the images that appear on television are *selected*; they do not represent 'reality' – they represent a reality. Second, television *assumes* a great deal about the world which is not then questioned. What is presented is a seamless web which actually depends on a set of specific assumptions. As a result, what appears on television seems to be common sense, what we already know. Situation comedy and soap opera, for example, generally depend on assumptions about how families – implicitly *all* families – are constituted and how they work. The course of the action is then worked out within those assumptions and most soaps would make no sense without them. It is important to note, then, that ideology in television is not really a content, a set of ideas, images or sounds. It is rather a set of *rules* that organize those ideas, images and sounds. The world of television texts is therefore a commonsense world in which much is taken for granted and the net effect is to exclude alternative possibilities and to present one meaning as the only real one.

By way of illustrating some of these ideas I summarize two studies from very different areas of television. Hurd (1981) seeks to understand how the 'ideological work' of police series on television functions. At one level this ideological work can be seen in what the dramas leave out. To start with, police series, though purporting to deal with the problems of law and order, actually leave two-thirds of the judicial process out – the courts and the prison system. It is as if the problems of conviction and imprisonment did not exist or, rather, were simply subsumed by the arrest of the villain. But it is not only these institutional sectors that are repressed. The typical plots function so that only policemen have characters. Everybody else – villains, the public, women – is presented as a series of stereotypes. Stereotyping encourages ideological treatment, in emphasizing particular features of a character type, especially by comparison with the policemen who are rounded characterful human beings. However, this still identifies only the 'more overt ideological results' in that it deals only with what lies on the surface.

Police series like *The Bill* or *Between the Lines* are obliged to make their reality convincing. To be convincing, they must 'incorporate the antagonisms and contradictions, real or perceived, of policing in England today' (p. 64) while at the same time displacing or concealing them. Police series must represent, but at the same time conceal, social contradiction. Hurd shows how representation-yet-concealment is achieved by considering the major oppositions identifiable within the programmes, the ways in which they are resolved within the drama, and their relations to the social, structural contradictions which they redefine. A variety of oppositions is identified, including police versus crime, law versus rule, authority versus rank, but it is the last which is probably the most important. So, the fictional police world is usually structured as an opposition between the comradeship of ordinary policemen on the one hand and the formal relationships of senior policemen on the other. This tension is psychologically plausible and therefore effective. Yet it diverts attention, in Hurd's view, from larger underlying conflicts in police work 'by divorcing the activity of policing from any class analysis of power relationships within society' (p. 68). The police series perform their ideological work by portraying social conflict in a realistic way but by ignoring deeper contradictions; conflict is transposed fictionally from one place to another.

O'Shaughnessy (1990) refers to these ideological functions as *displacement*, which represents the means by which social contradictions are hidden or diverted to other areas:

> Displacement occurs through omission; some problems and viewpoints are just not dealt with . . . It also happens through the privileging of certain issues over others. Gender conflict is often foregrounded . . . but

class and racial conflict are given less space. It occurs through 'mode of address': we are addressed as British families who are consumers interested in entertainment. This may be an accurate description but it's not the whole story; we could be addressed as workers or members of different classes, gender, and races. By focusing on categories which bind us together in unity, TV 'displaces' or hides our differences and potential social antagonisms. (p. 97)

Such ideological work is not only performed at one time. Most police series have to reflect shifts in society. For example, recent series have had to incorporate issues of gender by making women central to the plotting. That programmes of this sort mask social conflict does not mean that they do not change over time. There is an enormous gulf between *Z Cars* and *Prime Suspect* (see Clarke, 1992; and for a further discussion of ideology and television police series see Sparks, 1992).

A quite different example is provided by sport and its reporting on television. Clarke and Clarke (1982) point out that sport appears to be an entirely natural activity, the zestful enthusiasm of the innately talented with no meaning beyond healthful play. Actually, it is a socially constructed activity imbued with a variety of meanings which may be further enunciated by media reporting of sports events. The ideological force of sport comes not only from the meanings embedded in the activities, but also from the way that these meanings or values seem entirely natural and inevitable because of the association with 'uncontaminated' sport. Sport is ideologically successful because it can encode particular and distinct values by pretending to be something that it is not.

An important example that Clarke and Clarke cite is the involvement of sport with nationalism and, in Britain, specifically with Englishness.

By national culture, or nationalism, we mean an ideology which constructs the 'nation' as a distinctive and unique set of characteristics, traits and habits which make up both a natural character and a national way of life. It identifies those things that we, as English, are supposed to have in common. But the construction of nationalism also involves suppressing internal differences and conflict in order to be able to present "us" as a unity'. (p. 79)

The presentation of sport involves not only a construction of national unity but also a unity structured in a certain direction. There is a close association between the idea of being sporting and the British way of life. Indeed the British often like to see themselves as the teachers of other nations, bringers of sports like cricket, tennis and soccer to the heathen. So sport involves self-control, respect for the rules, reasonableness and fair play. Those who break the rules or aim to win at all costs are actively disapproved of. Sport is ideological in that it presents as natural and English a *particular* set of virtues and vices which is transferable to everyday life. As Whannel (1992) puts it:

> On English television, international competition is most commonly set up as Britain/England v. the rest. Characteristically this draws upon the ideology of fair play and sporting behaviour, whereby it is sporting Brits against the not so sporting rest. Foreigners are either quaint, funny and incompetent or, if they regularly beat us, take it far too seriously, benefit from levels of state and/or private support not open to the poor British, and probably use drugs. There is also a broader cultural frame at work that counterposes serious, competent Europeans and westerners with fun-loving, disorganized blacks and the third world generally. (p. 137)

The notion of preferred reading indicates that there is dominant meaning in a text but it does not necessarily mean that other meanings are not present. Indeed, many theorists argue that television texts are *polysemic* or *multiaccentual*; that is, capable of bearing many different meanings. There may well be a conflict over which meaning or 'accent' becomes the one that is dominant in the text and which organizes all the others. It is the assumption of many theorists of ideology in television that the meaning that emerges from this conflict is the one that concurs with the dominant ideology in general and which supports the current distribution of power in society. Other theorists argue that television texts are simply contradictory. However, the fact that television texts *are* polysemic or contradictory means that they can potentially be interpreted in different ways; some audience members may pick up not the preferred reading but one of the subordinate ones, a possibility explored in more detail in chapters 6 and 7.

If most television texts are polysemic but contain a preferred reading in accord with dominant power relations, there are also, of course, texts that are explicitly *resistant*. These contain a preferred reading that *opposes* dominant power relations or at least does not confirm them. Many examples of resistant texts in British television are drawn from single plays or series of plays written by authors in the dramatic tradition. *The Boys from the Blackstuff*, for example, clearly has a radical, critical edge – 'it is a serious drama which challenges conventional perceptions of society' (Millington and Nelson,

1986, p. 11; and see Tulloch, 1990a, for an extended discussion of radical British drama). As Kellner (1987) points out, comedy and documentary are also genres which can provide resistant views of the dominant culture and power relations.

Two final points need to be made about television as ideology. First, many of the examples that I have used so far are of single programmes or groups of programmes. There has been no attempt to describe the ideological structure of television *as a whole*. This, indeed, would seem to be a difficult enterprise, particularly since so many writers describe the experience of television as chaotic flow, without a single animating meaning. As pointed out earlier, in any one evening we can watch adventure stories, police series, situation comedies, Westerns, documentaries, current affairs, talk shows, soap operas and the news. There is nothing that guarantees that the ideological structures of these very different forms will fit in with each other. Thus, they *may* all have a preferred reading, but why should the preferred readings all support the dominant power relations in the same way?

Second, the discussion so far has all been about television *texts*. As I argued in chapter 1, a complete analysis of television has to pay due regard to texts, to the production context, and to the way that programmes are received by the audience. I will therefore be returning to the question of ideology in subsequent chapters.

Postmodernism

Postmodernism is now a term in common use. In general, it denotes large-scale cultural, and perhaps social and economic, changes that are said to be sweeping modern Western societies and which will fundamentally change their character. It is said to affect what is often called 'high' culture. Architecture and painting, for example, are postmodernist in that they break with the modernist traditions of the twentieth century. Popular culture is perhaps even more subject to the postmodernist revolution and, indeed, the way in which popular culture is no longer despised, as it was in the first half of the century, is itself taken as an indication of a postmodernist tendency. More fundamentally still, many theorists of postmodernism claim that its most important features have found their way into the culture of everyday life and now critically affect the way that we look at the world, not just as an artistic matter, but in our routine dealings in daily life.

If there is general agreement that there is at least a phenomenon to be debated, there is much less of a consensus as to the more specific features of postmodernism. Rather than try to establish a consensus, in what follows I will simply list six of the main features of postmodernism which are held to be applicable to television.

First, there is the claim that, as a society, we are progressively living, not in reality, but in *images* or representations of that reality. Indeed, there is no longer any difference between image and reality. For example, if we go to the Lake District, we do not see the mountains, the lakes, the streams, the grass and the sheep in a direct and unmediated way as Wordsworth might have done. Instead, we see these things entirely through the images created in television documentaries, films, advertisements and Wordsworth's poetry, all of which convey powerful representations not only of the Lake District itself but also, more generally, of rural life. As Fiske (1991) puts it, we live in an image-saturated society:

> The saturation is such as to produce a categorical difference, rather than one of degree, between our age and previous ones. In one hour's television viewing, one of us is likely to experience more images than a member of a non-industrial society would in a lifetime. The quantitative difference is so great as to become categorical: we do not just experience more images, but we live with a completely different relationship between the image and other orders of experience. In fact, we live in a postmodern period when there is no difference between the image and other orders of experience. (p. 58)

This view of the collapse of image and reality into each other is most closely associated with the work of Baudrillard (see especially 1983). For him, television is the major source of images in modern society, in creating a 'simulational culture'. Featherstone (1991) summarizes this view as:

> the loss of a sense of concrete reality as the consumer–television culture with its floating mass of signs and images produces an endless series of simulations which play off each other. Baudrillard refers to this as a 'hyperreality', a world in which the piling up of signs, images, and simulations through consumerism and television results in a destabilized, aestheticized hallucination of reality. For Baudrillard, culture has effectively become free-floating to the extent that culture is everywhere, actively mediating and aestheticizing the social fabric and social relationships. (p. 99)

Second, and in rather a different sense of image, contemporary societies are about creating an *image*, refining a *look*, presenting a *style*. Modern culture is concerned with surface appearance. As Ewan (1988) says, this amounts to an obsession with form rather than content. On the one hand, such concerns can lead to a certain celebration of sensuality. On the other, they promote consumerism as people try to buy a style or an image. Again, this depthless, superficial culture is reflected and enhanced in television. Grossberg (1987), for example, more or less defines television in terms of its superficial quality. *Miami Vice*, for instance is a show designed to stay on the surface, to be looked at rather than thought about, and which is indifferent to any values of any kind. '*Miami Vice* is, as its critics have said, all on the surface. And the surface is nothing but a collection of quotations from our own collective historical debris, a mobile game of Trivia. It is, in some ways, the perfect televisual image, minimalist (the sparse scenes, the constant long shots, etc.) yet concrete' (p. 28).

Third, postmodern culture breaks traditional boundaries. For example, it does not respect the division between high and popular culture or the distinctions between historical periods. Kaplan (1987) points to MTV as an example of this tendency. The pop videos played on MTV draw from every conceivable historical epoch and any cultural source, from fine art to advertising, for images.

> MTV, however, simply sweeps up these discourses and distinctions into itself, calling upon all the separate traditions, re-shaping and re-using them for its own ends, flattening them out into one continuous present of the 24-hour video flow. MTV also effaces the boundary between past and present in drawing indiscriminately on film genres and art movements from different historical periods; and also in the often arbitrary use of settings and clothes from the Roman, medieval and other past eras. The stance of the texts is that there is one time continuum in which all exists: past, present, and future do not indicate major time barriers, but rather a time band upon which one can call at will. (p. 144)

Kaplan believes that MTV stands for television generally. Certainly, some other television shows are pastiches, composites of elements from lots of different sources thrown together; there is no necessary respect for the authenticity of any one source. Many comedy shows, *French and Saunders* for example, take this form.

Fourth, postmodernist culture is self-referential. For example, the film *Maverick* includes a large number of references to other films. Not only are there scenes taken from other Westerns, there are also references to episodes in other, quite different, films in which the *actors* playing the leading roles have appeared. Television is particularly a medium which, to a large extent, feeds off itself. This can happen in several ways. Eco (1984), for example, describes contemporary television as neo-television in that it is constantly taking itself as its subject in chat shows or even news programmes. 'The principal characteristic of Neo-TV is that it talks less and less about the external world' (p. 19). Since many comedy shows depend on other television programmes for the material for jokes, it would be literally impossible for anyone to understand them unless they were frequent television watchers. For example, a person with little knowledge of television, assuming that there are any left, would not be able to follow programmes like *The Day Today* or *Knowing You, Knowing Me With Alan Partridge*.

Fifth, postmodernist culture does not follow the conventions of realism and narrative described in previous sections. Indeed, it often

plays with these conventions. *The Singing Detective* and *Twin Peaks* are cases in point. Other television series play with realist conventions in that they move from the realist depiction of a scene to filming the show being filmed. The action of *Full Wax*, for example, moves from the set in which the action takes place to the studio in which the set is placed, with its tangle of cables and equipment, and back again. Eco (1984) argues that, in the early days of television, producers went to a great deal of trouble to conceal the apparatus of production. Now, in neo-TV, the cameras are *meant* to be seen.

Sixth, postmodernist culture is fragmented. It is composed of a large number of bits which do not form a coherent entity. Kaplan's account of MTV is of a fragmented television form in which the images are not, as a rule, intended to create a meaningful whole. Similarly, Williams's view of the complete television experience as a *flow* of discrete and separate bits of television (Ellis's segments), discussed earlier in this chapter, makes much the same point. The *experience* is of fragments. For many audience members the fragmentation of the programmes, and of the sequence of programmes, is further broken up by the habit of channel hopping – moving rapidly from channel to channel without seeing any one programme completely.

The argument is, then, that television is an archetypical postmodernist form. It is so in its overall impact as a provider of images and its fragmented method of presentation. It is also postmodernist in its individual programmes in that they break boundaries, prioritize the superficial, are self-referential, and are non-realist and non-narrative. It is doubtful, however, just how significant or new these characteristics are. Cultural forms have always been self-referential and boundary breaking, for instance, and, to the extent that television is more prone to have these characteristics, it is more likely to be due to the increasing sophistication and skill of the audience than anything else. Furthermore, most analyses of television as postmodernist take as examples a fairly narrow range of programmes (mostly those watched by young people). The bulk of television, and the most popular programmes, do not, with a few exceptions, have the characteristics listed above. *Coronation Street*, for example, remains firmly in the realist, narrative tradition. Most important of all, however, whatever one may say about television as a postmodernist *text*, the critical feature is how the audience responds to it. This question is taken up in chapter 7.

3

The Genres of Television

The Concept of Genre

One of the factors contributing to the apparently chaotic quality of television is the very diversity of its output, as figure 2.1 and the list of an actual evening's viewing in the last chapter show. The concept of genre provides one way of exploring further the diversity of television texts. Ryall (1975) defines genre in the following terms: 'The master image for genre criticism is the triangle composed of artist/film/audience. Genre may be defined as patterns/forms/styles/structures which transcend individual films and which supervise both their construction by the film-maker, and their reading by an audience' (p. 28). Examples of genres are Westerns, gangster movies and musicals. This definition clearly refers to film, and contemporary notions of genre are heavily influenced by film criticism. However, the idea may be usefully applied to television, which manifests a wider range of genres – documentaries, news, game shows, soap opera, police series, thrillers, situation comedy, talk shows.

Ryall's definition presents genre in terms of an interaction between the text, the producer of the text, and the audience (see also Feuer, 1992). Every genre has its own particular rules and conventions which distinguish it from others. To some extent, these rules relate to content. Westerns are about the Wild West in the nineteenth and early twentieth centuries (see Ryall, 1970). Soap operas are about the relationships of characters, usually in a domestic setting. Certain kinds of character and event are therefore very unlikely to occur in certain genres. Domestic settings with everyday activities are unlikely to figure largely in police series, for example. Different genres will also have different narrative conventions (see chapter 2 for a discussion of narrative). Suspense, for instance, is an important narrative device in both thrillers and situation comedy. In the former, however, it works to resolve the disequilibium while in the latter it is resolved in laughter. Enigmas play an important part in thrillers and sometimes police series but are not usually an important part of soap operas.

Iconography and visual style can also be important in establishing a genre. Objects can function as icons or signs which are instantly recognizable as signs of that genre. The Western *Quigley*, for example, begins with a long sequence of packing a bag for a journey. No person is visible, just a series of objects – long boots, spurs, belt, bullets, sheath knife, rifle, saddlebag, holster. We instantly know that we are about to watch a Western (though in this case, oddly, a Western set in Australia!). The visual style of soap opera is also instantly recognizable. So, the credit sequences which start off each episode of *Coronation Street* and *Brookside* are very similar. They all show street scenes with people moving about carrying on with their everyday lives. Compare this with *The Bill*, whose opening sequence is of a police car moving fast and coming to a halt. In all these cases the viewer is sure before even getting into the programme what *kind* of programme is being watched. The specificity of visual style will continue into the programme itself. Soap operas typically use a great deal of close-up, which emphasizes their organization around the characters of *people*. Police series, on the other hand, in order to depict *action*, have more long shots taken from a distance.

The boundaries between genres are therefore apparently fairly firm. A science fiction/children's series like *Dr Who* will have different rules and conventions from a situation comedy like *Bottom*, which in turn will be different from a drama series like *Dr Finlay*. The most important genre distinction is, however, between fictional and non-fictional programming. As Corner (1991c) argues:

> Although this is not always a clean division in formal systems – certain principles of television 'grammar', for instance, apply to both – the levels of referentiality, modes of address, forms of propositional or more associative, symbolic discourse and the presence or otherwise of television's own representatives (e.g. presenter, host, reporter) serve to mark the two areas out into distinctive communicative realms. (p. 276)

For Corner, the characteristic relationship between television programme and the viewer of non-fictional output is in terms of *knowledge*, usually framed in direct speech from presenter to viewer. This is so even when the programme is devised as entertainment, as in a sports programme. In fictional television, on the other hand, the characteristic relationship is *imaginative pleasure*, particularly that derived from plotting and character.

Television producers set out to exploit genre conventions. It is clearly much easier to produce to a strict set of genre rules, to work to a formula. It also makes sound economic sense. Sets, properties and costumes can be used over and over again. Teams of stars, writers, directors and technicians can be built up, giving economies of scale. At the same time genres permit the creation and maintenance of a loyal audience which becomes used to seeing programmes within a genre. The apparently formulaic quality of television can often encourage critics to argue that television is an uncreative medium. However, this is not necessarily so, and distinguished television directors, script writers and producers have deliberately chosen to work within the constraints of genres *precisely* because they give a structure. Even children's programmes can provide opportunities. That series of *Dr Who*, for example, scripted by Douglas Adams and produced by Graham Williams attracted a great deal of critical praise.

Genres are a kind of complicity between producer and audience. The audience knows what it is getting. Indeed, part of the pleasure is knowing what the genre rules are, knowing that the programme has to solve problems in the genre framework, and wondering how it is going to do so. Audience members will wonder what is going to happen next, although much of what is bound to happen is known because of the genre conventions. Audiences will therefore come to a soap opera with a set of expectations set by the soap opera genre, and will derive pleasure from the way in which those expectations are realized. The normality of genre conventions also makes it possible to put on programmes that break or stretch the conventions. For example, the strength of those conventions makes parody possible. A good deal of television is dedicated to parody of other television programmes. *Knowing Me, Knowing You With Alan Partridge*, for instance, adopts the genre conventions of the talk show. This programme is funny mostly because we know what the conventions of talk shows are and enjoy seeing those conventions made explicit and exaggerated. Similarly, *The Young Ones* pushed the conventions of the situation comedy to their limits and, in doing so, created a cult audience attracted by the play with genre conventions (O'Shaughnessy, 1990).

Feuer (1992) suggests that there are three approaches to the social analysis of genre. First, the aesthetic approach concentrates on how genre conventions allow artistic expression and whether there are artistic benefits derived from transcending the genre. Second, in the ritual approach, genre can be seen as a cultural device whereby a society's common values can be expressed and social solidarity affirmed. Third, the ideological approach concentrates on showing how genre is an instrument of social control (see the discussion of ideology in chapter 2). By their very sameness, generic programmes repeat the same dominant message over and over again, and the genre conventions do not permit anything new or different to be said.

Television does operate generically but it is important not to overstate its dependence on genre, for a number of reasons. First, there are obviously differences *within* genres. As Feuer (1992) says:

> Originally a derisive term used to condemn other forms of drama as being hopelessly melodramatic, the term soap opera has been refined in a confrontation between such historical examples as the afternoon serial drama, prime-time serials, and British soap operas. British 'soaps', for example, cause us to question the equation of the term 'soap' with the mode of melodrama, because their own mode might better be described as 'social realism'; they possess none of the exaggeration and heightened emotion and elaborate gestures of their American cousins. And the middle-class, slowly unwinding, woman-centred world of afternoon soaps bears little resemblance to the fast-paced plutocratic worlds of *Dallas* and *Dynasty*. (p. 140)

One might well want to qualify this judgement since British soap operas appear to be changing and introducing story lines with a definite tinge of melodrama. *EastEnders* has always had a more melodramatic style than the other prime-time soaps, but *Brookside* has introduced stories in which people die of a mystery virus, and in *Coronation Street* a good deal of melodrama is extracted from the search for a kidney donor for Tracey Barlow.

Second, Livingstone and Lunt (1994) argue that a genre peculiar to television (and perhaps radio), the audience participation talk show, such as *The Oprah Winfrey Show*, is fundamentally ambiguous, partly because the genre conventions here are peculiarly open. This ambiguity manifests itself in the person of the host; 'is he or she the chair of a debate, the adored hero of a talk show, a referee, a conciliator, a judge, the compere of a game show, a therapist, the host of a dinner-party conversation, a manager, or a spokesperson? At times, the host plays any one of these roles, thus altering the roles of other participants and listeners' (p. 56). Indeed, just as audiences derive pleasure from genre conventions in seeing how their expectations are fulfilled, so they also find the amgibuities of genres pleasurable in another way, as they see how the conventions are manipulated (Connell and Curti, 1985).

Third, genres change their conventions over time. Police series in the fifties and sixties, for example, were largely concerned with the struggle between law and criminality within communities. Increasingly, from *The Sweeney* onwards, however, programmes like *Between the Lines* pit their heroes not only against criminals but also against their superior officers and the organization of the police force. The police hero now not only conflicts with the criminal but is also involved in a struggle against bureaucracy.

Fourth, and perhaps most important, the boundaries between genres are shifting and becoming more permeable. In fact, on one reading, it is almost as if modern television is characterized by a steady dismantling of genre. Again, there may be solid economic reasons for this change. New audiences are won by inventing new genres or mixing up old ones; the need for innovation produces a tendency to tamper with genre conventions. So, police series, like *Hill Street Blues*, take on more of the characteristics of soap opera. A number of writers believe that the important distinction between fiction and non-fiction is regularly crossed. This is done in the new genres of docudrama or infotainment. It is also done in the importation of the conventions of drama into news and documentary (see chapter 2). Connell and Curti (1985), for example, point to the way that news events are presented in terms borrowed from fiction. It is almost as if the audience can only understand the news by means of fictional conventions. Television's need for a constant stream of new programming means a perpetual tension between using genre conventions to retain audiences and keep costs down, on the one hand, and, on the other, breaking and crossing genre boundaries to attract new audiences and stay ahead of the competition. By comparison with film, therefore, television's use of genre is much less coherent. Furthermore, the fact that television comes at the audience as a flow of programmes, all with different generic conventions, means that it is more difficult to sustain the purity of the genre in the *viewing* experience.

Soap Opera

Soap opera must be one of the genres most associated with television, although the origins of the form lie in radio. Yet it is also the genre, with the probable exception of game shows and situation comedy, that has the lowest status within the television industry and, to some extent, outside it. Within recent years this image has changed. The press, for instance, especially the tabloid press, gives television soap operas a great deal of space. There are also publications devoted exclusively to soap opera, as the cover reproduced in Figure 3.1 illustrates. The same is true in other countries. In the United States, for example, the market for publications about soap opera is said to be about 40 million people and a column which updates viewers about the plots of twelve American soaps is syndicated in almost a hundred newspapers (Brown, 1994). Television critics in the broadsheet press can also take some soap opera seriously, especially *Coronation Street*. However, other soaps, imported Australian daytime programmes especially, are still treated with contempt. Here, a not uncommon image is that conveyed by the programme *Spitting Image*, which once represented the actors in an Australian soap as boards of wood, so poor was the acting thought to be.

At the same time as critical opinion is, to say the least, ambivalent about soap opera, the genre continues to be extremely popular with the viewers. It is not only a question of viewing figures: soap operas are often the longest-running programmes on television. An American soap, *Guiding Light*, has been shown since 1952 and *Coronation Street*, Britain's longest-running soap, first appeared in 1960. In their longevity, these soaps attract loyal audiences.

It is possible to discern four types of soap opera shown on British television. First, there are those British-produced programmes, *Coronation Street*, *Brookside* and *EastEnders*, which are shown at prime time two or three times a week. These are often noted for their gritty realism and depictions of everyday, and often working-class, life. Second, there are American imports, *E.R.* and *Chicago Hope* for example, shown in the evening and usually once a week. *Dallas* and *Dynasty*, shown some ten years ago, are probably the most famous examples of this type. Third, there are those programmes, largely imported, commonly from Australia, that are shown during the day. Examples of these are *Neighbours* and *Home and Away*. *Emmerdale*, shown in the early evening, is an example of

Figure 3.1 *Inside Soap* magazine, March 1995

the fourth category. Both these last two categories of programme tend to be made with low budgets and the plots are organized almost exclusively around family matters. While there are important differences between these four types of soap opera, the similarities are more significant. It is helpful to discuss the similarities and differences under two headings – *formal* qualities of the narrative style, and the themes dealt with.

Narrative form and structure

The most obvious characteristic of soap opera is the lack of narrative closure (see the section on narrative in chapter 2). Soaps do not have a beginning and an end like most novels or films. They are instead continuous serials composed of several different stories told simultaneously. Some of these individual stories may be brought to an end, perhaps by the resolution of a crisis, but the soap itself is rarely concluded. Even when a television company decides to stop the making of a particular soap, it may not always do so by bringing every story to a narrative conclusion (although in the case of *Eldorado* there was such a conclusion). One result of this absence of narrative closure is a lack of tension generated by the plot itself. Producers of soap opera sometimes get round this problem by the use of cliffhangers, referred to earlier. The intriguing thing about the use of cliffhangers in soap opera, however, is that often, because of information given earlier in the story, the audience already knows what the answer to the cliffhanger will be. For example, Grant in *EastEnders* learned of the infidelity of his wife Sharon with his brother Phil from a tape-recording. In a number of episodes he was prevented from playing the tape. Each time this happened the audience was kept in suspense as to what he would do when he found out. At the same time the audience already knew what was on the tape. As a rule it is not the *plot* that is providing the suspense here but the *characters*. Suspense is generated by doubts and uncertainties as to how the characters will deal with unexpected or difficult events and how they will develop and fill out as a result. In this respect, as Glaessner (1990) points out, soap opera is very different from a series (*Peak Practice* would be an example) and from a situation comedy (*As Time Goes By*). In the former, in each episode the narrative problem is resolved and the relationships between the characters have been restored to their former state. In the next episode the same protagonists will appear with much the same characteristics. In the latter, there may be some resolution of whatever crisis provoked the comic tension, but, again, the characters do not change or develop from one episode to another. Indeed the comedy often results from the very *un*changing nature of the characters.

The importance of character in soap opera is bound up with a second feature of narrative structure – the role of time. In series like *One Foot in the Grave*, the characters have no history and apparently no memory of what happened last week. In soap opera, such a history is of crucial importance to character development. Soap characters build up experience, acquire a *history*, which is shared with the audience, and they remember events in the past as do the audience. Consistency of character is therefore of much more importance in soap opera than it is in situation comedy. But it is not only history which is important in soap opera, it is also the passage of time in general. As Geraghty (1991) points out, it is a 'sense of endless but organized time which characterizes soap opera' (p. 11). Soap time is of an indefinite future which rolls forwards endlessly. Even events which might provide some end are the cause of more activity. A wedding, for example, does not close off the narrative but provokes further stories about setting up house, having children, or even divorce (Geraghty, 1981). Although endless, time is not haphazard. It is *organized* in such a way that it matches everyday life. There are fewer jumps in time than there are in other television fictional forms, a requirement often dictated by the needs of narrative resolution. Instead it is assumed that time is passing in *Coronation Street* in the same way as it passes in the everyday lives of the audience *and* is passing when the programme is not on. It is true that the American prime-time soaps (*Dallas* or *Dynasty* for example) do not depend so much on matching 'soap time' to 'audience time', but there is still a minimal attempt to do so (Geraghty, 1991).

A third feature of narrative structure in soap opera is its adherence to the conventions of *realism* (see chapter 2 for a discussion of this concept, especially the quotations from Jordan (1981) on pp. 28–9). The essence of the realist mode is that soap opera reflects how life really is lived. This, indeed, is the claim that the producers of soaps often make for their programmes. For example, the makers of both *EastEnders* and *Brookside* compared their realism favourably with the lack of realism in the settings of *Coronation Street* (Geraghty, 1991). As I pointed out in chapter 2, it is not really possible to accept that any soap opera can be the correct description of reality. They are all *versions* of the way that people live. The point is that realism is a *convention* whose techniques are designed to persuade the viewer that this is everyday life that is being portrayed.

At the same time, British soaps are not totally immersed in the realist form, since they often flirt with other forms – caricature and melodrama chiefly (see Longhurst, 1987). In the former, characters are presented not in a 'natural' way but as exaggerated portraits that unduly emphasize certain features. Particular characters almost always play that role. Reg Holdsworth, for example, carries vanity and self-seeking to extremes while pretending to a wholly inappropriate man-of-the-world image. Other characters may depart from realist conventions for a while only and may oscillate between realism and caricature even within a single episode. Mavis and Derek in *Coronation Street* exemplify this characteristic, both when appearing individually and in their relationship with each other. Melodramas present action not in a realist way but in an *excessive* way, bringing a great deal of emotion to every scene, far in excess of what is justified, an emphasis on the extraordinary over the ordinary. All soaps have melodramatic aspects. Close-up shots, for example, will dramatically emphasize what a character is feeling or expressing (Modleski, 1984). On the other hand, some soaps are much more melodramatic than others. American prime-time examples, such as *Dallas* or *Dynasty*, use melodramatic conventions much more than their realist British equivalents (Ang, 1985).

What are Soap Operas About?

It is not only the narrative structure that distinguishes soap opera from other television genres, but also the content, the kinds of theme that are deployed, and hence the kind of audience that is assumed. One may identify four major themes in soap opera, some of which will be emphasized more than others by particular programmes.

First, soaps describe the ordinary, everyday world. For the British soaps, this is stressed right from the beginning of each episode. As I have already said, the opening scenes are of ordinary street events with ordinary people doing everyday things – delivering milk, playing in the street. This is very much part of the realism described earlier. The settings used are those of everyday life – sitting rooms, cafés, pubs – and the action is largely mediated through conversations (the stuff of everyday life) that take place there. One might contrast this everyday quality with, say, police series in which it is the *extra*ordinary that is stressed. Again, there are differences between American and British soaps in this respect. American programmes, partly in association with their melodramatic qualities, are much more bound up with the unusual, whether it be high-level business dealings, which will be foreign to the everyday experience of most viewers, or trips in space ships, which are even rarer.

Second, the soap world is very much a woman's world. It is essentially organized around the private world of home rather than the public world of work. As I pointed out earlier, much of the action in soaps takes place in domestic settings. It is true that quite a few scenes are set in places of work or of public gathering – pubs or cafés, offices or factories. However, these public settings are not used to examine public *issues*, like class, wealth or the organization of power. They are instead utilized to show the relationships between characters who might not come across each other in private, domestic contexts. They are, as Longhurst (1987) points out, apparently public spaces which are really extensions of private ones. Even relationships between employer and employee are presented not so much as business, management or employee relationships but as opportunities for the development of personal issues (as in the relationship between Bet and her bar staff in the Rover's Return in *Coronation Street*). It is true that the American soaps, particularly *Dallas* or *Dynasty*, are much concerned with the intricacies of business. But again, this is presented in a particular way which essentially sees this public sphere *through* the concerns of the private. Therefore, the business dealings are personalized or heavily intertwined with family matters.

Soaps are concerned with the private sphere and they are also orientated around *personal and emotional* life. They are organized around the relationships, feelings and motivations of individuals, on the one hand, and the commentary that others make on these features, on the other. In our society, these are all seen as the province of women. As Geraghty (1991) says:

> For it is still women who are deemed to carry the responsibility for emotional relationships in our society – who keep the home, look after the children, write the letters or make the phone calls to absent friends, seek advice on how to solve problems, consult magazines on how to respond 'better' to the demands made on them. It is this engagement with the personal which is central to women's involvement with soaps. (p. 42)

Similarly, Brunsdon (1983) argues that in depicting a world interested in the conduct of personal life, soap operas presume a certain cultural competence on the part of their largely female audience. 'It is the culturally constructed skills of femininity – sensitivity, perception, intuition and the necessary privileging of the concerns of personal life – which are both called on and practiced in the genre' (p. 81). Without these skills of knowing about, and being able to judge, personal life, Brunsdon argues, it is difficult to appreciate soap opera fully.

Another way in which soap opera provides a woman's world is in its organization around very strong female characters. All soaps, especially the British ones, are full of strong women and weak, devious or immoral men. Soaps show that it is the women who are powerful in the private, personal sphere, and the story lines are largely, though not always, driven along by the actions or feelings of women. Again there is a contrast with 'males' tales' like thrillers or police series, in which men are the central characters who make things happen, who drive the narrative.

It is important to note that the women's world of soaps is presented *sympathetically*. The dilemmas of personal relationships and the significance of emotional life are given great importance. Again there is a contrast with males' tales, in which female qualities are often derided as mere hysteria and women are portrayed as inactive in the public sphere in which men move.

A third soap theme is the importance of the family and household, a feature clearly related to the first two themes. Although many characters are not involved in standard nuclear families (parents and children in the same house), they mostly do live with a partner, and story lines are organized around family problems which may involve many characters in different households. Indeed, in many British soap operas it almost seems as though everybody who appears is related to someone else. In *EastEnders*, for example, many of the characters are related in one way or another to the Beale family. In this emphasis on family there are differences between American and British soaps. In Geraghty's (1991) view, American soaps present a family structure that is essentially patriarchal in that men *appear* to be the dominant element. In practice, however, this patriarchal dominance is persistently challenged by strong women and is consequently always uncertain. British soaps, by contrast, have a matriarchal structure in which women are the active, dominant figures and men are weak and unreliable. Furthermore, as Glaessner (1990) points out, British soaps tend to locate families firmly in the local community. The net effect is to strengthen further the role of women by giving them an independent role in the community.

The role of community is a fourth theme found in soap opera, although almost exclusively in British programmes. They celebrate a community spirit in which, despite savage disagreements and quarrels, people do help each other. For example, in *EastEnders*, Pat took over the Queen Vic for Sharon after Grant's conduct forced her to leave. Indeed, it is almost as if the selfish or cantankerous characters reinforce the sense of community, since they can suddenly behave well when it is demanded of them, or collective sentiment can overwhelm or defeat their schemes. Such mutual help is supported, and made possible, by the detailed knowledge that the characters have of each other – a knowledge shared with the audience – and of the dense and close-packed way in which they live their lives.

A number of factors create this sense of community. Most obviously, a great deal of the action takes place between people who are not members of the same family but who are neighbours and friends. Individuals then function as 'characters' in the community rather than largely in the family as in American soaps. There are therefore weak men (Derek Wilton), strong, mothering women (Rita Fairclough), devious men (Barry Grant), headstrong younger women (Beth Jordache), erratic and immature younger men (Mike Dixon), and the grandmother and grandfather figures (Blossom and Jules from *EastEnders*). (Interestingly, it is very difficult to describe the roles that these characters play in the community in terms which are not ultimately derived from the family structure.) As Jordan (1981) points out, these character types may be played by several individual characters. Relationships between characters in the community take place directly between them, but it is very important that other members of the community comment on them. Gossip thus plays an important role and functions as another bridge between the audience and the soap opera, since the audience will also be commenting on the characters.

At the same time, the community has a long history. People do come and go, but it is assumed that most have lived there a long time. References are made to the past and, of course, the audience knows of that past. This history is strengthened by the sense of place. The British soaps are notoriously regional in their flavour; *Coronation Street* could be nowhere else but Salford, *EastEnders* the East End of London, and *Brookside* Liverpool. They are all invested with a powerful sense of regional and local loyalty which is signalled by the opening scenes of all three. *EastEnders* begins with a map of London, *Brookside* with shots of Liverpool with well-known local buildings, and *Coronation Street* with rows of back-to-back houses which could only be in the north. All these factors are reinforced by a less obvious feature – the strongly marked distinction between inside and outside (Longhurst, 1987). Despite the quarrels that regularly mark community life, and which provide much of the plot, the community is *internally* fairly harmonious. The world *outside* the community, by contrast, is a source of trouble and more serious strife. Events occurring outside the community have tragic consequences on its inhabitants; characters introduced from outside are often very disruptive; terrible things happen to characters who, even temporarily, stray outside the boundaries of the community. So, Pete Beale leaves Albert Square in *EastEnders* and ends up dead, while a virus brought back from Africa devastates Brookside Close.

The combination of a particular narrative structure and a particular set of themes produces in the audience, or is likely to produce in the audience, a sense of both distance and involvement. Audiences can be deeply engaged, talking about the characters as if they were real people and speculating on what will happen next. At the same time, they can also be distant from the soap, aware of the generic conventions, criticizing the acting, or discussing the plausibility of story lines. Audiences can, simultaneously, be inside the story, treating it almost like life, and outside, aware that it is, after all, just a story. For further discussion of this point see chapter 6. It is important to note that television producers are, themselves, well aware of this tension. As I have already indicated, besides the realism of the soap opera (drawing in) there is also melodrama and occasional parody (distancing).

Changing Soaps?

In the discussion of soap opera so far it is clear that there are substantial differences within the genre, especially between American and British varieties and between daytime and prime-time programmes. Some of these differences may be ascribed to cultural attributes and some may be attributed to differences in the types of audience. Audiences for soaps are changing and in ways that one does not entirely expect. Thus, it may be obvious that there is a higher proportion of men in the audience for prime-time soaps than for the daytime variety. Even for daytime soaps in the United States, however, 30 per cent of the audience is male, 45 per cent is young (18–34 years old) and 44 per cent of the women work full- or part-time (Brown, 1994).

Perhaps as a result of a changing audience, soap opera may be changing. Male characters are being treated more sympathetically, or at least their feelings, relationships and actions are investigated and dealt with as extensively as the women characters'. This has been particularly true in *Brookside* and *EastEnders* and in the American soaps. Young people figure more prominently, Bianca Jackson and Rachel Jordache for example, and a whole sub-genre of soaps, largely imported, has appeared to cater for the teenage market. There is more 'action' – religious cults and sieges in *Brookside, EastEnders'* frequent use of crime and criminals as plot devices. The soap world is no longer quite so safe. Lastly, the boundaries between the soap opera form and other genres are becoming more blurred, a general characteristic of television noted earlier in this chapter. For example, *Cheers* shows the soap world seeping out into situation comedy. As Geraghty (1991) notes, some of these changes may put at risk the continuance of soap opera as a woman's genre.

The reader should remember at this point that so far the discussion of soap opera has been confined to their *textual* characteristics. There is discussion of their production in chapter 5 and of their audience in chapters 6 and 7.

The News

News programmes on television are important. They have a high status within the television industry, so that there is competition to work in that area. They have a high public visibility, so that they may attract accusations of bias from many different quarters. They are broadcast several times a day and form a substantial part of television output. They attract substantial viewing figures. The main BBC news at 9.00 p.m., for instance, attracts an average of nine million viewers, although this can fluctuate a good deal depending on what is in the news at the time. Table 3.1 contrasts the viewing figures in a relatively quiet week in 1988 with the week in which a Pan Am jet was blown up by a terrorist bomb and crashed on Lockerbie, killing everyone on board.

This exposure to television news implies that many people are dependent on television for their ideas about what is going on in the world. As a source of international, regional and local news, television is more important than newspapers and radio. In a recent survey, 69 per cent of respondents mentioned television first as their main source of news (Gunter et al., 1994). Furthermore, television is thought to be more reliable. In the same study, some three-

Table 3.1   Quiet and busy weeks in television news

The Quiet Week (28 November to 3 December 1988)						
Programme	28/11	29/11	30/11	1/12	2/12	3/12
BBC 9 O'clock News (in millions)	9.4	7.9	6.5	5.9	7.4	7.4
ITN News at Ten (in millions)	5.4	8.8	8.1	8.6	6.6	7.5

The Not Quiet Week (19 December to 24 December 1988)						
Programme	19/12	20/12	21/12	22/12	23/12	24/12
BBC 9 O'clock News (in millions)	13.1	9.0	13.0	10.0	9.7	11.0
ITN News at Ten (in millions)	5.0	8.4	13.0	9.9	7.9	8.87

Source: Wallis and Baran, 1990, p. 58

quarters of the sample believed that television was the most complete, accurate, unbiased, quick and clear source of reporting of events of national and international significance. Even for events of regional and local importance some half of the sample made the same judgements, although newspapers were more significant for these events than for national and international news items. Gunter et al. also show that television is gaining over other media over time, especially over newspapers of all kinds, in public perceptions of reliability.

The starting point for any analysis of television news is the relationship between the flow of events in the world and the news programme. The latter is constructed out of the former. It is impossible to represent on our television screens the sheer multiplicity of events that occur every day even in the immediate locality, let alone in the nation or the world. News programmes have to *make sense* of this multiplicity of events, and in this way television is no different from any other news medium. This sense-making activity is a *construction*; it involves, for example, deciding what *is* news and what is not, or how to present a news item so that it can be understood by a very diverse audience.

This may seem a blindingly obvious point. Yet it is also one that is a source of misunderstanding between journalists who work in television and those who analyse it (see, Goodwin, 1990; Schudson, 1991). Journalists tend to see it as automatically an accusation of bias in reporting, while media researchers see it as a feature that is a necessary consequence of news gathering and presenting. The difficulties arise most acutely when arguing that the news is constructed in very particular ways with particular consequences.

One of the features of television news as a genre is therefore the necessity to make sense of what happens in the world. It is useful to refer to the devices used in this task by Fiske's (1987) term 'strategies of containment'. Four such strategies are of particular importance. First, events are selected for commentary because they fit into certain categories. Galtung and Ruge (1973), for example, argue that twelve factors determine whether events are newsworthy. I take the most important of these.

1   Newsworthy events tend to be recent and of a frequency that fits in with the production schedules of television. So, the news, on the whole, works to a 24-hour cycle. It tends to pick up events that occur in that cycle while frequently ignoring the *history* of those events. Thus, a government minister complained recently that television news reported the decision to close a hospital but paid no attention to the building of new hospitals.

2   There has to be a measure of *cultural proximity* in news items. What appears on British television has to be meaningful in terms of British culture.

3   Within the limits of the second feature, news items have to be surprising. What is newsworthy is what disrupts that which is assumed to be the normal course of life. Routine events are not of interest, but the sudden, unpredictable, or deviant are.

4   The more the event concerns elite nations or elite individuals, the more probable it is that it will become a news item. The concentration is on people and events in the public eye, not on the everyday, private sphere. As Galtung and Ruge point out, news about elite individuals is often taken as symbolic of what is happening to everyone in a society. The way in which television news picks out the extramarital affairs of Tory MPs and ministers has something to say about family life in general. 'Elite people are available to serve as objects of general identification, not only because of their intrinsic importance' (p. 66).

5   The more the event can be seen in personal terms, the more likely it is to serve as a news item. It is more newsworthy to treat an event as produced by a named (and photographed) individual than it is to see it as caused by 'social forces', for instance. So, the collapse of Baring's bank in February 1995 could be given more effective news value because it could be presented as allegedly the result of the activities of one trader, Mr Leeson.

6   Lastly, and in many ways most importantly, the more negative
     an event is in its consequences, the more likely it will be that it
     will become a news item. The news, as many often say, is fre-
     quently bad news. This leads to a stress on such topics as social
     conflict, crime, or natural disasters.

In sum, television news filters the welter of events in the world by
means of certain *news values*. If some happening fits in with these
values, it is likely to be reported. If it does not, it is likely to be
missed. It is important to stress again that the presence of these
news values is a *necessary* part of any news-gathering process. It is
literally impossible to cope with the flow of events without some
means of separating out the important ones. Of course, the use of
such filters will mean that, from time to time, television misses a
story which subsequently becomes important. An example of this is
given by Philo (1993). Philo is interested in explaining how the
Western media in general, and British television in particular, chose
to report the Ethiopian famine of late 1984 and 1985 so long after it
had been predicted. For up to a year some journalists and many aid
workers had been trying to call attention to the desperate plight of
the people of Ethiopia. However, the news values of television prevented any significant taking up of the story. Ethiopia is a third-
world country which is not culturally proximate to Britain.
Furthermore, it is difficult to make a story out of a *continuing* crisis.
The events could only become news when they could be sufficiently
dramatized, when something surprising (and negative) had happened which could be contained within the news-gathering cycle.
The result is that the relatively sudden elevation of the famine in the
news was a fairly random event triggered off by a particular journalist's activities and turning a continuous process into a news event.
Philo points to an important additional feature of the way that news
values worked in this case. Once one television network had covered
the story, it was covered by all the media. In a situation in which
television stations are competing with each other, they take their
news values *from each other*. Gans (1980) points to similar news values operating in American television news. In particular, he suggests
that ethnocentrism, altruistic democracy, responsible capitalism,
small-town pastoralism, individualism, moderatism, social order
and national leadership are all issues around which the news-gathering process is organized.

A second strategy of containment is *objectivity*. Television news
presents itself as a mirror of reality; it simply reports what is there.

In this sense, television news is simply borrowing the conventions of realism, discussed in chapter 2. The 'hand of the producer' does not appear in news programmes and events *seem* therefore to come at us unselected and uninterpreted. Fiske (1987) connects this feature with two other aspects of television news – authenticity and immediacy. What is reported, because there seems to be nothing else between us and the events, must be true – authentic. Further, partly because of the speed of news gathering, news reaches us very quickly; there is a real compression of time and space. It is worth noting that this naturalness, objectivity, of television does not happen automatically. As Winston (1993) points out, it has had to be worked at. Television producers have evolved a manner of presenting television news over a number of years. In its origins, television news owes more to the conventions of radio, the newsreel and the printed word, all of which gave the older news programmes a stilted, unreal feel which, to audiences reared on modern televisual conventions, seems very *unnatural*.

Thirdly, television journalists do not go out into the world unequipped. On the contrary, they go with a set of assumptions, or *frames*, which provide a way of organizing and filtering the information that they receive and which they then transmit in programmes. Frames may be defined as 'persistent patterns of cognition, interpretation, and presentation, of selection, emphasis and exclusion, by which symbol-handlers routinely organize discourse' (Gitlin, 1982, p. 7, quoted in Hallin, 1994, p. 81). For example, Hallin (1994) argues that a great deal of American television news until fairly recently was organized by what he calls a Cold War frame. Thus the reporting of the war in Vietnam in the 1960s and 1970s was presented with assumptions that the real story was that this was effectively a war between the United States (good) and the Soviet Union (bad). The issue was the stopping of communism not the legitimate rights of a small nation. The reporting of events in Central America, particularly El Salvador, in the early 1980s, on the other hand, was no longer determined by this frame. Journalists, heavily influenced by what had happened in Vietnam, now treated the Cold War account as just one among many, and were just as likely to see events as determined not by the hidden hand of Soviet Russia but by the desire of the people of El Salvador to improve their lot in life. The distinction between news values and framing is a little slippery. News values, however, determine *what* items will appear while framing determines *how* they will be presented.

A fourth strategy of containment involves the use of narrative.

Fiske (1987) argues for the utility of Todorov's theory of narrative (see chapter 2) in which 'a state of equilibrium is disrupted, the forces of disruption are worked through until a resolution is reached, and another state of equilibrium is achieved which may differ from or be identical to the first. This constitutes the basic structure of a television news story, just as it does of a sitcom or a cop show' (p. 293). For Fiske, news is told as a story 'in which the forces of disruption are explored and their conflict with the social order is enacted' (p. 293). Journalists thus have a mechanism for organizing their material for presentation, for imposing order upon chaos. It should be said that there is considerable disagreement about the narrative structure of the news. For example, in chapter 2 I discussed Lewis's view (1991) that television news is non-narrative because of its origins in the conventions of print.

The existence of these strategies of containment is related to the demands of television news as a genre. It has simultaneously to be informing, objectively giving information about the day's events, and entertaining. In addition, on some channels at least, it has to be capable of delivering an audience for advertisers; it has to be commercial. At earlier points in this chapter, I have argued that one of the features of television is the way in which the boundaries between genres are becoming blurred. This is true of television news. On the one hand, other types of programme, documentaries and drama-documentaries for example, are adopting the information objective. On the other hand, television news is adopting more of the conventions of other genres. The pressure to entertain in particular is causing changes in the way the news is presented. From the headlines at the beginning to the human interest story at the end, the news is meant to entertain, sometimes even at the cost of information.

News programmes are often accused of bias and these accusations can come from both left and right political perspectives. The following lines, written on the walls of a lift at BBC Manchester following John Major's appearance on *Desert Island Discs*, illustrate this conviction:

> Rich Tories cannot
> Pay a fee to
> Get their propaganda
> On the BBC
>
> But seeing what
> the BEEB will do
> Unfee'd, there's
> No occasion to.
> (quoted in G. Williams, 1994, p. 70)

It is very important to realize that bias is not necessarily the same as the strategies of containment that I have described so far. The notion of bias refers to a systematic distortion in favour of one interest. The strategies of containment *may* result in bias. For example, the techniques of framing may all run in the same direction, and favour, let us say, the interest of employers as opposed to trade unionists. Such a coincidence of framings is sometimes referred to as *agenda setting* (McCombs and Shaw, 1972). To the extent that the television news sets the agenda, it effectively tells the viewers what are the relevant issues, the frames, and it becomes very difficult to think outside them.

At times it is perfectly obvious that the television news is biased. In countries such as Britain this typically arises in wartime or in other national crises. Governments may indeed try to extend this war mentality to other crises such as large-scale strikes and suggest that the media, by being 'objective' and interviewing both sides, are not being patriotic. For example, Eldridge notes that the BBC was much criticized by the Conservative government for its 'objectivity' at the time of the invasion of the Falklands by the Argentinians. In the view of these critics, television news was simply unpatriotic in taking this stance. As Margaret Thatcher said in Parliament:

> I know how strongly many people feel that the case for our country is not being put with sufficient vigour on certain – I do not say all – BBC programmes. The Chairman of the BBC has assured us, and has said in vigorous terms, that the BBC is not neutral on this point, and I hope his words will be heeded by the many who have responsibilities for standing up for our task force, our boys, our people and the cause of democracy. (quoted in Eldridge, 1993, p. 9)

It is still some distance, however, from the demonstration of bias in this sort of circumstance to the claim that the television news is biased in general. I turn now to an examination of the debate surrounding one sustained attempt to demonstrate just this sort of general bias.

The Glasgow University Media Group

In a series of studies the Glasgow University Media Group (GUMG: 1976, 1980, 1982, 1985, 1993) set out to show how the television news is partial. As the first chapter of their most recent publication puts it:

> One of the questions pursued in the Glasgow research has been to ask what it is that takes place in British television news under the banner of objectivity, impartiality, and neutrality. The BBC's licence requires it to refrain from editorializing on its news programmes and the Independent Broadcasting Act of 1973 laid down the ruling that due impartiality must be preserved on the part of persons providing programmes as regards to matters of political or industrial controversy or relating to current public policy. (Eldridge, 1993, p. 3)

And the Group's answer to this question is fairly unequivocal: 'Our conclusion was that television is biased to the extent that it violates its formal obligations to give a balanced account' (Glasgow University Media Group, 1982, p. xi).

GUMG's conclusions are based on a detailed content analysis of a large number of news reports on industrial relations, the behaviour of the economy, and war and peace. In effect, they hold to the view of television news as agenda setting discussed earlier in this chapter.

> Our own view is that television cannot exclusively shape people's thoughts or actions. Nonetheless it has a profound effect, because it has the power to tell people the *order* in which to think about events and issues. In other words it 'sets the agenda', decides what is important and what will be featured. More crucially, it very largely decides what people will think *with*: television controls the crucial information with which we make up our minds about the world. (1982, p. 1)

The television news therefore both includes and excludes. It includes certain views and information and gives those a prominent position. At the same time it excludes other, perhaps contrary, opinions and thereby makes them invisible to the viewer. This process happens in a number of different ways. Most important, the news *defines the issue*, decides what is important, and organizes its presentation in terms of those news values. For example, during the 1970s there was a public debate about Britain's poor economic performance and, in particular, the high rates of inflation. There were several possible explanations for inflation but the television news preferred one to the virtual exclusion of others. GUMG's study of the first four months of 1975 showed that statements saying that wages were the main cause outnumbered by eight to one those reports that contradicted that view. As a result, great prominence was given to the argument that the way to reduce inflation was to keep wage settlements down. In this period, there were 287 occasions when arguments that wage restraint was the proper policy were presented as against the 17 times that contrary arguments were put. Similarly, in the late 1970s, there was extensive argument about the apparently poor performance of British Leyland, a company then manufacturing Austin, Morris, Triumph and Jaguar motor cars. There were two (at least) competing explanations of this – low investment by the company and disruptive behaviour by the workers, particularly their strikes. The television news preferred the latter explanation, as can be seen from box 2.

The particular definition of the issue adopted by the news will usually coincide with the official view of the matter. Official figures, whether they be company directors or politicians, are given more space and time to air their views and are treated with more respect by interviewers than, say, employees. At times, indeed, people like

Box 2 Findings of the Glasgow University Media Group

– In the 13 weeks of the Glasgow dustcart drivers' strike, which was reported in 102 bulletins and included 20 interviews, not once did a striker get to state his case nationally in an interview.

– In the same story from Glasgow, the causes of the strike were mentioned only 11 times out of 40 items on BBC 1, 6 times out of 19 on BBC 2 and 19 times out of 43 mentions on ITN.

– In January 1975 a widely reported speech by the Prime Minister which referred to 'manifestly avoidable stoppages of production' caused by management and labour was transformed in 29 later references, and made to apply to the workforce alone. This was part of the general view that 'the ills of British Leyland' could be laid substantially at the door of the labour force.

– In the coverage of the strike by engine tuners at Cowley, as against BBC 1's 22 references to Leyland's 'strike problem', there were only 5 references to 'management failings' and 1 to the Company's investment record. On BBC 2 there were 8 references to strikes as against 3 to management and 2 to investment; on ITN 33 to strikes, 8 to management, and none to investment.

– In the first four months of 1975 there were 17 occasions when views were presented on the news against the government's policy of wage restraint and lower wages as a solution to the economic crisis. There were 287 occasions when views supporting these policies were broadcast.

Source: Glasgow University Media Group (1982), p. 7

this, who may well be deeply involved, are seen almost as neutral commentators giving an objective view. Official sources and official statistics have a privileged position in the television news, in part because journalists are dependent on them for information. The corollary is that dissenting or oppositional opinions do not get such exposure. For example, in coverage of an industrial dispute involving dustcart drivers in Glasgow, which left a great deal of rubbish uncollected in the street, not one striker was interviewed although ten others, largely figures of authority, were, some of them several times. Of course, people who hold other views are occasionally represented on the news. However, 'information which contradicts the dominant view, if it appears at all, exists as fragments and is never explored by news personnel as a rational alternative explanation' (1982, p. 29). Alternative versions of reality are not then used to

structure interviews or organize the way in which an item is presented. Figures of authority tend to be interviewed in authoritative situations, in offices for instance. Others, especially if they are strikers,
will be interviewed in circumstances which scarcely lend weight to
what they say, in the street for example. Methods of news presentation of this kind are reinforced by the language used. Strikers are
characterized by television news as making 'demands', while the
management makes (the milder) 'offers'.

The work of the Glasgow University Media Group has been very
influential. Detailed rather than speculative, it has done a great deal
to inform the debate about the content of television news and, in
particular, about the ideological effects of that news (see the discussion of ideology in chapter 2). However, it has also been the subject
of fierce criticism, most prominently from two rival empirical studies, Harrison (1985) and Cumberbatch et al. (1986).

Harrison's book is a restudy of the television coverage of the
events on which GUMG based their work. It consists of an analysis
of the transcripts and other documents relating to the ITN news
coverage of strikes. At one level Harrison simply disagrees with
GUMG about the analysis of the data. He suggests that shop-floor
views are presented and background information is given. While one
of GUMG's most telling points was that the news does not explain
why strikes happen, and thus gives the impression that they are random events perpetrated by troublemakers, Harrison shows that the
news does present the viewer with the causes of strikes. The language of television reports does not all go one way. For example, in
the treatment of one strike, ITN news used the word 'threat' more
often applied to management activities than to labour. From this,
Harrison draws the conclusion that GUMG do not make clear what
yardstick is being used to make their judgements. 'One of the worst
difficulties in assessing the Glasgow critique is the repeated
condemnation of television in relation to standards that are never
clearly specified' (p. 68). Without such standards of judgement
GUMG's reading of the television news is just that, one partial
reading among many others.

There are more fundamental issues at stake in Harrison's disagreement with GUMG, however. First, Harrison agrees with the
group about the importance of news values. Of course journalists
work with some sense of what is important, which determines which
items are treated as news and which are not. However, Harrison's
point is that these news values do not cohere in such a way as to discriminate against trade unions and in favour of management. 'It is a

commonplace that news is more readily concerned with negative than positive occurrences, with events more than non-events, processes or situations' (p. 139). Trouble is much more likely to be reported than harmony. Under certain circumstances, such news values will also discriminate against management. To take a more recent example, television news in the early months of 1995 was preoccupied with the very large pay rises awarded to the directors of privatized companies. Second, television news is produced under great pressure and little time is given to each item. Harrison calculates that the average time given to news items covering industrial disputes during the period of this study was 70 seconds. However, this does not discriminate against trade unions, although it may well discriminate against the proper understanding of all news items. The difficulty created by the speed of news coverage is not the presence of a dominant frame organizing the presentation, but the absence of a frame at all. Third, any apparent partiality of the news may be rather a partiality built into what is being reported. If blame is to be attached, it belongs to society rather than the television programmes that seek to describe it. For example, trade unions are, as a rule, organizations that are much more public and accessible to the media than private companies, which tend to be rather more secretive. The simple result is that their doings will be more exposed to media investigation, and this is hardly the fault of the television producers.

One possibility that emerges out of the debate between GUMG and Harrison is that the television news has certain *central tendencies*. Broadcasters have interpreted the BBC Charter commitment to impartiality in terms of the need to defend certain features of British life. The BBC does not see itself as being impartial about parliamentary democracy, or terrorism, or religious or political extremism. Instead, it has a most definite view on these matters (see Schlesinger, 1978). The difficulty is that such a veneration of parliamentary institutions, however much it represents the consensus of opinion in Britain, may well have the effect of discriminating against extra-parliamentary politics of various kinds. In an influential piece on radio, although its conclusions apply to television with equal force, Hall (1973) argues that there is an unwitting bias in broadcasting which 'comes through in terms of who is or who is not accorded the status of an accredited witness; in tones of voice; in the set-up of studio confrontations; in the assumptions which underlie the questions asked or not asked; in terms of the analytical concepts which serve informally to link events to causes; in what passes for explanation' (p. 88). The bias can be mapped out by identifying three areas within which the news tends to operate. In the area of *consensus* there is widespread agreement about how to treat topics because they touch on the central institutions or values of British society. The area of *toleration* includes what Hall calls 'Home Office' issues, where widespread agreement is less sure. Social questions, abortion, single parents, divorce, all tend to receive tolerant and even sympathetic treatment simply because producers can assume a measure of public sympathy. Outside these topics comes the area of *conflict*, which will encompass travellers, squatters, strikers, terrorists, hijackers. In dealing with these issues, Hall notes, interviewers, presenters and reporters are much sharper and touchier:

> We are now at the crunch. For the groups and events upon which, increasingly, the media are required to comment and report, are the groups in conflict with this consensual style of politics. *But* these are precisely the forms of political and civil action which the media by virtue of their submission to the consensus, are consistently unable to deal with, comprehend or interpret. The nervousness one has observed in the treatment of these issues reflects the basic contradiction between the manifestations which the media are called on to explain and interpret, and the conceptual/evaluative/interpretative framework which they have available to them. (p. 90)

Gans (1980) makes a similar point about the way in which the American news occupies a middle ground:

> In its advocacy of altruistic and official democracy, the news defends a mixture of liberal and conservative values, but its conception of responsible capitalism comes closest to what I describe as right-leaning liberalism .. On the other hand, in its respect for tradition and its nostalgia for pastoralism and rugged individualism, the news is unabashedly conservative, as it is also both in its defense of the social order and and its faith in leadership. If the news has to be pigeonholed ideologically, it is right-liberal or left-conservative. (p. 68)

A second study which bears on the conclusions of GUMG is by Cumberbatch et al. (1986). This is an investigation of television treatment of the miners' strike of 1984 and 1985 and aims specifically to 'describe the arena of debate in which the strike took place as defined by the main protagonists on television news, and to examine the vexed issue of bias in the news' (p. 6). The authors did a detailed content analysis of all the BBC *Nine O'Clock News* and ITN *News at Ten* broadcasts over a one-year period from March 1984. In addition, they carried out two surveys of audience opinion in the middle of that period.

If there is any one conclusion that Cumberbatch et al. come to, it is that the issue of bias is complex and there are elements of both bias and balance in television news, depending on what measure of bias one uses. In certain respects, then, they agree with GUMG's conclusions that the television news can be biased. For example, television cameras tended to be placed behind police lines when there was any conflict with strikers. This appeared to emphasize the police point of view and gave the impression that strikers initiated violence. Interviewing was not even-handed and the miners' leader, Arthur Scargill, was almost four times as likely to be interviewed in a critical fashion as the Coal Board chairman, Ian MacGregor. In the use of statistics, television news had a tendency to bias, in that it favoured the Coal Board. In a particularly significant incident, the 'Battle of Orgreave', the television news blamed the violence on the behaviour of the pickets, when the police video showed that it was due to the use of police horses. Perhaps most important of all:

> throughout the strike there was a tendency for the news to emphasize the conduct of the strike – the epiphenomenon of union ballots, talks and negotiations and picketing violence – rather than the causes of the dispute. Thus the economics of coal production amounted to only 2.5 per cent of the issues raised, while pit closures and redundancies accounted for a mere 1.2 per cent. This is hardly surprising given the event driven nature of news. As with war, it is the movement and progress of campaigns and battles that are followed. The conduct eclipses the causes as the story moves on. Violence on the picket line is easier to represent visually on the news than a pit closing down. (p. 135)

This conclusion, that television news privileges events over causes, is precisely that reached by GUMG. In other respects, however, the news was found by Cumberbatch et al. to be balanced. Occasions of misrepresentation, such as that following the Battle of Orgreave, were, and are, very rare. No one issue, and certainly not violence on the picket line, predominated over others. In the kind of language used there was no obvious bias. So, potentially disapproving adjectives or verbs were not used any more frequently in connection with Arthur Scargill than Ian MacGregor. Most important of all, Cumberbatch et al. did not find that the television news set an agenda for viewers in the way that GUMG suggest it does. In particular, viewers gave a quite different priority to issues from that which the news did. For example, pit closures and redundancies as an issue were thirteenth in terms of frequency in news broadcasts, yet this issue was judged by viewers to be the most important one in the strike.

The debate about the methods and conclusions of GUMG has continued. The journal *Media, Culture and Society*, for example, published an exchange of views which largely concentrated on issues of method, especially the sources of data and the drawbacks of content analysis (Philo, 1988; Barker, 1988; Cumberbatch et al., 1987; also Goodwin, 1990). So far my presentation of the argument has been almost entirely conducted at the level of the television text. This leaves unexplained a number of issues. In particular we need to describe the social processes that generate strategies of containment and that produce bias, if it exists, *and* the way that audiences respond to news programmes. These processes will be considered in chapters 5 and 7.

The Representation of Ethnicity and Gender

So far I have effectively been emphasizing the *differences* between television texts by using the concept of genre. There may, however, be some themes that cut across genres, and two obvious possibilities are ethnicity and gender.

There have been considerable changes in the depiction of race and ethnicity on television. Tulloch (1990b) argues that news and documentary programmes in the fifties, sixties and seventies effectively defined black people as 'problems'. Framings were organized around the issue of immigration and the alleged impact that (black) immigration was having on the provision of housing, employment and education in Britain. News values stressed conflict and the violence that resulted from time to time. In a good deal of drama of that period, soap opera, police series, situation comedy, for example, black faces did not appear very much. When they did, it tended to be in stereotypical – and despised – roles as criminals or in 'background' roles such as servants, singers or bus conductors. One study cited by Tulloch found in a survey of television in a six-week period in the late seventies that West Indian actors accounted for 5 per cent of appearances while Asians made up 1 per cent, a significant underrepresentation of Asians by comparison with the whole population. At the same time, black people were not well represented in television *production* except in ethnic minority programmes.

There are indications that this situation is changing. More black actors are appearing in television shows and there are more black presenters in news and current affairs broadcasting. Perhaps even more important, however, is the way in which black characters are depicted on television. No longer so stereotyped, black actors are playing 'ordinary' characters. They are policemen and women in *The Bill*, Mick Johnson in *Brookside*, and Gita, Sanjay and Alan in *EastEnders*. The same process appears to be happening in the United States, although with one marked and very important difference. In a study of *The Cosby Show*, Jhally and Lewis (1992) say:

> What makes *The Cosby Show* particularly worthy of consideration is the fact that all its leading characters are black. Although . . . *The Cosby Show* is no longer exceptional in its nonstereotypical portrayal of African Americans, it has shifted the TV world toward a new vision, a world in which blacks, and, moreover, *realistic* blacks, can be members of upper middle class society. (p. 31)

The number of black actors appearing on American television has increased. In the decade from the mid-seventies to the mid-eighties, the overall percentage of black characters increased from 7 to 10 per cent. But, at the same time, these characters became steadily more middle-class. On the rare occasions when they did appear, working-class black people still occupied relatively stereotyped and deviant roles. To some extent this is an effect of the tendency for American television grossly to overrepresent middle- or upper-class people. In this respect, indeed, American television is very different from British, in that much of British television gives realistic and sympathetic portrayals of working-class life. The result of the American emphasis, Jhally and Lewis argue, is to increase realistic representation of black people but at the cost of suppressing the facts of the class structure in American life. Actually most African Americans are not middle-class, and the failure to represent working-class blacks realistically will have serious consequences:

> The increasing number of images of black upper middle-class life, including and propelled by the Huxtables, do represent a reality of some sections of the black population. But they also crucially hide and distort how

the majority of black Americans are understood. This distortion leads to
the emergence of a new set of regressive racial beliefs. (p. 70)

With this last reservation, the new way of presenting black people
on television effectively says to the audience that black people are
just like white people. The troubles and joys of Constable Datta
from *The Bill* are much the same as those of any other character. As
Jhally and Lewis say: 'White families must be able to appreciate,
understand, and identify with the Huxtables without forgetting that
they are actually looking at a black family. It asks white viewers to
accept a black family as "one of them", united by commmonalities
rather than divided by race' (p. 36). Of course, sometimes black
characters are involved in events in a particular way simply because
they are black. Usually this arises out of the attempt to portray
racism. One story in *EastEnders* had Gita and Sanjay being persecut-
ed by racist bigots, for example. Despite these events, the dominant
pattern of involvement of black characters in British soap opera is
simply as participants in the everyday, routine life of the square or
the close. Naturally this tactic also has the effect of suppressing cultural difference.

While it can be argued that there is a new view of black people in
television drama of various kinds, news programmes do not altogether share in it. American television news tends to associate drugs
with black people some 50 per cent of the time, although only 15
per cent of drug users are black (Jhally and Lewis, 1992, p. 60). In
general black people are disproportionately likely to be portrayed as
criminal or deviant in other ways. In British television news, this
sort of representation is partly due to the generic qualities of news
broadcasting and the kinds of news value and framing employed.
Riots make good news coverage and the interaction between street
protest and ethnicity has clearly become a standard way in which to
frame the debate, even if a news broadcast may say that a particular
disturbance did *not* involve black people. In this sense civil distur-
bances have simply replaced immigration as a news framing. It is
still the case that the net effect is to cast black people as partly the
cause of trouble (Braham, 1982).

Earlier in this chapter I described how television soap opera represents women. In many ways this genre is like other 'women's'
genres, such as romantic fiction or Hollywood women's films of the
thirties, forties and fifties (Modleski, 1984). As Geraghty (1991)
puts it, the emphasis is on a central woman character; there is a
division between male and female spheres; the woman's pre-emi-

nence in the narrative is based on her understanding of emotion; physical action is not central; personal relationships are crucial:

> The importance of the other worlds which are at the heart of women's fiction is that they offer models of both happiness and grief and the opportunity thereby to rehearse the extremes of emotional feeling; they establish utopias in which emotional needs are imaginatively fulfilled or, more frighteningly, distopias in which the values of women's fiction are undermined and destroyed. (p. 108)

However, soap opera clearly is not the only way of representing women in television. The traditional 'males' tale', as represented in police series such as *The Sweeney* and science fiction series such as *Dr Who*, or in the many Western, thriller or police films shown on television, offers a very different image. In these dramas, the protagonist is male, individualistic, and active in solving problems which beset those around him. These qualities are very deliberately contrasted with those of women. Women defined as good are typically passive and helpless, emotional and even hysterical. They may attempt to help the hero but often end up having to be rescued. Those women who are active all too often turn out to be bad characters. The active, forceful qualities of the male hero are therefore pointed up by the passivity of the women – or their evil activity.

One obvious feature of the representation of gender in both women's and men's television drama is the conflict between men and women. If in males' tales women are weak and inactive, in female ones men are devious and manipulative (Abercrombie and Longhurst, 1991). Many television dramas almost seem to be about gender conflict. Much situation comedy, for example, revolves around situations in which men and women are set against each other. Every episode of *Coronation Street*, for example, routinely pits the men and women of various pairs against each other in terms of gendered qualities. Even the stable marriages in most soaps take the form of a suppressed war between men and women. Indeed it would be possible to argue that television is largely *about* gender and this emphasis derives from the fact that television is a domestic medium.

There are indications, however, that, just as the stereotyping of black people is now less marked, so too is the representation of both men and women. I have already noted the changing role of men in soap opera. But many traditional male programmes are also giving a different role to women. Women police officers are increasingly being treated as colleagues, even superiors, in programmes such as *Prime Suspect*. Clearly, if such a process is occurring it still has some way to go. Interestingly, though, it may owe something to changes in the notion of genre that I noted at the beginning of this chapter. Many of the programmes in which gender roles are less stereotypically separated are also those in which there is some breakdown of the traditional genre boundaries. For example, *The Bill* is moving towards a fusion of soap opera and police series, in which male and female characters may continue to emphasize different qualities, but they will not be so sharply differentiated and will not attract such extremes of positive and negative evaluation.

4

The Television Industry

The Development of Television

The first television broadcasts were made in Britain and the United States in the late 1920s and early 1930s. In these early experiments the picture quality was poor and the transmission range inadequate. Even so, systematic broadcasting began in both Britain and the United States by the middle of the 1930s. In 1936 there were 3000 television sets in London and 50 in New York. The development of television broadcasting was somewhat interrupted by the Second World War, especially in Britain. After the war, however, there was a rapid acceleration and in 1947 there were 100,000 sets in Britain. By 1980 virtually every household in Britain had a set. This is not an uncommon pattern of the diffusion of consumer goods, as figure 4.1 shows. Although Britain and the United States were early pioneers in the development of broadcast television, demand for the service has grown rapidly world-wide. As table 4.1 shows, in 1965 there were 192 million sets in the world, while in 1986 there were 710 million. Growth in sets per thousand population has not been quite so rapid and television ownership is, as one might expect, very unevenly distributed across the world.

In its beginnings in Britain television was heavily influenced by the way in which radio broadcasting had been set up in the early 1920s. Radio in Britain was moulded by the ideal of *public service* (see Scannell, 1990, on which much of this account is based). This ideal came from two sources, the state and the broadcasters. The government of the day argued that control over broadcasting should

Table 4.1   Ownership of television sets

Continents, major areas and groups of countries	Total television receivers (in millions)			Television receivers per thousand inhabitants		
	1965	1975	1986	1965	1975	1986
World total	192.0	414.0	710.0	57.0	102.0	145.0
Africa	0.6	2.5	15.0	1.9	6.2	25.0
Americas	84.0	160.0	268.0	182.0	286.0	397.0
Asia	24.0	57.0	138.0	13.0	25.0	48.0
Europe (incl. USSR)	81.0	189.0	280.0	120.0	260.0	362.0
Oceania	2.4	5.5	9.0	137.0	262.0	360.0
Developed countries	181.0	373.0	564.0	177.0	325.0	472.0
Developing countries	11.0	41.0	146.0	4.7	14.0	39.0
Africa (excl. Arab States)	0.1	0.6	5.7	0.4	2.0	13.0
Asia (excl. Arab States)	24.0	56.0	130.0	13.0	25.0	45.0
Arab States	0.9	3.4	17.0	8.4	24.0	85.0
North America	76.0	133.0	209.0	355.0	564.0	783.0
Latin America and the Caribbean	8.0	27.0	59.0	32.0	84.0	145.0

Source: Sreberny-Mohammadi (1991), quoting UNESCO Statistical Yearbook (1988)

lie ultimately with the state, but that it should be an indirect control via a licence to broadcast which would put particular obligations on the broadcaster. At the time, the broadcasters, particularly in the person of Sir John Reith, the first director-general of the BBC, who held the post until 1938, had strong views about the kind of service radio broadcasting should be. It should educate, bring the nation together as a moral community, promote the highest standards of taste, and, by the provision of information and argument, help to create a rational democracy. In order to fulfil this mission, broadcasting should be a monopoly able to ensure that standards were met. These views were effectively accepted and the British Broadcasting Corporation came into being in 1927. Such a mission clearly brought the BBC into a very close relationship with the state and this was, and has continued to be, an awkward one, as the newspaper story reproduced in box 3 shows.

Television broadcasting, located in the BBC, continued in the tradition of public service from its first broadcasts in 1936. However, its monopoly position was undermined in the mid-1950s by the introduction of commercial television, funded by advertising rather than the licence fee which provided the revenue for the

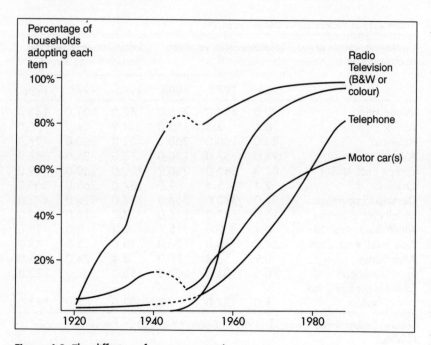

Figure 4.1 The diffusion of consumer goods
Source: Miles (1988), p. 38

BBC. This competition had a powerful effect on the BBC (see the essays in Corner, 1991a). Not only was there a change in the kinds of programme that were made – they became more 'popular' – but the share of the audience commanded by the BBC plunged dramatically, at one point as low as 20 per cent. Despite this element of commercial competition, however, the broadcasting of television still remained roughly within the public service tradition. Commercial television was regulated by an independent body – the Independent Television Authority – which was charged with the same kinds of public service aim that drove the BBC and was responsible for a high standard of programming. Indeed, the restrictions placed on commercial television greatly disappointed its advocates, who had hoped for more commercial freedom.

Many of the public service ideals also survived the movement to greater 'pluralism' in broadcasting in the late 1970s. This resulted in the formation of Channel 4 in 1980, which was charged with the responsibility of providing programming for minority groups not well served by the three existing channels (BBC 1, BBC 2 and

Box 3 PM backs Aitken in attack on BBC

Stephen Bates and Andrew Culf

The Prime Minister made it clear last night that he supported the stand of Jonathan Aitken, Chief Secretary to the Treasury, against alleged bias at the BBC despite misgivings from ministers about a renewed onslaught on the broadcasters.

Downing Street sources close to John Major said he was entirely comfortable with Mr Aitken's remarks. A senior Tory party source said: 'He supports those who have been seeking to persuade the BBC that they should act to uphold their statutory requirement to impartiality.'

Senior ministers, including accomplished media performers like Michael Heseltine and Douglas Hurd, believe a sustained campaign against the BBC could be counter-productive. Mr Aitken, speaking on Radio 4's World At One yesterday, renewed his attack, however, accusing broadcasters of arrogance and insisting he could cope with tough interviewing.

'The first person to make this criticism was the director-general of the BBC, John Birt, who criticised his own interviewers . . . I think there is a feeling around that some interviewers have got too big for their headsets,' he said.

Asked if his attack was motivated by uncomfortable personal experiences on the programme, he said: 'This is an extraordinary piece of misinformation and non-sense that I am personally unhappy. Far from it . . . I like the Today programme. I'm all in favour of interviewers who do put politicians on the spot.'

He received backing from John Gummer, the Environment Secretary and a veteran critic of the BBC: 'There is a distinction between tough questioning and the kind of questioning which does not give you the chance to answer and the kind of questioning which reveals particular views.'

Stephen Dorrell, the National Heritage Secretary, called for journalists to learn from their mistakes and asked opposition MPs: 'Is it really your case that all humankind is fallible except BBC interviewers?'

Chris Smith, Labour's heritage spokesman, accused some Tories of seeking to destabilise the BBC's coverage.

The BBC's defence remained robust. A spokesman said: 'We are determined to consider the agenda of programmes on an objective and impartial basis.' He denied that the BBC had sought to inflame the row by inviting Mr Aitken on to the World At One. The decision was taken by Kevin Marsh, the programme's editor.

'World At One took the view it was appropriate to invite Mr Aitken on to the programme to talk about the current state of the Tory party and the current public debate about politicians and the media.'

BBC radio's information office took 60 calls from listeners on Sunday, with 75 per cent supporting Mr Humphrys and 13 per cent expressing opposition.

Radio 5 Live's morning show, The Magazine, appeared uncowed by the Tory onslaught, devoting its phone-in to whether Mr Major should resign and interviewing John Carlisle, the Luton North MP, an outspoken critic of the Prime Minister.

Source: *The Guardian*, 28 March 1995 Reproduced by kind permission of *The Guardian*

ITV). However, the 1980s saw a major collapse of the moral, political, economic and social underpinnings of the ideals of public service broadcasting. As in so many other areas of social life, the government sought to deregulate – remove the controls over – the broadcasting industry and to bring in more competition, increasing the range of programming, all in the name of greater choice for the consumer of broadcasting. Many of these changes are enshrined in the 1990 Broadcasting Act, one of whose additional provisions was the creation of a third commercial channel, which is to be called Channel Five and is likely to start broadcasting in 1997.

It is important to stress that the changes in the broadcasting industry that began in the 1980s are fundamental and far-reaching. As Blumler (1991) says, they amount to:

the transformation of a major mass medium that had functioned in the same fashion for some thirty to forty years. Based on a single delivery system (broadcast air waves), television consisted of a small number of channels, programmed by a comparatively small circle of competitors for viewers' attention. The main sources of finance, lines of industry organization, and patterns of audience patronage were relatively stable. Those changes that did take place from time to time – in, for instance, the flow of revenues, distribution of audience favors, cycles of program, genre fashions, and regulatory controls – were all relatively minor, more marginal than systemic. In the last decade, however, a 'gale of creative destruction' has been unleashed on electonic media systems throughout the advanced industrial world (Schumpeter, 1942). An extraordinarily potent mix of technological, organizational, financial, and political factors has disrupted the prevailing, familiar patterns of such systems and forced their architects to re-examine and redeploy their resources. (p. 194)

This fundamental change has been produced by a variety of

factors in combination, as Blumler indicates. There are political and legislative changes that I have already described. There are important changes in the ownership and organization of media institutions and in the way that the work of television gets done. These are described in later sections of this chapter. There are also technological changes. The traditional means of supplying television programmes in both Britain and the United States is by broadcasting using the radio spectrum. The radio spectrum is a finite resource; if too many suppliers try to broadcast on it, the risk is that they will interfere with each other's transmissions. In both countries broadcasting of this kind was organized essentially by comparatively few organizations. From the 1970s onwards, however, this traditional technology was challenged by other means of supply of television.

The video-cassette recorder (VCR) was introduced and became largely a means of recording programmes for later viewing and for watching rented films. In 1985, 28 per cent of households had a videorecorder, while by 1990 59 per cent had one. Transmission via cable (laid underground) has also became increasingly important. This technology permits a much greater number of channels than broadcasting and has the potential to be used for a large number of purposes other than television. Negrine and Papathanassopoulos (1990) identify four phases in the development of cable. In the first phase, cable systems were merely used to relay broadcast television to homes that, for some reason or other, could not receive these transmissions directly. In the second phase, additional signals, usually from nearby areas, were retransmitted. This evolved into a third phase in which material not available from broadcast television was made available. This mostly consisted of films, although some cable companies have experimented with community programmes. Sometimes these programmes were provided directly by the cable companies, although more commonly they were re-diffused along cables having been originally provided to many operators by satellite. Some operators are just entering a fourth phase, in which they are exploiting extra revenues derived from advertisers or subscribers who are willing to pay extra for premium services such as recent films or sport. At the same time the cables are being used to provide more sophisticated communications facilities such as burglar alarm systems, teleshopping, and other forms of telephony.

Cable has proved fairly popular in the United States. More than half of the population has chosen to pay for cable services at a rate higher than the licence fee in many countries. The position in Europe is more mixed. In some countries the penetration is very high indeed. In Belgium, for example, 88 per cent of homes that have television are subscribers to cable. In Britain, the proportion is much lower at 15 per cent of homes with television, although by 1993 some fourteen million homes had the potential to be connected to cable television in that the cable passed their house.

The new technology that has attracted most attention, however, is satellite. Although satellites have high initial costs they can distribute over a very wide geographical area, as figure 4.2 shows. Despite a great deal of publicity, however, satellite systems have been slow to develop in Britain. It has been estimated that in 1992 some 10 or 11 per cent of homes with television in the United Kingdom had satellite dishes installed. The industry estimates that this will increase to some 30 per cent by the end of 1996 (*Cultural Trends*, 1992). It is very unclear what the outcome of the competition between cable and satellite will be. In many ways, cable has the advantage. It is a more reliable technology and it permits a much

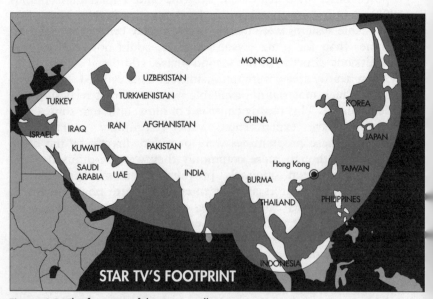

Figure 4.2 The footprint of the Star satellite
Source: G. Williams (1994), p. 35

greater range of uses. At present, however, and for some time to come, the real competition is not between satellite and cable, but between these two and *broadcast* television. British viewers, on the whole, have not taken to watching cable or satellite. Thus in 1990, each viewer in the country, on average, spent only 6 per cent of his or her total viewing time looking at cable, satellite or VCR replay *together*. The other 94 per cent was devoted to broadcast television from the four existing channels. Of course, this figure includes all those who do not have access to cable or satellite. Even those who do, however, do not seem dedicated to cable or satellite. For example, in those households equipped to receive satellite transmissions, 60 per cent of time was still spent viewing broadcast television.

The net effect of all these technological changes is that viewers have available to them a much larger number of channels. At the same time, the number of hours that viewers will be watching their television set has not increased, and certainly not in proportion to the number of different channels they can watch. It is very difficult to predict the effect that these changes will have, since, in Europe at least, they are comparatively new. Some lessons might be drawn from the United States, although one should be careful of such comparisons, for differences in national culture can be very important. Blumler (1991) describes five ways in which television production in the United States has been affected by 'a competitively driven multichannel television system' (p. 196). First, and most obviously, there is a great deal more competition between providers. Second, producers can no longer be sure what the audience is for their programmes. Further, there is clearly much more competition for limited audience attention and there is *some* evidence that audiences are 'channel hopping'; that is, they are not staying with any programme for any length of time but moving rapidly between different channels. Third, there is probably greater scope for innovative programming in an effort to establish a distinctive profile for a channel. There will, however, always be a tension between such programming and safer programmes which have a loyal audience. Fourth, television programmes are becoming more expensive to make, partly because of the competition for scarce programme-making talent. Fifth, it is not simply a competition for bigger audience shares or higher earnings, but also a struggle for control over other assets including the means of distribution of programmes. This Blumler describes as a struggle for power, one that is being conducted between very large media organizations.

The Structure and Funding of the Industry

Despite the technological changes of the past twenty years or so, the dominant mode of receiving television in Britain is still via the broadcasters. There are essentially three sectors of broadcasting – the BBC, independent television and Channel 4 – each of which is differently constituted and differently funded.

BBC 1 and BBC 2 are run by the British Broadcasting Corporation, which is a public body funded by a licence fee paid by everybody who owns a television set. The system has the advantages that it is a very cheap way of providing television, costing a few pence per viewer hour, and the fee is inexpensive to collect. Its disadvantages are that the level of the licence fee is decided by governments which are notoriously reluctant to raise it, although consumers regard it as a fair price to pay. It also bears down disproportionately on the poor since everybody pays the same fee. The BBC both transmits and makes its own pro-grammes, although under the 1990 Broadcasting Act, it is obliged to buy in a proportion of its programming from independent producers.

Independent television has a rather more complex structure. As figure 4.3 below shows, there are a number of separate companies involved in the broadcasting of television. Although each of these companies is responsible for distribution of programmes to a particular geographical area, they broadcast more or less the same pro-grammes. The obvious exception to this is the provision of local news. The independent television companies therefore form a network within which there is scope for some local variation. Programmes are provided to this network in a number ways. Most significant is the role of the larger companies, Granada and Central for example, in *making* programmes as well as broadcasting them in their own regions. These producing companies (sometimes called 'network' companies) supply programmes to the smaller regional companies through a complex accounting process. ITN is a separate company owned by the independent companies and is responsible for supplying national and international news programmes to the whole network. The independent television network was until recently supervised by the Independent Broadcasting Authority, which had a regulatory role. Perhaps most importantly, it awarded franchises to the companies to operate, and these franchises are periodically reviewed. The 1990 Broadcasting Act set up a new principle whereby there is competitive tendering for the sixteen new 10-year franchises. The Act determined that the award of franchises by the body that succeeded the IBA, the Independent Television Commission, should be made on the basis of cash bids. In general, the expectation was that the highest bid would be preferred, but the ITC has the right to prefer a proposal of high quality even if it is a lower cash bid. In the event, in 1991, a number of the existing companies lost their franchises amidst a good deal of acrimony and widespread concern that the bidding system would compromise the quality of British television, as companies tried to cover the costs of making high bids by spending less money on television programmes, which would therefore be of a lower quality.

Independent television is almost entirely funded by advertising, although there has been a growth of sponsorship, in which companies contribute to the costs of a programme in exchange for the appearance of their company name and logo at the beginning and end of the transmission. (Satellite television, on the other hand, attracts considerable sponsorship, up to 25 per cent of income.) In Britain, television advertising is worth a great deal – rather over £2.5 billion in the late 1980s, representing about 95 per cent of independent television's income for about 10 per cent of the available airtime. To some extent this gives television producers two audiences, the public and the advertisers, whose interests may, at times, be in conflict with one another. Advertisers simply want the largest audiences possible, while the public wants diversity and is not necessarily interested in watching programmes just because they attract large audiences. Pressure from advertisers on programme makers can lead to concentration on particular kinds of programme. This point is taken up later in this chapter.

Channel 4 is funded and controlled rather differently from both the BBC and independent television, although ultimately its revenues come from advertising. Set up to cater for minority tastes, it is owned by the Independent Broadcasting Authority, now the Independent Television Commission, the public body that regulates independent television. Channel 4 does not make programmes, but commissions or buys them in from external sources. Organizationally this makes it very different from the BBC and the independent sector in that it has almost no in-house production facilities. Programming can be bought from a variety of suppliers including the larger network or regional television companies, overseas producers, and small independent producers, many of which have been set up to make programmes for Channel 4. The latter arrangement in particular was supposed to encourage diversity in programming as well as keeping costs down. There are a large number of these small producers, probably many more than can be sustained by the size of the market in the long term. For example, Collins et al. (1988) estimate that, in 1985, 300 independent production companies supplied programming for Channel 4, but they supplied only an average of one hour each. Until recently, Channel 4 received all its income from the IBA, which in turn received a subscription from the regional and network independent companies. In return, the companies sold advertising on Channel 4 and their subscription was based on their advertising revenues. Now Channel 4 is in the position of selling a proportion of its advertising itself.

The structure and funding of American broadcast television differs again from the three British systems. In the United States, the distinction between transmission or distribution and production or programmes is raised to a matter of principle. Most of the programming is supplied by the three networks, the American Broadcasting Corporation (ABC), the Columbia Broadcasting System (CBS) and the National Broadcasting Company (NBC). The transmission of television is carried out by some two hundred local or regional stations. Some of these are genuinely independent of the networks while others have close relationships with one or other of them. Although most programming is supplied by the networks, local stations also transmit locally produced news programmes and material bought in from other sources. The system is funded by advertising in much the same way as the independent sector in Britain. There is also government regulation, although it is not as heavy as in Britain and does not concern itself with content as much. Instead, the intention is to inhibit the concentration of ownership in television. Thus the networks are not allowed to own a significant number of the local stations and there are regulations that stop local stations passing into the same ownership. Although the networks supply programmes, they are prevented from actually making them apart from particular kinds of factual programming. The result is that they buy in their material from production companies which are a great deal larger than those that supply Channel 4 and, more recently, the BBC. Further discussion of the way that these companies work can be found towards the end of this chapter and in chapter 5. There is also a Public Broadcasting Service in the United

States, funded by government grants, but it generally only attracts about 5 per cent of the audience.

The Ownership of Television

In Britain, as in many countries, most economic activity is conducted by companies that are in private ownership. It is a familiar argument that, in the twentieth century, the whole structure of the ownership and control of British industry has changed. A series of factors has contributed to this: firms have grown larger by merger and takeover; increasingly, businesses are owned not by single entrepreneurs or their families but by many shareholders; and large financial institutions, pension funds and insurance companies for example, have gradually assumed ownership of significant sectors of British industry by buying extensive shareholdings. Of these issues, the one that probably attracts most public comment is that of concentration of ownership – the tendency for firms to increase in size by merger and takeover. In some sectors of the British economy, tobacco or banking for instance, a few firms control almost all the market. The increasing tendency towards concentration – for a small number of firms to dominate the economy – causes a number of publicly expressed worries. Most notable amongst these is the concern that concentration leads to a decline in competition, the very feature that is so often used to justify private ownership of economic resources.

The way that ownership is concentrated in the media industries has prompted similar concerns, but it has also been argued that we should be *especially* concerned about how television, radio, newspapers and magazines are owned. The major reason for this is that these are the main media through which the citizens of a nation become informed about the issues of the day, and can have access to reasoned debate, and hence the media institutions are an important part of the democratic process itself. This is the principal reason that most countries have maintained some broadcasting capacity not in private ownership.

Concern about ownership of the media is as old as the media institutions themselves. It has long been recognized that the owners of newspapers can use them to promote their own political and economic aims. G. Williams (1994) argues forcefully for this position:

> Rupert Murdoch imposed political changes in his papers through his own personal intervention, regardless of the views of his readers. His papers moved to the right as he became increasingly right wing. For example, the *Sun* switched from Labour to Conservative in the February election even though half its readers were Labour supporters, and after 1975 developed into a partisan Thatcherite paper in opposition to the opinions of its readers (only 40 per cent of whom supported the Conservatives in the 1987 General Election). (p. 56)

According to Williams, political concerns also influence Murdoch's television policy:

> He has threatened to drop BBC World Service Television from Star TV and replace it with an international version of Sky News because of alleged bias against India and China. Murdoch is quietly acquiescing to political pressure from China and India, who do not like the BBC's coverage of dissident groups in each country. In September 1993 Murdoch demonstrated how far he would go to appease the Chinese when he sold control of the *South China Morning Post* to a 'close friend of China' because of its anti-Beijing editorial stance. 'We don't want Star to be shut down because of the opinions of some our editors', he said. (p. 35)

It is not only the simple fact of ownership that causes concern but the way in which ownership becomes more powerful as companies grow ever larger by the acquisition of other companies. Clearly, if there are political risks in ownership of the kind I have described, then they will be that much more serious if companies are larger and there are fewer of them.

Direct control of television output by an owner to serve political or economic ends may appear to be a fairly rare event. There may be more indirect influences, as when a television station promotes the products of other companies in the same ownership or when Italian television networks helped, successfully, to further the political ambitions of their owner, Berlusconi, in 1994. Other kinds of anxiety are produced by the concentration of ownership. Larger companies, with much greater financial resources, are more able to keep smaller competitors out of the market, especially as the costs of entering the television market are rising. More important, however, is the impact of more concentrated ownership on the diversity of programmes available. A fuller discussion of privatization and deregulation will follow, but one of the advantages that is often claimed for these processes is that they will encourage diversity by allowing companies to cater for small and specialized sections of the television audience, in much the same way as the market for magazines is composed of numerous specialized publications. In fact, privatization and deregulation have led to concentrations of ownership and a *loss* of diversity of programming. Privately owned television companies actually make more or less similar programmes, as they aim to maximize audience size. Neither does the presence of increasing numbers of channels produce diversity. As Dunnett (1990) argues:

> When it became possible to have dozens of television suppliers it was thought there might be considerable 'narrowcasting'. There would be a channel to serve each interest, the equivalent of an agony channel, a chess channel, a local news channel and so on. By and large this has not occurred. Instead there are numerous channels but each offers mass entertainment. (p. 57)

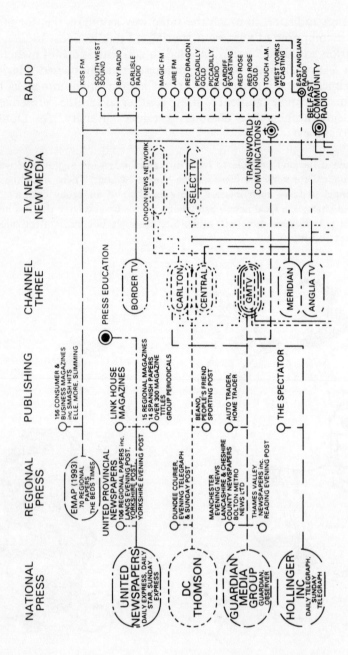

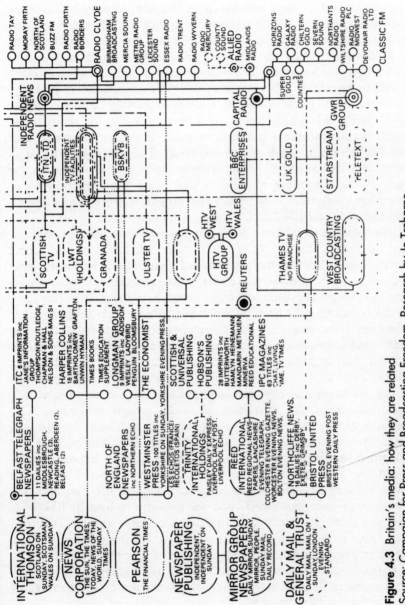

Figure 4.3 Britain's media: how they are related

Source: Campaign for Press and Broadcasting Freedom. Research by Jo Treharne

These are reasons to be concerned about ownership of television companies, but is their ownership in fact concentrated? In Britain, the commercial television network is composed of sixteen companies. Until recently, these companies could not take shareholdings in each other directly and it was impossible for one company to own more than one franchise. The possibilities for concentration of ownership in broadcast television were therefore limited. More recently, since the 1990 Broadcasting Act, cross-ownership of this kind has been permitted. Furthermore, it is now possible for there to be some concentration of interests between broadcast television and satellite television (cable is less involved). The chart reproduced as figure 4.3 demonstrates some of these links. For example, in the early 1990s, a number of mergers took place between commercial television companies – Meridian and Anglia, Carlton and Central, and Granada and LWT.

There is therefore some degree of concentration amongst companies involved in the supply of television in Britain. There are almost certainly some limits to this process, and a much more important issue is the way in which ownership patterns have changed not *within* television but *between* television and other branches of the media. Very large media conglomerates have been formed, which often bring together television, book, magazine and newspaper publishing, radio, film and video production. Some of these have taken on a high profile in public debate, often because of the entrepreneurs that direct them. Murdoch, Maxwell and Berlusconi, for example, are, or have been, all very much in the public eye and have extensive political connections. Figure 4.3, again, illustrates the formation of media groups in Britain. The Pearson group, for example, owns national and local newspapers, magazines, some of the largest book publishers, including Penguin and Longman, an interest in satellite via BSkyB, and an interest in television via Yorkshire/Tyne Tees TV. Similarly, News Corporation owns a string of national newspapers, including the *Sun* and *The Times*, large book publishers, and the majority interest in BSkyB as well as a small shareholding in Pearson. One must also note that this only refers to the British interests of these companies. Many of them are international and their British involvements are relatively minor.

Cross-media ownership of this kind causes a great deal of anxiety on a number of counts. As Michael Grade, the chief executive of Channel 4, said in a speech:

> If Murdoch's tentacles now attach themselves to a national terrestrial network, he will take an unbreakable stranglehold on our entire broad-

casting system. Unless Parliament acts, he will be unstoppable.

It is instructive to examine the charmed regulatory life of Rupert Murdoch as it unfolded after his Great Satellite Coup in 1990. The Broadcasting Act came into force immediately afterwards. It contained worse flaws than even the bizarre auction procedure or the damaging Channel 4 funding formula.

The strict percentage limits set by the 1990 Act were not applied to so-called 'non-domestic satellites'. How lucky for Mrs Thatcher's friend and supporter Mr Murdoch. He was now in the unique position of being free to build a multi-channel television business while owning more than a third of the British press. (*Guardian*, 27 April 1995)

Companies that grow larger by buying other companies not in their immediate field of interest are usually referred to as conglomerates. Murdock (1990) notes that there are three types of congolmerates active in acquiring media companies. Industrial conglomerates have their main area of interest in manufacturing but have diversified into the media. The most notable examples here are from Italy, where 70 per cent of the press is controlled by industrial companies, including Fiat. Service conglomerates are based in service industries such as retailing or financial services. Again, a good example here is Italian: Berlusconi's company Fininvest owns a national newspaper, a major cinema chain and three television networks, besides its interests in property, department stores, advertising and insurance. British media conglomerates tend to be of a third type, based solely or mainly in the communications industry. Indeed, many of them are selling their other interests in order to concentrate on the media. Reed International have sold their paper division, which is where they started, and Pearson have sold Doulton china.

A number of factors have combined to produce a concentration of ownership of this kind. First, companies are driven to grow in order to compete and the fastest way to grow is by acquiring other companies or, at least, by forming alliances with them. This tendency is compounded by the cost of the new technology and of the necessary marketing and promotion, all of which require the resources that only a large company can command. Second, the companies themselves believe that there are substantial economies to be made in owning several branches of the media. It is possible for one branch to promote the products of another, for television to advertise the appearance of a film or book, for instance. More important than these economies of marketing, however, are the potential economies in creative activity. Companies will argue that it is the same *kind* of resource that goes into producing a film, a television programme or a book and they might as well make the best use of that resource. So novels can be used as the basis for television programmes, which in turn can be issued as video-cassettes and/or audio-tapes and have extracts used in magazines. As Ted Turner, an American television entrepreneur, said:

> We're a lot like the modern chicken farmer. They grind up the feet to make fertiliser, they grind up the intestines to make dog food. The feathers go into pillows. Even the chicken manure is made into fertiliser. They use every part of the chicken. Well, that's what we try to do with the television product, use everything to its fullest extent. (Quoted in G. Williams, 1994, p. 73)

The most important motive force in the concentration of ownership in the media industries, however, is the action of governments over the past decade or so in attempts to introduce more competition and deregulation into the economy. In Britain, such attempts have been associated with the Thatcher governments, although there have been similar movements in many of the developed countries. As far as British television is concerned, the main policy changes are: removal of restrictions on ownership; loosening of some of the rules governing the conduct of television stations; and moves towards the commercialization of the BBC. For example, News International was permitted to buy a number of newspapers but also to operate a satellite television system – Sky – a cross-ownership of elements of the media previously forbidden. Again, as I have already pointed out, the 1990 Broadcasting Act allowed independent television franchises to come under the same ownership. There has been a progressive tendency for the independent television production companies, originally set up to provide programming for Channel 4 and now doing so for the ITA networks and the BBC, to merge. Some of the larger ones are even being bought up by the networks. Carlton, for example, has acquired Zenith productions. At the same time, restrictions on the conduct of commercial television, imposed in the name of public service television, are being removed. Lastly, the BBC is being encouraged, or forced, to become more commercial. Initially, this has taken the form of the development of peripheral services, which operate in the free market, and of the insistence that the corporation buy in a proportion of its programming from independent production companies. There are more radical proposals to make the BBC less dependent on licence fee income by opening subscription services or even by tak-ing advertising. While these moves to commercialize aspects of the BBC's activities do not directly lead to greater concentrations of ownership in television, they may do so indirectly in that they pro-vide further opportunities for already powerful media companies effectively to take shares in the BBC's market (by providing pro-gramming, for example).

Global Television

It is a commonplace of contemporary debate that people's everyday lives are becoming more global, more affected by events taking place very great distances away. Giddens has labelled this process 'time–space distanciation'. He defines globalization as 'the intensifi-cation of world-wide social relations which link distant localities in such a way that local happenings are shaped by events occurring many miles away and vice-versa' (1990, p. 64). At the same time as the world has become more global, it has also, it would seem, become more local. Thus, even in Europe, there is more emphasis on regionalism and local loyalties. Ethnic and regional conflicts are common and sometimes seem to have replaced national ones.

The media have played a major role in this process of globaliza-tion. Figures 4.4 and 4.5 show not only how media companies in France have a global role, but also how deeply entrenched foreign media companies are in French national life.

Of all the media forms, it is television that contributes most to a sense of globalization. Along a number of dimensions it has become truly international in its scope and effects. First, its *content* is inter-national. It is not only news programmes that depict events in far away places. Other programmes also use exotic locations and emphasize how British people are affected by international events. Further, television is, in effect, constructing a global audience. Certain events, the Gulf War or Tiananmen Square, for example, are played out in front of an audience drawn from every country. Gurevitch (1991) argues that such an internationalization of televi-sion creates a global public opinion and significantly affects the behaviour of the people who are involved in the events directly. For instance, the television coverage of the demonstrations in Tiananmen Square may have prolonged the demonstrations,

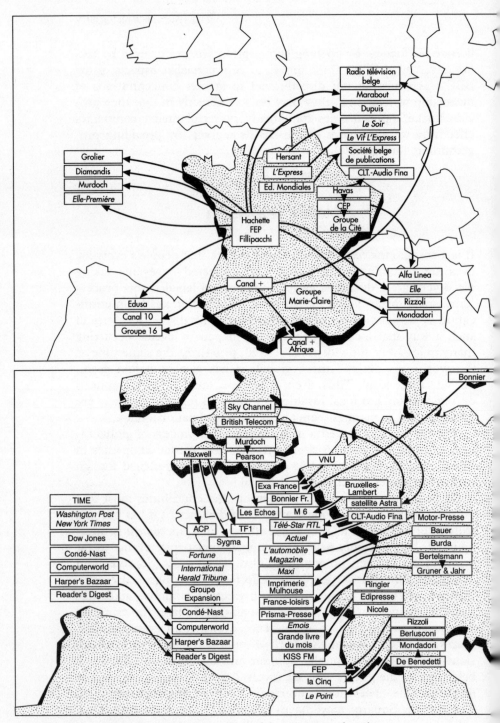

Figures 4.4 and 4.5 France and the international media
Source: Tunstall and Palmer (1991), pp. 138–9

constrained the behaviour of the Chinese authorities, and, via international opinion, significantly affected the attitudes of governments throughout the world to the Chinese regime.

Second, television can be *received*, internationally. This is partly a function of new means of supply, as the transmission range of the Star satellite illustrated in figure 4.2 above shows. In certain circumstances, the international scope of television transmissions can leave national governments powerless to regulate the content of the programmes that its population can receive. For example, in 1989 owners of satellite dishes in Britain were able to receive the transmissions of a company based in Holland specializing in soft-porn films. The company withdrew from a confrontation with the British government by encrypting its signals so that they could not be received in Britain. However, had they not done so, the British government would have been powerless to stop the transmissions (Negrine and Papathanassopoulos, 1990). It is also a consequence of the international growth in the number of television sets (see table 4.1 above). I have already noted that the distribution of television sets is very uneven world-wide; in countries like Britain, it is close to saturation, while in the non-Arab countries of Africa, there are only thirteen sets per thousand people. Nevertheless, a considerable proportion of the world's population have *access* to a television set, even if it belongs to someone else.

Third, the *ownership* of television production and distribution is becoming internationalized. I have already noted how the ownership of the media, including television, is more concentrated at the national level. The same is true of the international level, a process driven by the same processes of government deregulation, technological changes, and the perceived economies of concentration that are discussed above. In addition, other nations are catching up with Britain in the creation of a commercial television sector (as in Italy) while others are selling shareholdings in their public service television (as in France). The effect of these changes, largely in deregulation, is to create opportunities for the further growth of already large media companies on an international scale by the acquisition of other companies. These acquisitions can take a number of forms. There are vertical acquisitions in which companies in the same product but in different phases of its manufacture are brought together. For example, TVS, a British independent regional television broadcasting company, bought MTM, an American television production company. Alternatively, mergers can be horizontal, between companies involved in different products or active in different countries. Mergers between companies in Europe and the United States are particularly common. As Negrine and Papathanassopoulos (1990) say:

> What is of interest . . . is the manner in which individual media entrepreneurs and commercial media organizations have exploited the changing political and regulatory environment, and in the process have also speeded up the trends towards the commercialization and internationalization of broadcasting. In effect, decisions by individual media entrepreneurs, organizations, and politicians have singly and together brought about a greater linkage between media enterprises. Thus, deregulation in Europe has allowed entrepreneurs to move into new areas – Berlusconi into France and Spain, Murdoch into Spain, Maxwell into France and Spain, and so on. Similarly, organizations have fostered new linkages either as a defensive gesture or as a means of ensuring that their consolidated strength permits them to work in newer and different market sectors. (p. 130)

Table 4.2 gives details of the largest television/publishing groups in the world. Most of these own media assets covering a wide range, including television, music, books, magazines, radio and film, in many different countries. Time-Warner, for example, the largest company, is valued at $18 billion, has a labour force world-wide of

NEWSPAPERS	MAGAZINES AND INSERTS	FILMED ENTERTAINMENT	SATELLITE TV	BOOK PUBLISHING	TELEVISION	OTHER OPERATIONS	
UK:	UK:	20TH CENTURY FOX FILM	UK:	HARPER COLLINS	UNITED STATES:	NEWS DATACOM	100
The Times	Shoppers Friend	CORP.	BSKYB (50%)	UK, US & AUSTRALIA, INC:	Fox Broadcasting Company	NEWS GEM SMART CARD	80
The Sunday Times	The Times Supplements	COUNTRIES OF OPERATION:	ASIA	MARSHALL MORGAN & SCOTT	8 Fox Television Stations	SKY RADIO	71
News of the World	TV Hits	USA	STAR TV	PICKERING & INGLIS	LATIN AMERICA:	SPEKTAK PRODUCTIONS	51
The Sun	Inside Soap	CANADA		THE LAMP PRESS	El Canal Fox	REN-VIR (ANTENA 3) TV SPAIN	25
UNITED STATES:	UNITED STATES:	BELGIUM		WILLIAM COLLINS INTERNATIONAL	AUSTRALIA:	BROADSYSTEM LTD	100
The Boston Herald	Mirabella	UK		ALLEN & UNWIN	Seven Network	CONVOYS GROUP	100
The New York Post	TV Guide	SWITZERLAND		ANGUS & ROBERTSON			
AUSTRALIA:	FSI Division	MEXICO		GOLDEN PRESS			
The Australian	AUSTRALIA	GREECE		DOVE COMMUNICATIONS			
108 Regional Papers	12 titles	SOUTH AFRICA		COLLINS ANGUS ROBERTSON			
HONG KONG		PANAMA		KANANGRA			
Sunday Morning Post		KENYA		HARPER EDUCATIONAL (AUST)			
Wha Khi Yai Po		SINGAPORE		BOOK & FILM SERVICES (NZ)			
FIJI		MALAYSIA		HARPER COLLINS ASIA			
The Fiji Times		KOREA		CARTOGRAPHIC SERVICES			
Nai Lalakai		GERMANY		COBUILD			
Shanti Dut		PERU		DINOSAUR PUBLICATIONS			
PAPUA NEW GUINEA		PHILIPPINES		HILL MACGIBBON			
Post Courier		PUERTO RICO		POLLOCK SHIELDS PAINTING			
		TRINIDAD		ATLANTIC BOOK PUBLISHING			
		CHILE		COAT OF ARMS			
		AFRICA		ELEK BOOKS			
		DOMINICAN REPUBLIC		GRAFTON BOOKS			
		FRANCE		HARVILL PRESS			
		HONG KONG		MAYFLOWER BOOKS			
		TAIWAN		THORSONS PUBLISHING			
		INDIA		TURNSTONE PRESS			
		ITALY		THE ALTERNATIVE BOOKCLUB			
		ECUADOR		LASER CASSETTES			
		INDONESIA		AQUARIAN PRESS			
		PAKISTAN		UNWIN HYMAN			
		THAILAND		GEORGE ALLEN & UNWIN			
				UNIVERSITY TUTORIAL PRESS			
				WARWICK LEISURE			
				DOLPHIN BOOKCLUB			
				JOHN BARTHOLOMEW & SON			
				GEOGRAPHICA			
				TIMES BOOKS			
				INVINCIBLE PRESS			
				ROBERT NICHOLSON PUBLICATIONS			
				TRADER PUBLICATIONS			
				HARPER COLLINS (NEW ZEALAND)			

Figure 4.6 News Corporation
Source: G. Williams (1994), p. 36

Table 4.2 International media companies

Company	Revenue from all sources (1988 $million)	TV holdings	Selected other holdings	Main shareholders
Time–Warner (US)	*8,170	•HBO •HBO Video •Warner Bros TV •Warner Cable •BHC stations	•Time, Life, Fortune, Sports Illustrated, People •McCall's (50%) •Time-Life Books •Little, Brown •Book-of-the-Month •Warner Bros •Warner Home Video •Warner Bros Records, Atlantic Records, WEA International •DC Comics, Mad	Capital Guardian, Citicorp, Alliance Capital Management, Fayez Sarofim (all via Time); Chris-Craft, Capital Group, Sears Roebuck, Equitable Life (via Warner)
Bertelsmann (W. Germany)	6,380	•RTL-Plus (39%) •Canal + Germany (50%)	•Gruner & Jahr •Bantam, Doubleday, Dell •RCA Records •Ufa	Mohn family (89%) Gerd Bucerius (11%)
Fininvest (Italy)	**6,250	•Canale 5, Italia-1, Rete-4 •Tele-5 (45%) •Reteitalia	•Il Giornale, TV Sorrisi e Canzoni •Arnoldo Mondadori (7%) •Publitalia •AC Milan soccer club •Standa stores	Silvio Berlusconi family (100%)
Gulf & Western (US)	5,100	•Madison Square Garden Network •USA Network (50%) •Paramount TV	•Paramount Pictures •Simon & Schuster Famous Players	Capital Guardian Trust, Bankers Trust Jennison Associates
News Corporation (US/UK/Australia)	4,350	•Fox Broadcasting •7 US stations •Sky TV	•The Times, The Sun, Today, Boston Herald •Harper & Row (50%) •Wm Collins (42%) •Triangle Publications •20th Century Fox •CBS/Fox Video (50%)	Rupert Murdoch family (37%)
Capital Cities/ABC (US)	4,800	•ABC Network •ESPN (80%) •Arts & Entertainment (38%) •Lifetime (33%) •Tele München (NA)	•ABC Consumer Magazines •Fairchild Publications •Los Angeles •ABC radio	Warren Buffet (18.5%), Thomas Murphy, Daniel Burke

98   The Television Industry

Table 4.2 cont.

| Hachette (France) | 3,888 | •Télé-Hachette (production) •Channel I (facilities) | •Elle, Télé 7 Jours, Journal de Dimanche •Woman's Day, •Europe I radio | Marlis (51.5%) Groupe Fillipacchi (20%), Rizzoli Corriere (12.5%) |
| Gannett Foundation (US) | 3,315 | •GTG Entertainment •10 tv stations | •USA Today, 88 other dailies •16 radio stations •Gannett News Service | Gannett (10%) |

Notes: *Combined figure for Time Inc. and Warner Communications
    **Official 1987 figure includes extensive billings between Fininvest companies
Source: Negrine and Papathanassopoulos (1990), pp. 139–40

some 340,000 people, and is engaged in magazine and book publishing, music recording and publishing, film and video and cable television. As with all of the international media companies, Time-Warner is highly vertically integrated, bringing together all the stages of the production process and thereby generating substantial economies in production and marketing. It is also horizontally integrated, owning companies operating in related media fields.

Figure 4.6 shows in more detail the extent, range and geographical scope of holdings in television and related fields of one company, News Corporation.

The fourth aspect of the globalization of television concerns the *trade*, the imports and exports, in television programmes and products. Table 4.3 shows the pattern of British trade in television programmes from 1978 to 1985. The total amount of trade, both imports and exports, has risen over the period. As the last column shows, Britain is a net exporter of television programmes and is one of the world's largest exporters, although lagging a long way behind the United States. Britain is successful in this trade partly because the programmes are in the English language, partly because they are internationally recognized as being of high quality, and partly because of the efficiency of production stemming from the long history of the industry in Britain. The importance of the language factor is shown by the destinations of exports, about half of which go to North America.

British television companies make very serious efforts to sell programmes abroad, particularly to the United States, which has the largest and most lucrative television market. Sometimes this takes the form of selling drama series in their entirety for transmission in the form in which they were made. *Reilly – Ace of Spies*, for example, was

Table 4.3   Trade in television

	EEC	Other W. European countries	USA and Canada	Other developed countries[a]	Rest of world	Total	US and Canadian share (%)	Balance of trade[b]
1978	6	3	17	6	5	37	46	15
1979	10	4	18	7	3	42	43	14
1980	8	3	30	6	3	50	60	19
1981	10	4	21	8	4	47	45	10
1982	11	3	35	9	5	63	56	8
1983	11	2	47	11	6	77	61	8
1984	15	4	51	14	7	91	56	1
1985	14	6	65	16	9	110	59	28

Notes: [a]Other developed countries are Australia, New Zealand, Japan and South Africa.
[b]Receipts less expenditure.
Source: Collins et al. (1988), p. 63

sold to the American Public Broadcasting System (PBS), which takes so much British television drama that it has been said that PBS stands for Primarily British Series (Alvarado and Stewart, 1985). Alternatively, where there are a large number of episodes of a series, it can be sold to the independent stations in the United States for stripping, a technique of transmission in which episodes of a series are shown on successive days to build up an audience. An unlikely example of such a show sold to American television was the *Benny Hill Show*, but most British television is not produced in enough episodes to make stripping a regular possibility. Lastly, British television producers can try to sell formats, that is the concept of a programme rather than the programme itself. This will be used when a programme is too idiosyncratically British to adapt readily to the American market. The humour and language of *Absolutely Fabulous*, for example, fell into this category, but the American networks were interested in buying the format to produce an American version.

Fifth and last, television is *produced* internationally. Some of the processes involved here are most obvious in the production of news. Gurevitch (1991) identifies three kinds of international television news organization, all of which scarcely respect international borders.

1   There are the television news agencies, such as Visnews and Worldwide Television News, which distribute raw, unedited news footage from around the world.

2   Organizations like CNN or Sky News supply fully edited news programs by satellite.
3   Various regional broadcasting organizations, such as the European Broadcasting Union, manage the exchange of news stories between their members.

Satellite technology has accelerated the tendency to internationalize the production of television news. In the coverage of a news event the engineer responsible for setting up the satellite link is usually the first person on the scene, to be followed by the journalist who is to comment on the event. The result is that news gathering is so fast that the journalist often has to be briefed by his or her home base on what to say on arriving at the scene (Wallis and Baran, 1990). The general outcome of the internationalization of news production is the development, as Gurevitch puts it, of a 'global news room'.

It is also in the production of news that the tension between the global and the local noted at the beginning of this section is manifest. Wallis and Baran (1990) note, for example, the growing importance of *local* television news. In the United States, local stations will not only lead with local items, they will also give a local gloss to international and national stories by employing local experts to comment. Local news of this kind has proved very popular and contributes a large proportion of the stations' profits. The United States has a long tradition of local autonomy, but Wallis and Baran argue that the same process of localization of news dissemination is occurring in Europe too.

There is also an increasing tendency towards to the globalization of the production of television drama. As the costs of production rise with rising production values, television companies have an incentive to cooperate in the production of drama. These coproductions take a variety of forms from the simple sharing of costs to full-scale cooperation in production, often using locations in the participating countries. While the BBC and ITV generally pursue coproduction deals with the English-speaking Commonwealth and the United States, Channel 4 has also been inclined to find partners in European television companies. The majority of coproductions, however, remain within one language community (Collins, 1990). All these tendencies will, of course, be much enhanced by the internationalization of ownership noted earlier. International media organizations will be making programmes drawing on world-wide material for distribution world-wide.

These various aspects of the globalization of the media industries have clear implications in limiting national sovereignty. With broadcast television, it *seems* as though governments can control what kinds of programme are transmitted, although it is true that, in Western societies at least, governments do not want to be seen to be interfering too much with freedom of speech. But even with broadcast television there are limits to such control, given that so much programming in many countries is imported. The government of Spain, for example, may not like the fact that one-third of its television programmes are imported from other countries, making the content of a substantial part of the television schedule beyond its control. However, given popular demand, and the enormous expense of home-produced television, it has little choice. With satellite transmissions, of course, it is even more difficult to maintain national sovereignty over television. As figure 4.2 above shows, the signal from a satellite can cross many borders. In these cases effective control is difficult, being restricted to internal controls over what people watch (difficult to enforce) or international agreements involving television companies over what is transmitted (difficult to agree in the first place).

Even more significant in many people's eyes is the fact that so much of the programming that fills the schedules of broadcast, cable or satellite television is of American origin. The United States is much the largest exporter of television programmes in the world. It has the largest home market, which enables American programme makers to cover their costs easily and make a little extra profit by offering programmes for export at low cost. Although the export of programmes makes up a relatively small proportion of total American output (some 2 per cent by value), it is still worthwhile effectively dumping material on other countries. Other national television systems, especially the ones in newly developing countries, will have real difficulty in making their own programmes to anything like the standards employed by American producers. As a result, they have to import to satisfy home demand (to at least one-half of total programming in many cases). The cost differences can be very large. For example, in 1992, the BBC spent an average of £38,000 per hour on programmes bought in, including those imported from the United States. To produce its own drama programmes cost the corporation an average of £481,000 per hour, almost thirteen times as much (Tunstall, 1993). The globalization of television appears to mean the dominance of American television made by American companies. It is not only direct importation that is in question. Even when smaller countries do make their own programmes, they frequently copy American models as being the only ones available. These might be attempts to copy *Charlie's Angels*, for example, or, more likely, the borrowing of programme genres like game shows or quiz shows. Even the news in most countries adopts a form taken from American examples. In most countries, news broadcasts involve a news reader using direct address interspersed with reports from the field.

Arguments like these can provoke the claim that the globalization of television is in fact a process of *cultural imperialism* (Mattelart et al., 1984; Tomlinson, 1991) in which American-owned companies come to dominate world television with American programmes. (And in this context it is interesting that the United States *imports* only a tiny proportion – about 2 per cent – of its television programmes.) As a result, there is a widespread feeling that indigenous cultures will get swamped by American culture. This feeling is expressed by third-world societies which are just beginning to set up their television systems. It is also expressed by first-world societies, in Europe for instance, which have mature television systems but still feel that the independence and authenticity of their culture is at risk. One outcome of this can be an attempt to control the importation of American-originated programming, since so many of the other features of the globalization of television are beyond the control of individual nation states. A number of developing countries have restricted American imports, or vetted the content of imported material, or devised policies intended to promote a national television and film production industry. The European Commission has also tried to place quotas on the importation of American material or to insist on a minimum percentage of productions of European origin. These policies have had only a limited success, and are fiercely opposed by the transnational media companies and the American government as being in restraint of free trade.

In any event it might be argued that the cultural imperialism thesis is a little overstated (Collins, 1990). Although the United States continues to dominate international trade in television programming, other countries are beginning to develop a television industry and become exporters. As Sreberny-Mohammadi (1991) comments:

Empirically there is a more complex syncopation of voices and a more complicated media environment in which Western media domination has given way to multiple actors and flows of media products. More nations of the South are producing and exporting media materials, including film from India and Egypt, television programming from Mexico and Brazil. For example, TV Globo, the major Brazilian network, exports telenovelas to 128 countries, including Cuba, China, the Soviet Union, East Germany, earning export dollars for Brazil, and its productions outnumber those of any other station in the world. Indeed the flow of televisual materials from Brazil to Portugal is one example of how contemporary cultural flows reverse the historic roles of imperialism. (p. 121)

A large number of countries, both European and third-world, are developing active television industries, and are beginning to become exporters. This will particularly be so where population size and language are favourable. Both India and Brazil are large countries with a potentially vast home market and they are both important producers of film and television. Rajagopal (1993), for example, points to the crucial role of the state in promoting indigenous national programming. Spanish is a world language, which puts Mexico in an advantageous position. At the same time as there is at least an incipient cultural pluralism in television production, American media companies themselves are being challenged. Table 4.2 above shows that, although most of the largest media companies world-wide are indeed American, some are not. Furthermore, foreign companies are beginning to move into the United States. The Japanese, especially Sony and Matsushita, have been active in buying up American companies, and British, German, Dutch and Australian enterprises are also well represented.

Ultimately, the successes or failures of cultural imperialism will depend on the ways in which audiences take to foreign-language programming. There is some evidence that audiences prefer their own local (as opposed to global) programmes. As Tunstall and Palmer (1991) put it:

Yet towards the end of the 1980s, it also became evident that there was a contrary trend – the prophecies of more channels and of 'television without frontiers' were in some respects self-disproving. Foreign language material in general remains unpopular. The great popularity of *Dallas* in Europe around 1980 had no television equivalent by 1990. Popular channels required extra advertising revenue, while both popular viewer demand and regulatory pressure persuaded those channels to invest in more domestic programming. Some of this domestic programming was Italian, French, German, Dutch copies of American game show formats. American programming by 1990 still occupied a vast number of scheduled hours, but increasingly these were at low audience times like 3 a.m. or 3 p.m., or on new channels, often with very low audience shares. (p. 3)

English-speaking audiences, especially American and British, are particularly prone to prefer programmes in their own language. Collins (1990) uses Hoskins and Mirus's (1988) term 'cultural discount' to refer to the loss of attractiveness when a television programme is shown to an audience to whose cultural and/or linguistic experience it is alien. For British and American viewers, therefore, there is a substantial cultural discount attaching to television programmes in a language other than English. As Collins points out, it is one of the major achievements of the American television and film industry that it has developed programming which reduces cultural discount. Only part of this is due to knowledge of the English language throughout the world. It is also a question of culture. It is therefore arguable that, for many British viewers, there is a lower cultural discount attaching to American programmes than there is to some programmes produced in Britain, particularly if they have a strongly regional or 'high culture' flavour.

Such audience preferences, together with government attempts to resist 'Americanization', may well create substantial incentives to produce more television locally. In turn, this will force the international media companies to recognize local and national cultures as market niches and to produce for those niches or to acquire local television production companies which will do so. As Miller (1993) argues, international media companies now understand 'that shifts in the global political economy require a de-domiciling of corporate thought and planning to include local cultural contours as one more configuration to be parcelled as a "market niche"' (p. 104). While such a tendency may place limits on cultural imperialism, it is worth remembering that the international television marketplace will still be dominated by large, transnational, integrated media companies. There may be less *cultural* imperialism, but that does not mean to say that economic imperialism is reduced.

The Political Economy of Programme Making

In the television industry the production of programmes and their distribution are often located in different organizations. For example, Channel 4 is a distribution agent which buys in programmes from independent producers. Distribution is a relatively inexpensive activity and, once transmitting equipment is in place, running costs are comparatively low. Production costs, on the other hand, are very high, although they vary by the type of programme.

Table 4.4 shows how very expensive drama is and how very cheap imported programming can be. If production values are lowered, costs can be reduced even further. For example, in the United States the game show *Wheel of Fortune* costs about $7000 for each programme, while Brazilian soap operas can be produced for as little as $3000 dollars per episode (Dunnett, 1990). Television of any quality, however, is costly and that cost is increasing rapidly. Between 1978 and 1985, for example, the cost of new programming on British television rose by an average of 18 per cent per year (Collins et al., 1988).

Of course, television producers try as hard as they can to reduce these costs. They may try to raise the proportion of the cheaper types of programme, studio-based situation comedies, talk shows or daytime soap operas, for instance. They will shy away from producing one-off programmes, but will try to create series wherever possible, which give economies of scale in a number of respects. They will try to sell programmes to other countries to recoup some of the costs of production, although, as I showed above, this is not wholly effective. Repeats will also obviously save money even though they also attract public criticism.

Cost reduction is important to any television organization whether it is privately owned or is public service. More generally

Table 4.4 Production costs per hour of BBC 1 and BBC 2 network productions, 1992

Programme type	Percentage of total hours produced	Percentage of total cost	Average cost (£000) per hour (first showing)
Drama	4	21	481
Light entertainment	8	13	161
Features and documentaries	17	18	94
Average of all network first showings			90
News	7	6	77
Current affairs	17	11	59
Sport	15	7	40
Acquired programmes	21	9	38

Source: adapted from Tunstall (1993), p. 20

than this, however, most television stations in the world are businesses interested in profit maximization. Even public service television is affected by the ethos of business because it has to compete with television organizations that do function as businesses. An important question, then, is how the need to function as a business in pursuit of profit affects the kinds of programme being produced. As Golding and Murdock (1991) argue:

> Take for example, the increasing reliance on international co-production agreements in television drama production – these arrangements impose a variety of constraints on form, as the partners search for subject matter and narrative styles that they can sell in their home markets. The resulting bargain may produce an americanized product which is fast moving, based on simple characterizations, works with a tried and tested action format, and offers an unambiguous ending. (p. 27)

Television is expensive to produce and the public reception of any programme is always uncertain. Television managers simply do not know whether a new show will prove popular or even that an old one will continue to do well. The result is that a major issue for television executives is the *management of risk*. Besides keeping costs down, they must also try to prevent a programme from being a failure. As Gitlin (1983) argues in a study of prime-time American television:

> Uncertainty is the permanent condition of show business, as of much of the entire business system. As soon as capital pays its lip service to risk (for which profit is its just reward), it gets busy trying to minimize it. 'The marketplace', the intended recipient of the product, is an abstraction and an imperfect guide. It cannot tell the anxious executive what to do. Therefore, the TV industry, like others, tries to develop ways to control both supply and demand – supply in order to smooth its workings, demand so that it remains of a sort the networks are set up to satisfy. (p. 14)

Gitlin points to a number of ways in which television managers attempt to control risk. First, and most obvious, they try to create successful shows which attract large audiences. The larger the audience, the more advertisers will have to pay for advertising space in the commercial breaks and the more money will accrue to the television company. It is, however, one thing to want successful television programmes but quite another to know how to create them. Gitlin found that television managers all had some theory of success in television. Programmes had to have strong characters; well-known actors were important, as were strong scripts. These theories were, however, all extremely vague and, in effect, nobody has a clear idea of how to create a television success. This problem is compounded by the relationship between the people who actually produce the programmes and the network executives who are ultimately responsible for buying the programmes and distributing them. The former see themselves as the creative element with the talent to produce success if left to themselves. The latter, who have ultimate control, are frequently more worried about containing the risks posed by the producers. Gitlin cites many cases of pilot programmes altered by the executives who wanted a happy ending, a 'light', 'bright' or 'joyful' tone, and an uncontroversial content. In doing this the network executives were attempting to minimize the risk that audiences would be lost. In turn, of course, they were also giving up the potential opportunity of gaining audience share by putting on quite new programmes.

A second strategy is to try to duplicate programmes that are successful by a variety of means. The crudest method is simply to show repeats of popular shows. This can be both cheap and effective and, if a long enough period is left between original showing and repeat, it can always be presented as classic television. Alternatively, one television producer can attempt to make a copy of a programme that is successful on another channel or network. It is very rare for copies to be remotely as successful as the original. As Gitlin points out, copies are usually only surface-deep. What is often missed is the 'aura' of the show, the feeling of the original conception, which cannot be captured just by story lines or by the use of particular kinds of actor or location.

Lastly, spin-offs from successful programmes may try to capture some of the original aura. At its simplest, this consists in making series after series of a show that has proved that it is popular. Often the initial success is unexpected as in the case of *Auf Wiedersehen, Pet* or *Minder*. Single plays that have hit a public nerve are also sometimes made into series in their own right. Spin-offs of these kinds very frequently stem from the popularity of particular characters or performers or producers. Television executives often believe that the secret of success lies in the charisma of performers, and the same actors are used as often as possible. Again, producers that have delivered success in the past are often called upon to do it again. All these strategies of duplicating success are clearly intended to minimize risk. There is little that is new in television because the new runs too many financial risks.

In the determination of the success of a television programme, audience response is all-important. One way of minimizing the financial risk posed by new programming is to test out the responses of a sample audience before the programme is broadcast. This is a technique commonly used in American television but not so common in Britain. People are recruited, often in the street, to act as an audience for pilot programmes and are asked subsequently what their opinion of the programme is. In a rather similar attempt to control or predict audience response, television producers may make programmes that are designed to appeal to a particular audience segment, young professionals, for example, that have an appeal for advertisers. In the industry jargon, the producers are delivering the demographics for the advertisers. Underpinning these tactics is a wish to control the audience (reduce risk) by measuring it (Ang, 1991). I return to this point in more detail in chapter 6.

5

Television Production

The focus of this chapter is on the *organizations* that produce television rather than on the television industry as a whole. In many ways the production of television is like the production of manufactured goods. It is a very complex process with a high degree of division of labour; the production process is broken up into a large number of stages, some of which may be subcontracted. A considerable degree of standardization is involved, the repeated use of particular sets, for example. Each stage is carried out by skilled people who specialize in that activity. This fragmentation of the work process requires active and detailed coordination by management. Partly as a result, the relationships of production are hierarchical, with final authority vested in the management. However, unlike many other production processes, whether in manufacturing or service industries, this also has a strong sense of team work. As Ellis (1982) says:

> Broadcast TV adopted the studio production methods that were developed in the classic Hollywood cinema, and imitated by film industries elsewhere. However, it represents a considerable refinement of these methods towards a more industrialized kind of production, directed towards the production of series and serials rather than the single 'prototype' film that was typical of the classical cinema. Broadcast TV also involves a different form of production financing from cinema. Its financing is characteristically a concern of the broadcast institution as a whole, rather than that of any individual programme or series. TV's industrial production involves a detailed breakdown of work as far as possible into separate functions that require a considerable amount of skill; a corresponding management structure to co-ordinate this divided labour; a

production geared towards repetition; and a financing that is geared to the total output of a given period rather than running on a programme-by-programme basis. (p. 211)

The Producer

Television is a producer's medium (Newcomb and Alley, 1983). He or she acts as the link between the creative and commercial aspects of television. Producers are managers – and wield substantial power – but they are also collaborators in the creative process, a difficult balance to strike. As one observer of the British television industry puts it:

> The producer role encompasses elements not only of the civil servant but of a latter-day Renaissance Man, capable of playing all the parts. The producer ideally should be good with both words and pictures, the two main building blocks of television. He or she needs some basic grasp of TV technology, of tape against film, of sound, lighting and sets; requires (usually extensive) specialist knowledge of the particular programme genre, such as drama or news; needs to be able to juggle ideas against finance; needs plenty of sheer energy; needs some performance skills – the ability to enthuse and activate others during a long working day; and needs diplomatic skills to smooth ruffled egos and to persuade outsiders to do things at different times and for less money than they would prefer. (Tunstall, 1993, p. 6)

An American study of producers defines the role in similar terms:

> All of this suggests that the role of the producer is an exceptionally complex one. Like his audiences, his critics, and his clients, he knows the history of the entertainment form in which he works. He realizes that it will be in his own interest to minimize shock and innovation. But he also realizes that it will do him no good to stay mired in convention, to practice only with careful copies of someone else's new ideas. He cannot afford to let new trends and social attitudes go unnoticed, nor can he easily accept every shift in the wind of opinion, follow every cult to its illogical conclusion. He walks a narrow bridge toward a dreamed-for success. (Newcomb and Alley, 1983, p. 33)

The producer organizes and manages, making sure that the various elements of the production system are there at the right time and that the whole process is carried out within the budget. For some producers this may be a detailed, day-to-day matter, while for others it may involve more remote control. At the same time, producers are actively involved in the creation of programmes, often responsible for the original idea and working closely with writers. For example, Julia Smith, an established drama producer, was asked in 1983 by the BBC to produce a new soap opera. It was she, together with the script writer Tony Holland, who produced the idea that was subsequently to become *EastEnders*.

In this combination of management and creativity, the activities of producers are very like those of similar people in other branches of the media, all of which involve the management of creativity. For example, the commissioning editor in book publishing is responsible for making sure that all the processes involved in producing a book work smoothly together and within budget. But he or she is responsible as well for thinking of ideas that would make good books, for finding the authors who would be capable of turning those ideas into words on the page, and for encouraging, advising and helping the author as work proceeds. Film producers are also not unlike television producers in being the bridge between financial and management constraints and the creative process of making the film. However, cinema also tends to give more power to the directly creative people, especially the director of the film. Television as an industry works to much more demanding timetables and has to produce more material within more restricted budgets. These exigencies tend to demand much tighter management in general and hence favour the role of producer.

There are, however, several different ways of being a producer. Perhaps most significantly, producers can function at different levels. For example, within the British television networks there is a distinction between the series producer, who will be in daily detailed contact with programme making, and the executive producer, who will have overall responsibility for several programmes or series and hence will not have any detailed involvement. Similarly, in the production of some American daytime soap opera (see table 5.1) there is a distinction between the supervising producer, in charge of several series and with overall budgetary and personnel control, and (confusingly) the executive producer, who is involved in a much more detailed way with the production of a single series. The executive producer will work with the writers and will handle logistical or personnel problems. At a level further down, line producers will deal with such matters as rehearsals, planning how each episode will be shot, and organizing actors and technicians.

Table 5.1 Soap opera production

Procter and Gamble Productions, Incorporated		
Executive in charge of production		
Supervising producer		

Advertising Agency Personnel
Production staff for Guiding Light
Executive producer – 1
Producers – 2 (line producers)
Associate producer – 1
Assistants to the producer – 2
Production assistants – 2
Casting director – 1
Assistant casting director – 1
Production office coordinators (secretaries) – 3

Creative staff/talent
Headwriter – 1
Dialogue writers – 4–5
Actors –   Contractor actors (approximately 30–35)
Day players
Under-fives   hired on a daily basis
Extras   (number varies)
Directors – 4

# Technical staff	# Stage crew	# Support staff
2 technical director	2+ electrician	2 music supervisor
2 video director	2+ carpenter	2 set designer
2 audio engineer	2+ prop	2 set decorator
6 cameraperson	2 studio supervisor	2 stage manager
4 boom person	2 prod. supervisor	2 hairdresser
4 utility person	maintenance	2 make-up
2 music cartridge		1 costume designer
operator	*Advisors*	1 assistant designer
2 videotape editor	1 legal	3 wardrobe
2 lighting director	1 medical	

+ Head plus assistants
Source: Intintoli (1984), p. 123

Not all producers will work for the major TV networks (see the section, 'The structure and funding of the industry', chapter 4). Increasingly in Britain television production is moving out to independent companies which sell programmes to the BBC, Channel 4 or the ITV companies for transmission. In the United States, this process is further advanced, with the networks effectively acting not as producers of television programmes but as buyers and sellers of programmes made elsewhere.

In saying that television is a producer's medium, it is clear that the producer has a great deal of power vis-à-vis others involved directly in the production process. Even if not responsible for the creative success of individual programmes (see comments on *The Boys from the Blackstuff* later on in this chapter), producers are, collectively, responsible for the *kind* of television that is produced in Britain. Furthermore, the attitudes that producers have to their craft have traditionally dominated the higher reaches of the management of the British television industry. As Tunstall (1993) points out, former producers have gone on to very senior management roles in the BBC, Channel 4 and the ITV companies. At a lower level, producers will set all the important creative constraints within which writers, actors and directors will work. For example, Smith and Holland, in their initial work on *EastEnders*, decided that the soap would be located in the East End of London, devised the main story lines, and created the characters, besides generating the 'feel' that the programme would have as a depiction of life in an inner-city area with a large number of social problems. In creating the main structure of the programme in this way, Smith and Holland relied on their own artistic judgement. The audience research that the BBC subsequently conducted was essentially used to justify decisions that had already been made.

The power of the producer is very much confirmed by an American study of television producers conducted by interviewing a number of well-known producers (Newcomb and Alley, 1983). Although these men stressed the importance of consultation and collaboration, it was nevertheless clear who was the boss (see box 4).

As the extracts from the interviews in box 4 indicate, producers, even very high-level producers in this case, keep very substantial and detailed control. As Mantley says, this is largely because of the requirements of TV production. With the need to produce a great deal of programming very quickly, a firm system of control is necessary. The result of this system of control is that the audience can often recognize a producer's style in different programmes or series.

These interviews are taken from a study of American producers. A British study, conducted by Tunstall (1993), comes to similar conclusions. Tunstall distinguishes several levels of programme decision making in both the BBC and ITV. At the apex are the channel heads. Next down are departmental heads in the BBC and

Box 4 The producer's medium
Interview with Quinn Martin

People compare me to the old moguls of the movies. And I am really a controller. I believe in control. When I say I am a benevolent dictator I really mean that. I was always brought up that the guy at the top had the responsibility of control. Now that is an offshoot of my environment. We're all products of our environment. I grew up in this town and grew up seeing strong father-figure images: Mayer, Cohen, Warner, Zukor. So I patterned my style without even thinking about it. To me, coming out of films, it was just natural for me that that's the way you did it.

Q. *Will you comment on the thesis that television is a producer's medium?*
I don't think there's any question that in television the medium is a producer's medium. I very strongly controlled the creative content of everything that came out of this shop. We laughed when I used the term benevolent dictator but I do believe that it's necessary to have a single focus or point of view. Once that is established I give people a lot of freedom. But there is a stamp that is placed on each show. You create a point of view in terms of story, look, casting, everything else. Then people can go do as much as they want. But I still OK'd every idea for every show before it started.

Interview with John Mantley

Q. *Do you believe that the focus for creativity and power in television is the producer?*
That's right. Not in motion pictures. Motion pictures have come to belong to the director. Television is a producer's world, not because we make it so, but because of the exigencies of television. A director comes in to me and he is handed the script six working days before he shoots, twelve working days if it's a two hour show. In many studios in this town, or in many operations, the director is not allowed to change that script. He has to shoot it the way it is. I never expect that. I sit down with the director, and if he's got a problem with the script, I try to resolve the problem. If his suggestions are not as good as what is there, but are not really destructive, most of the time I will give him what he wants, because he's alone down there in the cut and thrust of shooting, and he has to feel secure with his material. If his suggestion is bad, of course, I won't use it.

Q. *Do you do the same with actors and writers?*
There is no time to do anything with actors. I mean, if a man – a good actor and a responsible actor – has a real problem with a scene and feels he can't handle it, then I will talk to him, sure. And I have made changes. But I will not allow an actor to pick at a script on the

sound stage. That just upsets everyone and destroys the show. I also let directors cast their shows. I sit in on the casting and I read with every actor who appears on one of my shows, because I can tell when I read with the actor whether they're going to be good on camera or not. That knowledge is very valuable to me and the director. I have only one rule in casting: I will not let a director use any actor that I feel is wrong for a given part, because I think that puts too great a burden on both actor and director. They have to 'sell' me, and they shouldn't have to do that. So if it comes to the point where I say, 'I really can't see this actor,' I will say, 'Okay, let's find someone we agree on' . . .

That's why this is a producer's medium. There is no way (in TV) the director can control, to any great extent, the material he gets because he's hired sometimes a year in advance and he, in most instances, has to take the script he's given. That was never true, as I've indicated, on *Gunsmoke*, because I always had many scripts in advance (until I got down to the last three or four shows, and then every director understood, whether he liked it or not, he had to do the script given him). But, before these last few shows, I always presented an unhappy director with two or three other scripts and let him choose one he wanted to do. The show was so well organised that I could switch from one script to another in mid-stream without

any serious problems.

But that's why this is a producer's medium, and that's why, more than anybody in any other medium, I think, the taste, the energy, and the creative powers of the producer are so important. The fact that a one-hour show must be shot every six days does not allow much time for a democratic society! The truly involved executive producer hires the line producer, the executive story consultant, the director, the composer, and, in concert with the director, the guest cast. He also makes the final cut, okays special credits and, in the first season, creates main and end titles. Incidentally, that list of authorities holds true for all executive producers, but not all of them become that involved in all of those areas. And there are executive producers in this town who just come in at eleven and look at the dailies and scribble a few words on the script and go home. When that happens, nearly all the functions that I perform are then relegated to the line producer. So you can't tell by a man's title what he actually does.

Q. *He is a producer, at whatever level – he's going to be a producer.*
That's right. Norman Lear used an interesting term the other day for the people that we are talking about. He called them 'strong' producers, and I think that wherever they come in, that's a good designation.
Source: Newcomb and Alley (1983), pp. 57 and 104–7

directors of programmes in ITV. Below that are executive producers in the BBC and department heads in ITV. The next level down, consisting of series producers or editors, is the one that interests Tunstall most, since this is the highest level of decision making which still has daily contact with the content of programmes. Series producers, in turn, have responsibility for managing producers or assistant producers.

Series producers exist in what Tunstall calls 'private worlds' defined by the genre of the programmes that they make. Producers of different genres will have very different backgrounds, images of their audience, and styles of work, and their output attracts very different amounts of prestige. Producers of documentaries, for example, are generally elite recruits with university degrees, often from Oxford or Cambridge. Documentaries are expensive to make and projects can take a long time to come to fruition. They frequently have an international orientation and are often the subject of co-production deals with other countries to cover the expense of production. The producers concerned stress the necessity of their being emotionally involved in the subjects being documented, and they have a strong belief in television as an institution serving and educating the public. Perhaps as a consequence of all these features, documentary production is a high-prestige sector of television.

In this sense, as in others, documentary producers are very different from sports producers. The reporting of sports not only has a relatively low reputation in the television industry, it also attracts criticism in that it is claimed that sports producers have too close a relationship with sports personalities and organizations. This tight involvement with the sports that they report may contribute to the privacy of the sports producers' world which is more cut off from the rest of television than other branches. Recruitment takes a non-elite form. Only a minority of sports producers have a university degree and the majority have come up through the ranks or from sports journalism. They are all sports fans and in this sense, as in others, they are very close to their audience.

Comedy producers, on the other hand, take very little notice of audience research. They trust their judgement and back artists and programmes that make *them* laugh. Like drama producers they have a very great respect for writers; at the core of comedy are funny scripts and characters. The prestige of comedy is low in British television, although, with the rise of alternative comedy, that may be changing. This uncertainty of status may be related to the changing recruitment pattern of comedy producers. Alternative comedy producers tend to move from university into radio comedy, where they acquire script-writing experience, and thence into television. Mainstream producers are older, typically have come into television from the theatre, and then have worked their way up through the television hierarchy.

Light entertainment, including quiz shows, chat shows and game shows, has the lowest prestige of all in that it is thought to be simply the repetition of formulae. At the same time, programmes of this kind attract relatively high ratings and, of all producers, light entertainment specialists pay most attention to audience research. Programmes of this kind are also very cheap to make, requiring little or no rehearsal, and using members or the public or guests who do not charge. The major cost, indeed, is the host or presenter. Again, the backgrounds of these producers reflect the lower prestige attached to their output. Few have a university education; most have worked their way up from the technical side of television. All pride themselves on having an unusually good feeling for popular taste.

For Tunstall, despite the variations in the producer's role from genre to genre, they all have considerable power and autonomy. Indeed, in his view, they are gaining in these respects, an issue taken up in the section 'Changing systems' later on in this chapter. But their autonomy is still effectively limited by their superiors, who take strategic decisions. In the British system, these decisions are taken by individuals not committees. However, most of these senior posts have so far been taken by ex-producers, which has made sure that production considerations (including questions of programme quality) have remained very much to the fore. British television, in other words, is 'producer-driven'.

One of the ways in which producer power is most noticeable, and most necessary, is in the maintenance of coherence in series and serials. Directors, actors, writers and other production staff may participate in only one or a few episodes of any series. There must be some means of ensuring consistency of style, character and plot across many episodes spanning perhaps many years. The producer fulfils this function; he or she is the guardian of the *image* of a series. With very long-running series it may not be one person who carries out this task, but rather the office of the producer. For example, in *Coronation Street*, the office will have an important role in maintaining the style of the programme, and it employs a biographer whose task it is to ensure consistency of character and plot (Dyer et al., 1981). Audiences will expect the various conventions of the series to be maintained. These conventions will relate to all aspects of the series – the consistency of character over time, the plausibility of plots, the signature tune, the camera style, the interior decor of the Rover's Return, the objects present on the set.

The maintenance of a coherent image over time may not be an easy matter and disputes may occur over what this image is and how it may best be sustained. For example, the very long-running series *Dr Who* had several producers, and several different actors playing the central role, from its first transmission in 1963. Each of these tried to set his own stamp on the programme while keeping within the conventions established by the series. It was felt, however, that one producer in particular had stepped outside the boundaries. In his hands, the series became more intertextual; that is, it persistently referred outside the programme to other television programmes, films and books in the lines spoken by actors, the objects present on the set, and the story lines themselves. In the eyes of other members of the production team and of vocal fans in the audience, this led to parody of the programme. *Dr Who* was no longer the kind of television show that it had been since its inception (Tulloch and Alvarado, 1983).

This discussion of the importance attached by the television industry to questions of image is clearly connected to the issue of genre noted in chapter 3. Of course there are *specific* characteristics of, say, *Dr Who* or *Coronation Street* which producers strive to preserve intact. There are also the conventions of soap opera or science fiction genres within which these programmes fit. Producers have to maintain the genre boundaries, which help the audience and, incidentally, make production easier because it becomes more routine.

The Production Team

So far, I have argued that television is a producer's medium chiefly because of the exigencies of television production – the volume of programming required, the speed at which it has to be produced, the tight financial constraints, and the generic consistency that is demanded. The more significant these constraints, the more powerful is the position of the producer. They are probably at their most significant in the very demanding production of American daytime soaps which appear daily. As Intintoli (1984) points out, a greater emphasis on profit in the production of the soap *The Guiding Light* led the production company to strengthen the authority of the producer. For some years, in effect, writers had run the show but they were displaced. Intintoli describes the effect of this pattern of producer control:

Directors and actors are limited by the authority structure, pace, and nature of the work. Their exclusion from story conferences, their limited knowledge of future story, and the breakneck production schedule generate a great deal of frustration and pressure. Having to work very quickly with often less than satisfying material that has to meet the approval of the production hierarchy (and audience) limits the variability and innovativeness of performances. Professionalism largely means meeting organizational requirements. It also, importantly, means that 'form' again takes precedence over 'content'. (p. 157)

The production conditions, and consequent producer power, in *The Guiding Light* are extreme and American television in general gives more power to producers than its British counterpart, as we shall see in a moment. Furthermore, different conditions in different genres (or in the film industry for that matter) will give more control than others to artistic personnel at the expense of the producer. In addition, despite the importance of the producer, the production of television is still a collaborative exercise involving a large number of people with a wide range of skills. To make successful television at all it is critical that the collection of people brought together should function as a *team*. For example, when Euston Films (the makers of *The Sweeney, Minder* and *The Flame Trees of Thika*, amongst others) was set up as a production company, the founders had the importance of the team spirit very much in mind. They were reacting against the American system of giving the producer all the power because they felt that that did not give the audience good television. There was no point in employing talented directors and technicians and then not giving them their head. Staffing was arranged so that there was time for director and technicians to discuss problems on location before filming began. This not only saved time in filming, it also 'promoted a cooperative team-spirit amongst the unit' (Alvarado and Stewart, 1985, pp. 45–6).

Team working of this kind can be so strong that it is not always possible to tell who has made a particular contribution. In effect, the issue of authorship has been obscured. For example, in the extremely successful series of television plays, *The Boys from the Blackstuff*, although the original script was written by Alan Bleasdale, the actual lines as delivered, or the gestures used, were arrived at by contributions from the actors, the producer and director as well as the script writer. As one of the technicians, the lighting cameraman, on this series put it:

It all comes down to a team. It's not all down to one person. The whole thing about *Blackstuff* was that you'd got a bloody good writer, bloody good actors and it was sorted in that way. The production team come together in terms of Philip and myself, the camera operator, even the assistant and the grips. Everybody is working towards a set end and that produces a style in the end, it really does! I mean I produced the lighting and camera operation side – just remember it's Liverpool, the locations you're using and remember the style is because of those locations. If you're filming in Oxford say, it will be totally different. The style isn't just made by one person deciding: the style evolves under Philip's [the director] eyes and supervision. (Millington and Nelson, 1986, p. 123)

One way of describing the production team is by distinguishing above-the-line from below-the-line personnel. Although there may be some variations between genres, included in the above-the-line category are the producers, both series and executive, the director, the writer or writers, and the actors. Below the line come the technical personnel – camera operators, lighting and sound technicians, film and video editors, make-up artists, musicians, costume and set designers, production administrators, property buyers.

In television drama, apart from the producer, whose role I have already described, the most important position is that of the writer. As one of Newcomb and Alley's (1983) producers said:

We produce for two reasons. One is to protect the material. And the second is that we have discovered that producing is an extension of writing. The day before they're going to shoot it you walk on a set designed for a character you've written. You say to the art director, 'the man we've written would not have these paintings. He would not have that dreadful objet d'art sitting there. It's much too cluttered for a man of his sensibilities.' (p. 145)

In many ways this is scarcely surprising. Writers, after all, do not just produce the dialogue, they also effectively provide the structure of the programme. Like the producer, they are as well an important element in the continuity so critical to series and serials. This is especially significant in soap opera. It is often said that what makes any particular soap popular is not the quality of the acting or lavish production values, but the story and the characters. It is the writer who is mainly responsible for narrative and characterization. In addition, and more importantly, many have argued that television is peculiarly dependent on writers, unlike film for example, because it is very much more verbal. It is about *talk* and the pictures essentially illustrate the talk. Here is a writer explaining:

> The television screen is small. The picture doesn't overwhelm the audience, as in the cinema; the sound doesn't come washing round the living room in luscious stereophonic waves . . . People *listen* to television. It's much more like radio with pictures than it is like movies. In modern movies, the words are often deliberately inaudible; the director wants to tell his story with pictures and sound, not pictures and dialogue. He is interested in large-scale dramatic effects, in impressions, not in the sharp particularity of dialogue. But in TV large-scale effects simply don't work; the screen won't take them. What the screen will take is people talking comprehensibly to each other. (Mitchell, 1982, p. 56, quoted in Millington and Nelson, 1986, p. 53)

This is an important point, although it is unlikely that it is only the size of the television screen that is the significant feature. More relevant still is the fact that television is an essentially *domestic* medium. Television is addressed to everyday life and, as such, is more about talk than it is about dramatic events. This point is taken up further in chapters 2 and 7.

Clearly the position of writers does vary from genre to genre. As Murdock (1980) points out, the notion of the writer as the individual, free, creative artist sits uneasily in television organizations which are commercial in orientation, even in the BBC. Success in the ratings requires continuity of character, well-established settings, and themes and plots that are not going to surprise the audience too much. As Murdock points out:

> To achieve this consistency the producer and script editor often furnish prospective writers with detailed specifications of what is required. In the case of *Upstairs, Downstairs*, for example, writers were given the story outline of the episode they were responsible for, told where it would fit in the series and whether it was to be a comedy, tragedy or drama and provided with detailed sketches of the main characters. The emphasis was firmly on craftmanship rather than authorship, professionalism rather than creativity. (p. 27)

Such constraints are particularly characteristic of series and serials, many of which can potentially be exported. This industrialized writing reaches its apogee in American daytime soap opera. As Allen (1987) notes:

Over the more than three decades of televised soap operas, elaborate systems of production control and division of labor have been devised both
to maintain production schedules and to keep production costs low.
Scripts are turned out on an assembly-line basis, dictated by the need to
produce five hours of new material each week. The show's head writer
determines long-term story developments and provides a written summary of the action to occur in each episode. This outline is then turned over
to associate writers, who fill in the dialogue to be spoken. (p. 143)

At the other extreme, single plays on British television are not so
subject to market pressures of this kind. The writers of these dramas
are, as a result, more autonomous and more able to say something
artistically, morally or politically contentious. At the same time, as
many commentators note, British television as a whole continues to
give the writer a central place (Bacon-Smith, 1992).

There is no single model of the production team and its internal
relationships that applies across all television production. Between
the genres, or sub-genres, of television there are differences in the
organization of the production team which reflect different production conditions and artistic traditions. For the purposes of the discussion that follows I distinguish between daytime soap opera,
prime-time series, serials and soap opera, and prime-time drama.

As implied above, daytime soaps tend to be produced by methods
that are effectively industrialized, manifesting a high degree of division of labour and specialization and a demand for rapid and cheap
production. In the hierarchical system that results, as I have already
noted, producers are pre-eminent. Next most important are the
writers, who are frequently organized by a head writer.

The roles of supervising producer, executive producer, and headwriter
clearly make the major decisions within the production organization . . .
The three roles also monitor the episodes that are taped and aired. This
can have a direct impact on the daily production process, particularly as
their observations are communicated to the line producer who oversees
each day's taping.
The relative authority of the writer and executive producer is particularly
important in shaping performances. Since, as a writer put it, 'they always
need you tomorrow', and the show is dependent on a writer's knowledge of
future story (which may not be revealed to other executives), writers have
tended to garner a great deal of power. (Intintoli, 1984, p. 135)

The rest of the above-the-line team, the director and the actors, are
not as important. Directors have little freedom to take their own ini-

tiative and develop the artistic qualities of the programme. They are limited by direct control from the producers, who will often specify how each scene is to be shot, by the speed with which they have to produce each episode, and by the fairly rigid conventions of the soap opera concerned. From the point of view of the producer, the ideal director is someone who is inventive, but within fairly narrow limits, so that the writer's task is not made more difficult and the next director who works on the programme will not be presented with problems of continuity. Actors, similarly, are not that important. It is not all uncommon even for actors who have played characters for some time to be replaced. In daytime soaps, therefore, there is not as much identification of the actor with the part that they play. In prime-time the actor is much more important. At the same time, performances are tightly constrained by writers and producers. As with directors, actors have to work within strict time limits, often being presented with a script at the last minute with little time in which to learn lines. These constraints can lead either to a certain distance from the show, and the display of considerable cynicism, or to frustration as actors feel that the character they play is being misread by the writers. Actors, in other words, have a not unnatural tendency to believe that they are the guardians of their character. Conflicts between actors, on the one hand, and writers, producers and directors, on the other, about how characters are likely to behave, think or dress are not uncommon. In daytime soaps, however, these conflicts are almost always settled in favour of the writer, and the actor simply has to live with the decision (Hobson, 1982; Intintoli, 1984).

The structure of the production team in prime-time soap opera (*Coronation Street* or *EastEnders* for instance) or other prime-time series (such as *Minder* or *Between the Lines*) is rather different. The pace of production is much slower – an episode of *The Sweeney* took four or five times as long to produce as one of *The Guiding Light*, for example. Budgets are much more generous, allowing a great deal more attention to be paid to production values. A major effect of these lesser constraints is that greater freedom is given to the creative elements of the team, the writer and the director particularly (Alvarado and Buscombe, 1978). The writer's role is critical as with daytime soaps. The director also becomes more prominent. As one interviewee in Alvarado and Stewart's (1985) study of Euston Films said:

> The directors actually felt that they were making something worthwhile. Consequently, you could attract good directors, and once you could

attract good directors you could attract good writers because it became
their project . . . When people are hired by Euston Films they know they
are going to make something worthwhile and they will have control. They
will have a benign producer above them because things are made on a
very tight budget, but they will have an artistic control over their project
. . . All the other series were made almost on a factory basis where the
director had very little power and very little say in what was done: he shot
the schedule and that was that. (p. 47)

Other forms of prime-time drama, single plays or serials, for
example, give even more freedom to writers, directors and actors. In
a set of plays which in effect form a serial, like *The Boys from the
Blackstuff*, the writers have primacy as they have in the other genres
discussed so far. For programmes of this type, however, an additional reason for the dominance of the writer is the historic link
between the theatre and television in Britain. Despite this, however,
the script is not absolutely sacrosanct as it is in American daytime
soaps. It is, instead, a working document which is refined by others
as the production proceeds. The writer, in effect, becomes a collab-
orator involved in a team effort; he or she does not have sole artistic
control. Producer, director and actors will have an input into script
changes. Sometimes these will be motivated by artistic considerations (that a character would not say that, for example) and sometimes by budgetary or technical considerations (that a scene is
technically not feasible or a particular effect is too expensive).
Indeed, in the standard contract between the writer and the BBC
there is provision for the necessary rewrites to make the script
acceptable for production, although the writer has control over
these rewrites. The director and actors will have an input into the
production over and above their participation in script changes. To
some extent the director's role is invisible in that all his or her
inputs are realized by other people – actors, cameramen and so on.
None the less the director has to make the script happen by direct-
ing the other people. In *The Boys from the Blackstuff* the director was
responsible for introducing a distinctive visual style, for insisting
that a more feminine element be introduced, and for making
changes to dialogue as filming proceeded. In this series of plays the
actors also made important contributions. They did not simply play
the parts as written, and it was not a matter of acting with particular
intensity or conviction. Actors also made suggestions about the
script, about the dialogue, and the fact that so many of them were
familiar with Liverpool (where the series was shot) and with the

writer's earlier work gave them a particular insight into the plays.

In prime-time drama of this kind the collaboration between direc-tor, writer and actors may conceal the role of producer, which is so much more prominent in other genres. Even in *The Boys from the Blackstuff*, however, the role of producer is crucial. He was not only responsible for the usual budgetary matters, he also appointed the production team. Ultimately, he was also the only person who had the authority to sort out conflicts within the production team, par-ticularly those between writer and director.

In reviewing the balance of power in production in television, therefore, it is possible to say that, although television is a produc-er's medium, in some genres writers, directors and actors have more power than in others. In these cases television production is less hierarchical and more collaborative. For much television, therefore, it is an exaggeration to say that the producer is the sole guardian of the style and image of a particular programme, as was implied in the earlier discussion. These vital components of the success of televi-sion are also the product of teamwork. All members of a production team, from producers, writers and actors to members of the techni-cal staff, are somehow imbued with the knowledge of what makes for the distinctive personality of a particular television show.

In discussing the ways in which television production teams work, I have minimized the role of performers in drama produc-tions. This is only half true. There is no star system in television as there is in cinema and probably very little identification with per-formers on television as there is in cinema (Dyer, 1979; Stacey, 1994). On the other hand, television does seem to have performers who, while not being stars, are *personalities*. Medhurst (1991), in writing about Gilbert Harding, a television performer of the 1950s, finds it difficult to refer to Harding as a 'star':

> I think it's something to do with the fact that most film stars have an aura of mystery, of otherworldliness, of sexual desirability, that is enhanced by the size of the screen and the darkness of the cinema. To visit a cinema in the golden decades of Hollywood was to enter a palace, a temple, a sacred site of surrender and completion. To watch television is to enter the living room. Television performers are too available, they're on too often . . . Gilbert Harding, then, was the first paradigmatic television per-sonality. He wasn't, after all, enacting a fictional role, but trading on an aspect (however heightened) of his own personal attributes. (p. 73)

These personalities are central to a particular programme, viewers will know them by name, and programmes will become simply vehicles for them. Such personalities are found in comedy (Victoria Wood, Lenny Henry) and in game shows (Michael Barrymore, Cilla Black) particularly. The phenomenon is not so common in other branches of television such as drama, documentary or news.

Lusted (1991) argues that successful television personalities are challenging of the status quo and disruptive of social order. This is the function they perform for the audience and is therefore very different from the film star's capacity to excite identification. Tolson (1991) argues that so developed is television's personality system that some chat shows and talk shows (*The Dame Edna Experience* of the mid-1980s, for example) have turned to self-reflection and self-parody. The personality performer parodies the fact of personality on television (see the section 'Postmodernism', chapter 2, for a similar argument). When performers become personalites, they can gain considerable financial power. This is reflected in their pay, which can be very high. In 1987 the world's highest paid TV personality was reportedly Bill Cosby, who had earnings approaching the $100 million mark (Dunnett, 1990). Perhaps even more significantly, these personalities increasingly often have their own production companies which make and market their programmes. *Absolutely Fabulous*, for example, is produced by French and Saunders Production.

Producers and Audience

So far I have been looking at television production in terms of production *systems*. Television is produced for audiences and producers will have particular audiences in mind. This may be an explicit process – programmes are designed deliberately to attract certain audience sectors, perhaps for advertising purposes. Less explicitly, however, all producers will have some notion of who they expect to watch their programmes. Ideas of the audience will depend to some extent on what programme makers are trying to do. Thus, a producer working in public service television, BBC 1 for example, may well have a notion of the audience member as a citizen, who needs to be informed and educated as well as entertained. Rather different will be the conception of an ITV producer for whom an audience member is a consumer towards whom advertising has to be directed. Both, however, have an interest in maximizing the size of the audience, even if it is an audience of a particular type, for that is the main way of judging success.

The origins of *EastEnders* lay in the BBC's need to reach a new early evening audience.

> Many of the specific production decisions – about the location and set-ting of the serial, about the balance of the characters, about publicity and scheduling, and about the themes and storylines – were to a certain extent informed by ideas about the type of audience the programme was aiming to reach, and by assumptions about what would interest and entertain it, and thereby keep it watching. (Buckingham, 1987, p. 23)

The programme is, of course, very popular but that popularity, that interest in maximizing the audience, was not seen as inconsistent with the BBC's mission as a public service institution. Quite the contrary: the producers saw it as their mission to bring high-quality soap opera, which dealt with real social issues in a responsible way, to as large an audience as possible.

The same association of a belief in quality with an interest in audience response is manifest in the production of *Dr Who*. Producers of this programme would have an abiding interest in maintaining the size of the audience and in designing episodes that would increase that audience, perhaps by attracting both a 'mass' and a 'serious' audience. Many of the conflicts within the production team were generated by debates as to the likely impact of plot or character innovations on audience loyalty. At the same time a producer could say:

> We have that special relationship with our audience – *Doctor Who* pro-ducers and *Doctor Who* people. We've not been obliged to observe the strictly commercial criteria that say a producer on American television has had to observe when everything has to be reduced and ironed out and made to actually work . . . That's not the way that British television works . . . Certainly not the way that the BBC works . . . So it's a pecu-liarly British institution and a reflection if you like of British society, of British audiences and British television . . . If the Americans had been given the basic format of the Doctor they would have given you a won-derfully logically worked out 'quirky' hero who was always the same, and you would have been able to see around all the eccentricity and predict it . . . The reason we get away with it is because our audiences are more indulgent . . . We suddenly woke up and realised that it wasn't a kid's programme but there was something in this sort of Englishness that was

valuable and prized by the audience. (Philip Hinchcliffe, quoted in Tulloch and Alvarado, 1983, p. 178)

The producer here is using a particular model of the audience – its 'Englishness' – to reconcile what he wants to do artistically with the series with the need to maximize audience figures.

A rather different example of the way that conceptions of the audience enter into the production of television is provided by Espinosa's (1982) analysis of a script or story conference for the American television serial *The Lou Grant Show*. The final script from which an episode of a television serial is shot is the product of a series of meetings – or story conferences – on successive drafts of the script. For *The Lou Grant Show* those present included the executive producer or producers, the story editor or editors, and the writer for the particular script under consideration. Espinosa found that, in constructing the text over the period of these meetings, the participants were effectively (though perhaps without being aware of it) using a set of rules concerning the relationship of the script to the potential audience. There were four such rules. The first rule – 'Engage the audience' – simply means that the producers should make sure that the audience stays in front of the television. Audience engagement is facilitated by creating characters that the audience can identify with, making sure that the plot is one that the audience can follow, and using the display of human (recognizable) feelings. Anything that jeopardizes audience engagement must be questioned. Second, the producers felt they had to keep in mind the audience's knowledge of the world. For example, in a story involving terrorism, the writers have to trade on the audience's knowledge of real-life terrorism which they have learned about from the news. At the same time, the story lines have to recognize audience knowledge of television itself and of other types of programme that might deal with terrorism but in an entirely different way. The third rule is that producers have to meet the audience's expectations for the show. This is partly a question of genre, which is discussed in chapter 3. So individual shows cannot stray too far from generic conventions. Furthermore, a particular programme will set up its own conventions (as in the *Dr Who* example discussed earlier). One way in which this is manifest is in the consistency and regular appearance of the central characters. Lastly, writers and producers have to work to the rule 'Don't divide the audience'. Issues, those involving ethnic conflict or rape for instance, are avoided because they will invite controversy and put off at least part of the audience that might be offended by the treatment of the issue. The further assumption is that the audience as a whole is put off by controversy.

These examples show the way in which producers of television programmes have some notion of the audience in mind when they are deciding what to produce. Indeed, they must have such a conception in order to make decisions at all. It is an image of the audience that provides the basis for deciding on one programme rather than another. As Ang (1991) points out, it is not easy for television producers to get at the audience directly, for it is a dispersed mass hidden in millions of private homes. Therefore, what they have to construct is an 'invisible fiction' (Hartley, 1987) of the audience, which may or may not bear much relation to its actual characteristics.

Television producers will try, in varying degrees, to measure the audience in order to produce a more accurate model of how audiences are responding to programmes (a discussion of various methods of audience measurement is provided in the next chapter). All television companies measure their audiences, often in very sophisticated ways. Two of the most used indices are audience size and audience appreciation (how much the audience has liked a programme). Television professionals pay a great deal of attention to the 'ratings' even though they are widely regarded as misleading. Indeed everyone involved with a programme will have a powerful interest in the ratings as a measure of how well they are doing. As a producer on an American daytime soap said:

> The writer will call every Thursday (the day the ratings come out). He might say, 'Hi, it's a nice day. I got the script on the way.' Then 'Did you get the ratings? Did the ratings come in yet?' The actors may not want to get into specifics but they will come up rather timidly and say, 'How are we doing?' (Intintoli, 1984, p. 184)

In a study of British television (in the BBC) Burns (1977) found a similar concern with ratings:

> The shock of a reported AR [audience rating] figure of 63 for a programme in a 1963 comedy series which had touched 75 was enough to disrupt the first hour or two of rehearsal of a subsequent production. Very little work was done. The atmosphere of dejection deepened with every new arrival. Clusters formed around the leading actors, the floor manager, and the assistant floor manager, with the producer circulating between them and the telephone. 'This', it was explained to me, 'is what it's like on a morning you've got a low audience figure.' For cast and pro-

duction team, it was 'the figure'. Even after rehearsal began, the figure returned to the centre of the stage during waits: '63 – and I thought it was such a bloody good show.' The whole gathering was, in fact, engaged in a more preoccupying task than rehearsal for the next show: the search for a reassuring explanation. It was found eventually in the concurrence of a sports film on the commercial network. (p. 177, quoted in Ang, 1991, p. 147)

Ang argues, however, that not only is audience measurement inaccurate, but its real purpose is to provide an *image of a controllable audience* so that producers can continue with their day-to-day work (see also Cantor, 1987). In Ang's view, the television institutions are not really interested in accurate description of the untidy reality of audiences because this would interfere with their attempts to construct a streamlined product.

> This suggests that if television institutions need to know the audience in order to establish and maintain a relationship with it, they are generally not interested in getting to know what real people think and feel and do in their everyday dealings with television. Indeed, institutional knowledge about the television audience inevitably abstracts from the messy and confusing social world of actual audiences because this world is irritating for the institutions, whose first and foremost concern is to seize control over their own conditions of existence . . . Institutional knowledge is driven toward making the audience visible in such a way that it helps the institutions to increase their power to get their relationship with the audience under control, and this can only be done by symbolically constructing 'television audience' as a objectified category of others that can be controlled. (p. 7)

This point can be illustrated by the production of *EastEnders*. Although this programme was designed to fill a gap in the BBC's early evening schedule, and was therefore nominally fairly tightly targeted, data on the audience was not actively used in its development. Furthermore, the evidence that was available was actually ignored. The programme makers may have been enthused by good ratings but they did not use them as any kind of guide. Instead they relied on their own judgements about what made good programming, and the major source of contact with the audience was their visits to the pub or discussions with the tea-lady. So, producers and script writers had to have some idea of the audience in order to produce programmes at all. To make a show with a degree of realism they valued their contacts with everyday life, with street talk. But they did not value detailed audience research, which would, in their view, only get in the way of the creative process. In a sense, what the producers of *EastEnders* do is to reflect what they *imagine* to be the audience's concerns back at them. There is a contrast with the ill-fated *Eldorado*, the production of which did use audience research.

One obvious implication of Ang's argument that television producers operate with a model of the audience for their particular programmes which is created to make the production of the programme easier, to create a controllable production situation, is that there may well be a gap between this model and what the audience actually thinks and does. With the advent of new, and more fragmented, audiences created by new technologies of cable, satellite and videorecorder, this gap may potentially be even larger. (See chapters 6 and 7 for a more detailed account of the new audience.) Of course, this gap means that producers frequently misjudge the audience to such an extent that programmes flop badly. At other times, however, it is distinctly possible that there is a gap between producers' model of the audience and the actual audience, but the programme works. And that is the test with which most producers operate. If programmes work, there is no need to revise the audience model, whatever detailed audience research shows. For example, Lewis (1991) shows that audiences do not in general understand the news. There is a gap between the model of the audience employed by the news producers and the expectations and capacities of the audience. However, people still continue to watch the news, not least because they feel that they 'ought' to, and producers continue to produce the news in the way that they feel is appropriate.

Television producers have a rather more direct means of trying to control the audience. This takes the form of scheduling; that is, the decisions about at what time, on what day and in which season to run a programme. This is a competitive activity. Schedulers from BBC and ITV (and now also satellite and cable) will try to win market share from each other by ingenious placing of popular programmes. This can lead to 'ratings wars'. For example, Michael Grade, who was in charge of scheduling *EastEnders* when it first appeared, originally put the programme at 7.00 p.m. followed by a popular programme to try and keep viewers with BBC throughout the early evening. At this time it clashed with *Emmerdale Farm* (as it was then called). Then followed a duel:

I put *EastEnders* at 7.00 because *Emmerdale Farm* was not networked. As
a response to it going at 7.00, ITV for once got its act together and networked *Emmerdale Farm*. That was a blow, but I knew – from my knowledge of ITV – that *Emmerdale Farm* went off the air in the summer for a
number of weeks, and I only had to wait for that window, and then I
would be away. What they did was that they somehow squeezed extra
episodes and repeats, so there was no break in the clouds. So I thought,
this is crazy, this is silly now, I'm going to have to move it. And because
of the sort of press we have in this country, I didn't want them rubbishing
the show – 'panic move' – they'd have written that as a failure story. I
had to dress the presentation of that move in such a way as to protect the
show, so I gave all kinds of reasons for the move, trying to disguise the
fact that I was having to move it because it had reached a plateau and
wasn't moving off. (Michael Grade, quoted in Buckingham, 1987, p. 22)

Grade subsequently moved *EastEnders* to 7.30 p.m. In this position
it had less competition and this allowed it to build up its very large
audience.

Ratings wars of this kind are much more common in the United
States, where the networks are locked in a far more vicious commercial struggle for audience share. Although still competitive, British
scheduling is rather less aggressive. All British broadcast television
providers are still within the public service tradition, the differences
in funding method means that audience share is not *that* important,
and there are in any case agreements between BBC and ITV which
moderate the worst excesses of competition (Paterson, 1990).

Despite this gentlemanly moderation, the practices of scheduling
do represent the intrusion of some market principles into the programming decisions of British television producers. Thus, John Birt,
now director-general of the BBC, made his name by proclaiming
the primacy of the schedule. According to this doctrine, the schedule should be decided and then programmes should be commissioned to fit particular kinds of audience and particular time-slots.
The practice before was to produce good programmes and then
decide what was the best time to put them on.

Scheduling is therefore part of the strategic planning process. It
involves balancing programming against finance against time-slots
and is very much the province of senior management. Schedulers
use a number of techniques to improve the likely audience for their
programmes. For example, a programme that is likely to be less
popular will be placed between two programmes that do attract substantial audiences – so-called 'hammocking'. Alternatively, if a programme wins a large audience, the next programme can be expected

to 'inherit' a substantial proportion of that audience through audience inertia. Sometimes, through a process called 'pre-echo', audiences will begin to watch a programme regularly simply because it precedes one that they particularly want to watch and they have sampled it by turning on a little early. It used to be thought (though no longer) that there was substantial channel loyalty and once an audience had switched on to one channel, they would stay with it, again out of inertia. There are also a number of constraints that schedulers have to cope with. For example, the evening news on both BBC and ITV is a fixed point and the schedules have to be constructed around it, as is done with other programmes so popular (*Coronation Street* and *EastEnders* are examples) that the audience has got used to them and they cannot be moved. Constraints of this kind will limit other programme possibilities. For example, 'adult' drama, particularly that involving violence or other moral risk, on the independent channels cannot be broadcast before 9.00 p.m. because the family viewing policy insists that children should not be exposed to this sort of programme and they will be safely in bed at that time. However, the evening news is at 10.00 p.m. This means that drama has to fit into the hour between 9.00 p.m. and 10.00 p.m.

Scheduling clearly involves a model of audience behaviour. The schedulers have to make assumptions about what the audience is doing at various times of day. Paterson (1990) argues that these assumptions largely have to do with *family* behaviour. As he says:

> The policy is rooted in normative assumptions about the family. In the early evening, domestic life is assumed to be devoted to meals and the audience is understood to be unable to concentrate for long spells. Television is in the control of the child audience with parents available intermittently until about 7.30 p.m. From this time the mother is thought to control television, which functions for the next 90 minutes as the focus of the family. After 9.00 p.m., when the rules on content are less strict, children's viewing is seen as the responsibility of the parent. Control of the television set is shared between the adults with the father assumed to take a much more central role in programme choice. (p. 33)

Such a view of the way that families work may be well out of date. In any case family structures and ways of behaving are so very diverse that it would only have applied to a minority of households. Nevertheless, programme planners have to make some assumptions about the lives of their audiences in order to schedule at all.

Changing Systems

It will be clear from much of the discussion in this book that television is in flux. There are new ways in which television programmes are transmitted, there are new regulatory regimes, and new audiences are being created. These features are being reflected in new ways of organizing production.

At the beginning of this chapter I stressed the way in which television production was like the production of manufactured goods in a factory. It is a complex process with a high degree of division of labour; the production process is highly fragmented. This fragmentation of the work process requires active and detailed coordination by management and, partly as a result, the relationships of production are hierarchical, with final authority vested in the management. Television organizations in Britain are vertically integrated, incorporating within the organization all the functions needed to produce, market and distribute television programmes. In the 1990s, however, this form of organization is beginning to break down under the impact of economic and legislative changes.

Some insight into these changes may be gained from an account of similar changes in the film industry in Hollywood. Christopherson and Storper (1986) argue that, until the late 1940s, films were produced in Hollywood by a factory-like process – the studio system. The studio was set up as an assembly line for large-scale production of a standardized film product. Film production crews carried out separated, specialized tasks and their skills were virtually handed down from father to son through apprenticeships. Scenes were shot not in chronological order but in batches, using the same actors and sets in order to maximize efficiency. Such a system needed fairly detailed management control and this gave the central place in film production to the producer rather than the director or any of the other artistic roles. The studios stabilized their markets by vertically integrating production of films with their marketing, distribution and exhibition. In particular, the studios owned or controlled a substantial proportion of the cinemas and were thus able to guarantee an outlet for their production.

This was, then, a stable world. The studios' scale of output kept their costs down, their workers had steady employment, and markets were kept firm. All of this prevented serious competition, since it was difficult for any new company to become established. In the forty or so years since the late 1940s this system has gradually changed. The process was initiated by a court decision in which the studios were forced to divest themselves of their cinema chains. This deprived them of their guaranteed market and greatly increased the risks of making films. The second major force for change was the appearance of television, which slowly established itself as an important competitor for the consumers' time and money. As a result, the studio system gradually started to crumble. Throughout the 1950s the studios increasingly turned to independent producers to make films, which would then be rented out to distributors by the studios. Initially this was an attempt to gain a greater variety of films (achieve product differentiation) but it also had cost advantages. Both the levels and security of employment of production and other staff declined. More production was also undertaken outside the United States, partly in an attempt to create films which could have an export market. These processes accelerated from 1970 onwards as the studios had their worst year ever. The major studios shrank in size to cut down their overheads. They sold off land and disposed of much of their production facilities. An increasing proportion of film making was hived off to independent production companies, which in turn subcontracted to smaller specialized firms. These independent firms were effectively carrying much of the risk previously shouldered by the studios. The result is that the film production and distribution industry is now composed of a multitude of specialized units, which are no longer all within the same organization.

Until the early 1980s the television industry in Britain was a little like the early film industry. BBC 1, BBC 2 and ITV had the field to themselves with no real competition; they had stable and relatively well-funded markets. They were large, integrated companies, which, as a rule, carried out all production in-house. They were also responsible for distribution. They offered secure employment to their staff. Producers did not feel market pressures directly and had little idea of the make-up of their audience. As Tunstall (1993) sums up:

> Television producers lived a sheltered life within a system based on consensus and cartel. There was a consensus between the political parties and between broadcasters schooled in the BBC and ITV versions of public service. The trade unions also played a central role, favouring good-quality British programming, a broad mix of programming genres, and strict quotas of cheap programme imports. The unions got secure employment for their members, with extremely generous levels of manning and overmanning. (p. 8)

By the early 1990s this picture of the television industry was being changed by a variety of factors, chief among which were the appearance of Channel 4, competition from satellite and cable, and government requirements for a proportion of independent production in the main channels. The first three of these issues – Channel 4, satellite and cable – have already been discussed in chapter 4.

Channel 4 pioneered a new form of television production modelled on the book publishing industry, in which producers commissioned programmes from independent production companies. One obvious effect that this had was to encourage the development of an independent sector rather like the independent film companies that had developed in Hollywood. In 1980 the independent sector was tiny. By 1990 one thousand firms were independent television producers. The great majority of these are extremely small, but between ten and fifteen are large, with turnovers of over £5 million. It is likely that there will be some concentration in the sector as the larger companies take over the smaller.

The boost to the independent sector given by the formation of Channel 4 was further enhanced by the 1990 Broadcasting Act, which stipulated that one-quarter of BBC and ITV production had to be carried out by independent production companies. The four new ITV companies which won franchises in 1991 all began broadcasting by buying in programmes from independents. Together with the move to independent programming went other features reminiscent of the Hollywood experience. Employment in the main channels was reduced. In 1987–8 the ITV companies were employing 17,000 people to run a single national channel, and in 1993 that number had shrunk to 11,000 (Tunstall, 1993). Instead of having life-long employment, staff were employed on short-term contracts, especially junior production personnel. With so much production shifted out-of-house, BBC and ITV had a surplus of studio space and this was sold off. At the same time, and in concert with the Thatcher government's policy, there was an attack on trade union power.

It is still too early to tell what the effect of these changes will be. Life as a producer will undoubtedly be more insecure than it once was. However, as Tunstall (1993) points out, this does not mean that producers will lose power in general. Indeed, it may make them more autonomous, as more work is subcontracted to independent producers. In-house producers may also become more powerful. In 1992, for example, the BBC introduced its policy of 'producer choice', which gave producers more financial influence by allowing

them to decide whether to use in-house production facilities or to
go outside.

A contrary view to that taken by Tunstall is advocated by Cottle
(1995). He suggests that Tunstall has altogether too optimistic a
view of the power held by producers. The changes in technology,
the deregulation of television and increased commercial pressures
which were described in the last chapter have seriously reduced the
autonomy of the television producer, compromised the quality of
what they produce, and shifted real control up the hierarchy. The
last point is particularly important, for it 'is the way in which the
"big" decisions are taken by senior corporate personnel concerning
such fundamental concerns as whether to commission or not, the
degree of resourcing to be made available, and considerations of
scheduling' (p. 162) that is fundamental, in Cottle's view, to the
operation of British television.

6

The Importance of Audiences

As we have seen in the previous chapter, audiences are important to television producers, even those who work in public service television. Producers will work with an image of the audience in their minds, although that image may bear little relation to the reality.

Images of the television audience also inform wider public discussion of the medium. One common image is that of the passive viewer, slumped in front of the set mindlessly watching. Male versions of this couch potato have a can of lager in one hand and a bag of crisps in the other while they watch sport. Female versions are addicted viewers of every soap available. Such images of the passive audience are often associated both with particular ideas of the quality of television programmes and with theories of the effect that such viewing practices have. So, passive viewers are said to prefer trivial programmes and producers pander to them by offering such programmes. The combined effect of triviality and passivity is addiction and a lulling of the critical faculties.

The image of the passive viewer therefore connects up the content of programmes (trivial), with a mode of viewing (passive), with a set of effects on the audience (narcotizing). Similar sorts of assumption are at work in popular speculation about the effects of television on particular sections of the audience. For example, there is a persistent public debate about the effect of violent programmes on vulnerable sections of the audience, especially children.

Assumptions about audience behaviour of this kind are to be found at every level from everyday conversations through articles in the press to academic debates. As an academic example, a once-influential, though somewhat elderly, view of the effects of the popular media in general is to be found in the work of Adorno (1991). His view of the industries of culture is that they encourage mass deception and control consumers. They provide an 'affirmative culture' to 'regressed listeners'. Modern mass culture is standardized but pretends to be novel and can be contrasted with a genuine, pre-capitalist or early capitalist popular or folk culture. Most important of all, it encourages passivity in the audience and does not stimulate a critical social practice. 'By craftily sanctioning the demand for rubbish it [the culture industry] inaugurates total harmony' (Adorno and Horkheimer, 1979, p. 121). Modern sound movies, for example, stunt the 'mass media consumer's powers of imagination and spontaneity' (ibid., p. 126) by making the moving images so real that spectators are drawn into the movie world without any real thought. A similar, but more recent, critique of television has been put by Postman (1986), and is discussed in chapter 1.

Such views of the television audience as these take their meaning from a contrast with some other, preferred model of television watching. In this, audiences are active and critical of what they watch, they do not watch mindlessly, and they are perfectly capable of turning the set off to do something else more improving. Indeed, we probably all think that this is *our* mode of viewing; it is always *other* people who are the couch potatoes.

I have stressed that all these discussions flourish on assumptions about television audience behaviour. It is the purpose of this chapter, and the one that follows, to investigate these assumptions in more detail.

The History of Audience Research

It is customary to divide the history of academic research into television audiences into three phases: effects, uses and gratifications, and decoding.

Within the effects tradition, which lasted from about 1940 to 1960, the hypothesis to be tested was that television had direct effects on its audience. For example, it might be proposed that television election broadcasts had a direct effect on the way that audiences voted or that violence on television had a direct effect in producing violent conduct amongst the members of the audience. Actually the bulk of research within this tradition disconfirmed the hypothesis on the whole. Television, and the media generally, were found not to have direct effects and to be less powerful in moulding beliefs, attitudes and behaviour than other factors, such as personal influence. *Some* studies have found effects in certain circumstances. However, as Lewis (1990) points out, these studies tend to isolate a very specific media influence acting in particular ways, and it is unclear how generalizable the findings are to other circumstances and to the long term. For example, Hartmann and Husband (1974) found that the media played an important role in creating racist attitudes in all-white residential areas, mainly because they were the only sources of information.

In many ways, however, the general finding of no effects is not very surprising since the model of media effects that underpins it is very simple. The likelihood is that the whole process is much more complex. Audiences are not blank sheets of paper on which media messages can be written; members of an audience will have prior attitudes and beliefs which will determine how effective media messages are. Further, other intervening variables will mediate between audience and message. For example, Katz and Lazarsfeld (1955) showed how the media may have an effect through a 'two-step flow', in which influential people are affected by media messages and then pass on that effect, in a mediated and diluted form, to others. The research methods of the effects tradition also tended to produce an oversimplified model. They were usually based on experimental procedures, the ideal of which is to measure an audience's attitudes before and after an exposure to the media. Such a method necessarily considered media effect as a very *short-term* matter to do with change in *attitude*. The next phase of audience research, the uses and gratifications approach, therefore tried to look for longer-term changes; to consider audience members, not as isolated individuals, but as functioning within a social context; to take into account the content of the media; and to study not narrow attitude change but the wider knowledge, conduct and beliefs of the audience.

The uses and gratifications approach (particularly influential from the 1960s to the 1980s) was more fundamentally informed by a different way of seeing audiences. Its advocates claimed that, while the effects tradition looked at what television did to audiences, the uses and gratifications approach looked rather at what audiences did with television. Instead, therefore, of seeing the typical audience member as passive in the face of television, the uses and gratifications approach treated her or him as an active subject. The viewer in this scheme was treated as having certain needs, generated by a range of social processes, which television satisfied. The audience member is active in the sense that he or she chooses to watch television programmes, and makes sense of those programmes in ways that meet his or her needs. One early influential formulation of the approach stresses that it is concerned with:

> (1) the social and psychological origins of (2) needs, which generate (3) expectations of (4) the mass media or other sources which lead to (5) differential patterns of media exposure (or engagement in other activities), resulting in (6) need gratifications and (7) other consequences, perhaps mostly unintended ones. (Katz et al., 1974, p. 20, quoted in McQuail, 1987, p. 234)

McQuail (1987) has pointed out that this early formulation of the uses and gratifications approach depends too much on a concept of needs which has turned out to be difficult to operationalize in actual empirical research. He therefore prefers a reformulation as follows:

> (1) Personal social circumstances and psychological dispositions together influence both (2) general habits of media use and also (3) beliefs and expectations about the benefits offered by media, which shape (4) specific acts of media choice and consumption, followed by (5) assessments of the value of the experience (with consequences for further media use) and, possibly, (6) application of benefits acquired in other areas of experience and social activity. (p. 235)

Within the last twenty years or so, the uses and gratifications approach has itself been subject to criticism. For example, it has been argued that in several of its manifestations it has *too* active a notion of the audience member. It almost seems that audiences have complete autonomy in relation to television. While much effects research started off with the assumption, which it then proved to be incorrect, that members of the television audience were almost powerless in the face of television, uses and gratifications research at times seems to go to the opposite extreme and assume that audiences are all-powerful. Another line of criticism is that the uses and gratifications approach does not provide a good account of meaning, of the way that audiences read or interpret television programmes.

It is this last criticism that the third school of television audience research – the decoding approach – is designed to address. A prevailing assumption of this approach is that watching television is essentially a process of decoding (Hall, 1980). Audiences are looking for the meaning in the television programme in much the same way as a spy will extract the meaning from – or decode – a message from his or her controller. The implication that television programmes are something of a puzzle is deliberate, although it is also important to note that audiences are not conscious of the decoding process that they use; extracting the meaning from a programme is an everyday, taken-for-granted process. It is even more important to realize that, perhaps unlike the spy's message, there are several possible meanings in a television message and therefore several different ways of decoding it.

The process of decoding takes place within a social context. How one 'reads' or interprets or gives meaning to a television programme depends on social position and the situation within which the programme is seen or talked about. One of the first empirical studies in the decoding approach was by Morley (1980). Morley was interested in exploring how the process of decoding differed by social group. His method was to show a programme of the current affairs documentary *Nationwide* to different groups of people (twenty-eight in all), each of which represented a social position. So, for example, he had a group of black students in further education, a group of bank managers and a group of shop stewards. Following the showing of the programme there was a discussion in the group of the issues dealt with. Different groups had very different reactions. Morley classifies these reactions into three types: dominant, negotiated and oppositional. If a section of the audience responds in the dominant mode, they are using the values, attitudes and beliefs that are dominant in society. If they use oppositional modes, they are, as the term implies, employing a way of thinking that contradicts the dominant mode. Other groups within the audience using the negotiated mode are neither oppositional nor dominant but have a meaning system that can live with dominant values without believing or accepting them.

The division of the audience into these three blocks, however, still oversimplifies the social structure of the audience, as figure 6.1 shows. For example, both black students and shop stewards had oppositional ways of thinking and saw *Nationwide* as biased against the working class. However, they were also very different from each other. The black students essentially withdrew, considering the programme to be irrelevant to their concerns. The shop stewards, on the other hand, tended to be actively critical, seeing *Nationwide* from a radical working-class perspective. Similarly, amongst those

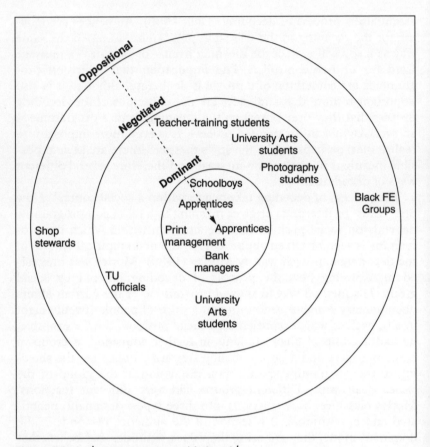

Figure 6.1 Audience responses to *Nationwide*
Source: Morley, 1980, p. 136

adopting the dominant mode there are great differences. Bank managers were traditionally conservative. Apprentices, on the other hand, tended to be much more cynical about people appearing on the programme, whoever they were, but at the same time held 'dominant' attitudes on the evils of trade unionism or of the social security system.

In describing different approaches to the study of television audiences, it is easy to exaggerate the differences between them. Indeed, all three approaches are trying to get at similar questions and, as Curran (1990) points out, there is a strong tendency for each new school of audience research to reinvent the wheel. To the extent that there are differences of approach, they more often concern methodology rather than issues of substance. The effects tradition tended to use the experimental methods of psychology or large questionnaire surveys on attitudes. The ideal was to produce quantitative data under controlled circumstances, which permitted detailed statistical analysis and a relatively high degree of validity and reliability in results. The decoding method, on the other hand, tends to use interview methods on very small samples. For example, a characteristic strategy is to tape-record a group of viewers discussing a programme and then to try to analyse the conversation that results. The ideal here is to understand in depth the meaning that participants give to the television experience and not necessarily to produce results with a high degree of reliability and validity. It is qualitative rather than quantitative. The uses and gratifications approach, on the other hand, tends to adopt both kinds of method. There are also variations in the theoretical models of the audience that are adopted.

Audience Measurement

The television industry needs to measure audiences to establish the level and nature of audiences for programme monitoring and for the selling of advertising airtime. Since 1981, the Broadcasters' Audience Research Board (BARB), jointly owned by the BBC and the Independent Television Association, has been in charge of audience research for the industry. BARB is responsible for specifying and approving measurement systems and commissioning research of various kinds, which it does by periodically appointing a research contractor. Since 1991, measurement of audiences has been done electronically by means of the Peoplemeter. This is a device placed inside the television set which can record when the television is on and what channel is being watched. It can also record who is watching, since each member of the household (and visitors) presses a button on a handset to indicate that he or she is watching. In addition, the meter will report data on videorecorder usage, including its use in recording programmes off the television for viewing later on (so-called time shifting).

A great deal of care goes into the construction of the sample of households that will have a Peoplemeter installed. The full sample of 4500 households nationally is actually constructed by aggregating sub-samples from each ITV region. Each of these sub-samples is designed to represent different household structures, made up by the interaction of three variables: stage in the life-course (for example, does the household have children), occupational and educational status of the head of the household, and household size. The result is that twenty-four different types of household are represented, allowing very detailed statistical analysis. (For further discussion, see Sharot, 1994.) The result of this carefully controlled measurement system is a programme rating, which may be defined as the proportion of the total relevant population that sees that programme. For example, a rating of 25 per cent for *Coronation Street* amongst adults in the Granada region would therefore mean that 25 per cent of adults who are able to receive Granada transmissions in that region watched *Coronation Street*.

In addition to the data gathered by the Peoplemeter, BARB also carries out other kinds of research. For example, audience reaction – to what degree audiences like the programmes they watch – is studied by asking a panel of viewers to fill in weekly diaries and scoring each programme on a scale of 1 to 6. An appreciation index is calculated, which gives the average score expressed as a percentage of the maximum possible (an average of 6 would represent 100 per cent). Again, because the panel of respondents is chosen to reflect various demographic factors, detailed statistical analysis of audience appreciation is possible.

The Constitution of the Audience

Measurement systems of the kind that I have described produce a great deal of detailed information about the audience, although it tends to cover a relatively narrow range of topics that concern programme makers and advertisers.

Television commands a great deal of its audience's time and interest. There are seasonal variations in this total; the amount of time we spend on average watching the television is about half as much again in winter as in summer. Women watch more than men. There are also differences between the social classes in the amount of television viewed, as table 6. 1 illustrates.

As table 6.1 also shows, the total of hours of viewing has declined over the years. This decline is particularly significant as the amount

Table 6.1   Hours of viewing

	1986	1987	1988	1989	1990
Social class (hours:mins per week)					
ABC1	20:47	20:54	20:14	19:48	19:31
C2	25:18	24:40	25:25	25:00	24:13
DE	33:11	31:47	31:44	30:57	30:13
All persons	25:54	25:25	25:21	24:44	23:51
Reach (per cent)					
Daily	78	76	77	78	77
Weekly	94	93	94	94	94

Notes: Viewing was of live television broadcasts from the BBC, ITV and
Channel 4.
Percentage of UK population aged 4 and over who viewed TV for at
least three consecutive minutes.
Source: *Social Trends* (1992)

of programming available to audiences increased over the period.
The result was that each channel commanded a smaller amount of
audience time. Part of the reason for this loss of audience was the
increased use of videorecorders. During the 1980s video use was
not recorded by the measurement systems then in use. As we have
seen, since 1991 the Peoplemeter has been able to measure such
use; currently homes with VCRs record some five hours of
television per week, about half of which is played back within a
week.

Even if it has declined somewhat, television viewing represents a
substantial commitment of time for most people. Table 6.2 shows
the amount of time in minutes that people take in various leisure
pursuits in the home. Television is by a very long way the most popular such pursuit, occupying almost twice as much time as all other
leisure pursuits combined. Indeed, television takes up more of our
time than *any* activity other than sleeping and working.

Because television is, in general, a leisure pursuit, viewing practices have a well-marked daily rhythm. Between 10 and 15 per cent
of the population will be watching during the day until the mid-
afternoon. From then on the audience builds up until it reaches
almost half of the population at the peak time of between 8.00 p.m.
and 10.00 p.m.

From a sociological point of view, perhaps the most interesting
finding from the audience measurement systems concerns the kinds
of programme that people watch. Table 6.3 shows the amount of

Table 6.2   Leisure inside the home (minutes per average day)

Activity	Men, full-time employed			Women, full-time employed		
	1961	1974–5	1983–4	1961	1974–5	1983–4
Radio	23	5	3	16	3	2
Watching TV	121	126	129	93	103	102
Listening to music	1	3	1	1	1	1
Study	0	1	3	0	0	2
Reading book/ papers	28	19	24	13	13	20
Relaxing	20	31	16	27	31	14
Conversations	2	7	14	1	7	21
Entertaining	5	6	6	5	10	7
Knitting, sewing	0	0	0	14	8	7
Hobbies, etc.	8	7	12	3	7	11

Source: adapted from Gershuny and Jones (1987), p. 47

Table 6.3   Viewers of the main programme types by socio-economic background

UK adults 1985	Average viewing hours per week	Percentage of time spent viewing						
		Entertainment				Demanding		
		Light e'ment	Light drama	Films	Sport	Drama, Arts, etc.	Infor- mation	News
Social class								
ABC1*	23	16	24	11	9	4	18	10
C2DE	30	15	26	12	9	3	17	9

Note: *Better-off and longer-educated, professional, managerial, etc.
Source: Barwise and Ehrenberg (1988), p. 26

time that audiences spend on different types of programme, and what kinds of programmes those of different socio-economic background watch (defined in terms of occupation and education).

The proportions of time spent watching different types of programme are almost constant across the different groupings within the audience. In many ways this is a remarkable finding. In other fields of activity, generally speaking, one finds that different social groups have different social behaviours. For example, the middle class have very different tastes and leisure pursuits from the working class; women and men tend to have very different kinds of job. Yet all social groups watch a remarkably similar mix of types of television (see Barwise and Ehrenberg, 1988; Goodhardt et al., 1987).

Table 6.4   Viewing of the main programme types by viewers of different programmes

UK adults 1985	Percentage of their other viewing time spent viewing						
	Entertainment				Demanding		
	Light e'ment	Light drama	Films	Sport	Drama, Arts, etc.	Infor- mation	News
Viewers of the average programme of:							
Light entertainment	15	26	11	9	3	17	9
Light drama	15	27	12	9	3	18	9
Films	14	26	13	9	3	17	9
Sport	15	26	11	10	3	17	9
Drama, Arts, etc.	15	26	12	9	3	18	9
Information	15	26	11	9	3	17	9
News	15	26	11	9	3	17	10
Average	15	26	12	9	3	17	9

Source: Barwise and Ehrenberg (1988), p. 28

The two groups do, however, watch different *amounts* of television. The result of this is that the 'lower' social group watch more hours of demanding programmes in each week. Similar results obtain for other sub-groups within the population, men and women, old and young, north and south. There are some differences but they are still only slight. For example, women watch a higher proportion of soap opera than men and men watch more sport than women. This general lack of difference shows up in another way. Commonsensically, one might expect that those who watch, say, *Coronation Street* would have a different pattern of viewing from those who watch, say, *Panorama*. Again, this turns out not to be true. As table 6.4 shows, viewers of any one programme category, sport for example, spend about the same amount of time watching light entertainment as do viewers of light drama. More specifically, those who view *Coronation Street* will spend about the same amount of time watching programmes like *Match of the Day* as those who watch *Panorama*. In other words, there is almost no tendency for people to focus on one programme type.

In general, then, different social groups have remarkably similar viewing patterns. The same lack of social differentiation is found by looking at the problem from the opposite perspective, not which programmes different groups watch, but what the makeup of the audience is for different programme types. Again, as table 6.3 shows, the demographic constitution of the audience for any one programme type is much the same as for any other. As before, sport is the exception in that a much higher proportion of men watch it compared with other programme types.

It is important, clearly, for the television channels and networks to try as hard as they can to retain their audience and not allow it to go to competing channels. I have already explored, in chapter 5, some of the scheduling tactics that are employed. A great deal of television is produced as serials or series, both drama and documentary. From the point of view of the television producers this has several advantages. It helps to lower costs (see chapter 4) and it should contribute to the retention of audiences who will, it could be assumed, remain loyal to a particular programme week after week. On the face of it, audiences do appear to be loyal. After all, successive episodes of *Brookside*, for instance, do attract roughly the same audience rating. However, surprisingly, it turns out that this audience is not composed of the same people. In Britain, about half of the people in the audience for one episode watch the next one. This figure varies very little for different types of programme, for serials, or series, or programmes with the same format. Although this seems to demonstrate a lack of viewer commitment to what may be favourite programmes, Barwise and Ehrenberg (1988) argue that there is still some loyalty. Even with levels of repeat viewing of 50 per cent, it is more likely that someone who watched one episode of *The Bill* will see the next one than someone who did not. Furthermore, it turns out that the main reason why people do not watch successive episodes is that they are not watching the television *at all*. Of those who do watch at the same time each week, the majority are watching the same programme that they watched the previous week.

One of the implications of the relative lack of viewer loyalty is that many viewers do not see every episode of long-running serials. For example, 30 per cent of the audience for the critically acclaimed serial *Jewel in the Crown* saw one episode of the total of fourteen, 6 per cent saw four episodes and only 2 per cent saw all fourteen. Although there were a good many frequent viewers of the serial, most audience members were effectively dipping in and out. So, even if very few people saw every episode of *Jewel in the Crown*, a fairly large number saw at least one episode. This is usually called *programme reach*, a concept which refers to the proportion of the audience that ever watches an episode of a series or serial.

So far the discussion has concentrated on what people actually do watch rather on what they want to watch. For a variety of reasons, members of the television audience may not actually watch what they want or like to watch. Most viewing takes place within households round one set and there will necessarily be a good deal of negotiation about what to watch, which will result in some members of the household giving up their preferences.

The industry uses a comparatively simple method of measuring audience satisfaction, the appreciation index. Viewers are asked to indicate their appreciation of programmes by putting them into one of six categories. The bottom one, 'Not at all interesting and/or enjoyable', is given a score of zero, while the top one, 'extremely interesting and/or enjoyable', is given a score of 100. The intervening categories go up in steps of 20. The scores of individuals are then averaged to produce an average appreciation index for the programme. Appreciation indices (AIs) do not vary a great deal between different programmes – generally in the range 60–80. There are some relatively unsurprising relationships between appreciation and viewing patterns. For example, for entertainment programmes, people who frequently or regularly view a programme often tend to like it better than those who do so more rarely. Rather less expected is the relationship between audience size and audience appreciation. As table 6.5 shows, in general, programmes attracting lower audiences are also less liked. Part of this is due to the fact that the more popular programmes attract more frequent viewers who generally give higher appreciation indices. There is also considerable variation between individual programmes; some minority programmes can be extremely well liked. However, the finding does to some extent undermine any commonsense assumption that minority interest programmes will automatically attract a band of followers who greatly like the programmes.

For more 'demanding' programmes, documentaries or news magazines for example, the pattern is rather different. Programmes of this type, with similar audience size to entertainment programmes, will attract higher AIs. Furthermore, there is no relationship between audience size and AI for this type of programme.

Earlier on in this section I presented data which appear to show that people do not 'specialize' in particular types of programme; viewers of *Coronation Street* are not any more likely to watch *EastEnders* than are viewers of *Newsnight*. This, however, records what people actually watch; it does not record what they want to

Table 6.5   Audience size and average audience appreciation

Audience size (percentage rating)	Audience appreciation
25+	74
20–24	70
15–19	69
10–14	67
1–9	65

Source: Barwise and Ehrenberg (1988), p. 52

Table 6.6   Programme clusters

Programme cluster	Examples on ITV	Examples on BBC
1. *Sports*	World of Sport Professional Boxing	Grandstand Match of the Day Rugby Special
2. *Current affairs*	Today This Week Aquarius	Late Night Line Up Talk Back 24 Hours Panorama
3. *Light entertainment* (a) Serials	(a) Coronation St. Peyton Place Family at War	
(b) General	(b) Opportunity Knocks Golden Shot This is Your Life Mike & Bernie	(b) Z-Cars Owen M.D. Galloping Gourmet
(c) Sit. comedy	(c) Please Sir On the Buses	(c) Now Take My Wife Here's Lucy
4. *Adventure*	Public Eye Callan Jason King Hawaii Five-O	Ironside The Virginian
5. *Children's*		Magic Roundabout Blue Peter
6. (*Not named*)	Thunderbirds	Star Trek Pink Panther Monty Python Top of the Pops

Source: Goodhardt et al. (1987), p. 104

watch. Data derived from programme preferences show that there *are* distinct clusters of programme (Goodhardt et al., 1987). That is, there is a tendency for viewers who like one programme of a type also to like another. Six programme clusters are identifiable. Table 6.6 shows what they are with examples of programmes taken from 1972. It should be noted that this is not an exclusive classification in which people like one type of programme and not others. It is simply based on groupings of above-average likings. These clusters correspond to commonsense categories, with the possible exception of the last one (sometimes referred to as cult programmes).

Why then should there be a clustering of viewers' *liking* of programmes when there is no such clustering for their *actual* viewing? The main reason has been referred to earlier. Within families watching television there has to be some negotiation about what to watch at any given time and, as a result, some people will end up watching programmes that they do not especially like because other family members do like them.

The Nature of Television

Barwise and Ehrenberg (1988) argue that this data on television audiences indicates that television is a mass, low-involvement medium. Many of the markets for consumer goods are segmented. For example, the readership of different magazines, newspapers or books varies by social class, age, gender and so on. Thus the *Sun* has a much more working-class readership than the *Guardian*. On average, the readership of *Bella* is younger than that for *Good Housekeeping*. Television, however, as we have seen, is quite different. Programmes do not appeal to particular social groups. For almost any programme the make-up of the audience is the same. Television is truly a mass medium.

Television does not involve its audience to the extent that other media can. It is usually watched in distracting circumstances in the home, while a lot of other activities are going on. The result is that people do not always concentrate intently on the television and, indeed, the medium frequently does not demand such attention. In this respect, it is unlike print media, especially books, that do require a greater attentiveness and which are often used in more conducive circumstances such as solitary reading. The same is true of film, whose conditions of reception are modelled on the theatre, in which it is (in the twentieth century at any rate) inappropriate to do something else while the film is on. At the same time, television is poorer than print at conveying information efficiently. The result of these features is that we use television for relaxation in an almost casual way, so that we frequently watch whatever is on. The low-involvement quality of television is also shown in the lack of loyalty to series or serials, so that only half of the audience will watch next week's episode having watched this week's, an absence of channel loyalty, and the non-association between particular social groups and types of programmes. Barwise and Ehrenberg summarize:

> There is abundant evidence from audience research that people rarely go to much trouble to watch particular programmes. The fact that we are lit-tle involved in most of what we watch explains, for example, the low use of VCRs relative to the total amount of television viewing, the steady day to day size of the total television audience regardless of what is being shown, the low repeat-viewing of all programme series, the often fairly moderate levels of audience attention and appreciation, and the tendency for people to avoid watching demanding programmes. (p. 124)

In discussing the habits and behaviour of television audiences so far, I have relied on a particular style of audience research, which aims to provide quantitative evidence based on direct measurement systems like the Peoplemeter or on standardized questionnaire or diary methods. Such methods are particularly powerful in certain respects, in providing reliable and valid data. However, they also have their drawbacks. First, they do not get at the television experi-ence as a whole but rather at the individual programme or given sets of programmes. It is arguable that, generally, audiences do not watch programmes. What they watch is *flow* (see chapter 2). The set is switched on of an evening and the household sits in front of it, not particularly attentively perhaps, and indulges in a flow of televi-sion experience. Some audience members may even zap quickly between channels, not paying very much attention to any one pro-gramme. Second, there is now abundant evidence that audience members attend to television in very different ways at different times. Sometimes they give the set their full attention and some-times they do not. Frequently they are not even in the room when the set is on. The methods of audience research that I have described so far cannot distinguish between such very different modes of appropriation. Third, and most important, most of the vital questions about television audiences concern what audiences actually make of the programmes that they see, what meaning they give them. We want to know, above all else, how people talk about television, how television affects them, how they interpret what they see. Such questions will apply even if it is accepted that television is a low-involvement medium. I return to their discussion in the next chapter.

The Powerful Audience

So far, I have discussed the ways in which the audience may be undifferentiated but also the ways in which it is segmented on classical sociological lines – by social group, social class, for example, or gender. There are other ways in which the audience is divided up, however, and in this section I consider the proposition that some sections of the audience are more powerful than others.

When producers make television programmes, they have in mind, to varying degrees, the domestic audience. They are also aware of other groups that have, for various different reasons, an interest in the kinds of programme that are put out. The government of the day, for example, often has an uneasy relationship with the media in general because of its obvious interest in the portrayal of its policies and the comment on its conduct. In the case of the BBC this relationship is particularly difficult, as I showed in chapter 4. Because of the national and international prestige of the BBC, its role as a public service broadcaster, and the government's control over the level of the licence fee and hence the corporation's income, there will always be the suspicion that programmes are influenced by government pressure. In the spring of 1995, for example, as box 3 above shows, a number of government ministers made attacks on the BBC's alleged anti-Tory bias. The BBC then scheduled a full-length *Panorama* interview with the prime minister, John Major, to be broadcast three days before local elections in Scotland. The opposition parties took the corporation to court in Scotland to try to get the transmission postponed on the grounds that it infringed the BBC's own rules concerning equal treatment of all political parties before elections. The courts ruled that the transmission of the programme, without any attempt to balance it by interviews with the leaders of the other parties, was indeed an infringement of the

BBC's own rules and, as a result, the programme was transmitted after the election. At the time, many commentators surmised that the corporation knew that the decision to broadcast the interview would cause the trouble that it subsequently did, but went ahead because it had been intimidated by the prior attacks from government ministers on its alleged lack of objectivity. This is but one recent example of attempted or actual government intervention in broadcasting. The post-war history of British television is actually peppered with incidents in which producers or managers have been influenced by the reactions of politicians (see, for example, Tracey, 1977).

Influential people and families can also form a powerful part of the television audience to which television personnel have to pay special attention. Tulloch (1990a), for example, describes the history of a television series, *The Last Place on Earth*, a semi-fictional account of Captain Scott's expedition to the Antarctic. The advance publicity for this series indicated that the script, written by playwright Trevor Griffiths, would present a portrait of Scott that was somewhat at variance with the prevailing image of him as a British hero. Scott's family attempted to influence the content of the series and recruited other influential people to bring pressure to bear on the television company responsible, Central Television. Concessions of various kinds were made to the protesters, although the programme was transmitted in several episodes. As Tulloch argues, the influence of Scott's family and associates was even more prominent in the debate that followed the screening of *The Last Place on Earth*, for press comment largely took the line that the programme had traduced Scott's justified reputation as an heroic polar explorer.

Besides pressure from government and powerful individuals, interest groups of all kinds will attempt to influence television organizations. They may want publicity for their causes or, conversely, they may want to stop adverse notice. They may, indeed, want to influence the content of television directly. Mary Whitehouse's National Viewers' and Listeners' Association for example, has represented a section of the audience which broadcasters have had to take special notice of (Tracey and Morrison, 1979). Whitehouse and her organization have been influential in mounting a critique of television organizations, the BBC in particular, as not embracing a firm enough moral code in their programming. In her view, they have helped to encourage a permissive moral climate in which individual freedom is the prime virtue. Whitehouse used these beliefs in her attack on the BBC over *EastEnders* (Buckingham, 1987). She argued that this programme, in its language, the topics that it dealt with, and the violent behaviour it occasionally depicted, violated the 'family viewing policy' and should not be shown before 9.00 p.m. in case children saw it. The BBC took Whitehouse's comments very seriously, although it is unclear how they actually affected the programme's content. The corporation's responses took the form of stressing first, the soap opera's moral commitment and, secondly, that it simply reflected real life in the East End of London.

Powerful sections of the audience may make themselves felt by direct contacts with television managers. They may also become visible, and hence enter into the calculations of programme producers, via publicity in newspapers and other media. Newspapers, indeed, take an extensive interest in television. A great deal of space in the tabloids is devoted to discussions of the events, characters and actors in television soap opera for instance. Buckingham (1987), in a survey of press coverage of *EastEnders* in a relatively quiet month in November 1985, found that the *Daily Mirror* carried seventeen separate stories in that month on *EastEnders* alone, the *Sun* had nineteen and the *Daily Star* twenty-six. The story reproduced from the *Sun* as figure 6.2 is entirely typical of the press coverage of soap opera.

As Brunsdon (1984) points out, newspaper comment on soap opera is in fact part of the pleasure of watching, and being involved in, the programmes:

> 'True stories', usually by cast and ex-cast, and usually in the popular Sundays or weeklies, promise to take the lid off the fiction. Autobiographies by people like Pat Phoenix and Noele Gordon offer glimpses of the relation between personality and character . . . Some of this material can be thought of as 'soap opera as news'. Exposés are certainly national news. But so are illness, death, legal prosecution, accidents, marriage and divorce of the actors and actresses. Often, these stories of 'real life' run as a kind of sub-text, or parallel soap to the one we watch on television. This sub-text is not kept separate when watching. The knowledge you have about particular characters 'in real life' feeds into and inflects the pleasure of soap watching. (pp. 82–3)

For television producers this volume of press comment is a double-edged weapon. On the one hand, it is often very good publicity. On the other, to the extent that newspapers are critical of television, it is one more constraint to take into account. For example, the now defunct soap opera *Crossroads* was the subject of a good deal of press

◎ ANOTHER CORONATION STREET EXCLUSIVE ◎

I Bet I can take over The Rovers

Simply the bust . . . Faith, left, raises a pint and poses on the bar just like Bet. Faith reckons she'd be a perfect replacement   **Faith picture: STEVE LEWIS**

By CHARLES YATES

FUNNYGIRL Faith Brown wants to get serious — as the new queen of Coronation Street.

Street fan Faith leapt in with an offer to the show's bosses after hearing that Julie Goodyear may quit as pub landlady Bet Gilroy

She said yesterday: "I can knocker the leopardskin spots off Bet — just let me prove it!"

Faith, 50, is desperate to take Julie's place in the Rovers Return.

Faith, whose boobs are a Bet-style 41ins, said "I've been a Coronation Street fan since the show started — I've never missed an episode.

"When I heard Julie was set to leave the show I couldn't believe my ears. I'd love the part — and I'm

Julie in war of words with her telly bosses

happy to audition for it. I'm no prima donna. People know me as a comedian, singer and impressionist but I want the chance to prove I'm a serious actress too.

"I've got the perfect credentials to replace Bet — I'm blonde, busty and I can pull pints as well as fellas!"

She added: "I'd like to be bitchier than Bet, but just as glamorous."

And she has dreamed up the perfect entrance line — as Alec Gilroy's new wife. She said "He

where I was the ship's entertainer."

Faith put in her bid after The Sun revealed last week Julie may quit.

Yesterday Julie was locked in a battle of words with Street chiefs. She has refused to agree to a statement prepared by Granada saying she's happy to carry on as Bet

Julie, 53, celebrates her 25th anniversary in the Street next month, but is disillusioned with the show. The star, who is on holiday in Lanzarote, has written her own version of the statement. She wants to

say she is having a "smashing holiday and intends to return soon to negotiate her contract."

Julie also wanted to add that she had not demanded more money on top of her £150,000-a-year contract.

Last night a Granada insider said: "There is almost a war between Julie and Granada over the statement.

"The show bosses want the statement to make it clear she has had a fantastic 25 years in the Street and that she wants it to continue.

"Julie, on the other hand, has different ideas. She wants time out to make a film and undertake other projects for at least a year.

"But she is resigned to the fact that she will not be allowed to do that and sees herself leaving."

When The Sun revealed her plans to quit last week, thousands of readers rang to protest and urged her to change her mind.

Figure 6.2 Tabloids on soaps
Source: *The Sun*, 7 April 1995 © News International

comment (Hobson, 1982). But at the time of the sacking of the leading actress, Noele Gordon, and also at the time the whole show was cancelled, newspapers treated the soap opera as a major story, involving extensive participation by television managers in public debate. The same is true of the more recently scrapped *Eldorado*.

The way in which the press feeds off television and television in turn responds to the press can lead to a kind of spiral of concern in which the various elements of the media create public interest in an issue. When this is limited to stories about television itself, as in the examples above, it may not have any wider social effects (although there are public concerns from time to time about the impact of television programmes on children). However, for issues going beyond television itself, the interaction of television with other branches of the media can create a 'moral panic'. The classic study of this phenomenon is by Cohen (1980). Cohen argues that, at certain times of social stress, societies get into moral panics about a particular social issue or group, during which a great deal of attention is focused on the behaviour of certain social groups. His study concentrated on the conflicts in southern seaside towns between mods and rockers. However, its conclusions could well apply to many social groups and issues: black immigrants, travellers in the West Country or raves, for example. The media have a major role in amplifying the panic, and because of this media attention, the agencies of social control – the government, the police and the courts – are driven to devise new policies to control the groups concerned. This gives a further turn to the screw in that government action, or police attention that results in arrests and convictions, is reported on television, on radio and in the press, further fuelling the sense of moral panic. This is an additional example of the way that television becomes part of the phenomena it is attempting to report. It suggests that television has effects, but these operate on particular sections of the audience who are in a position to influence events. As Gurevitch (1991) says:

> The enhancement of the roles, and the powers, of television can be traced to its emergence, in the era of instant global communication, as an active participant in the events it purportedly 'covers'. Television can no longer be regarded (if it ever was) as a mere observer and reporter of events. It is inextricably locked into these events, and has clearly become an integral part of the reality it reports. (p. 185)

The International Audience

In chapter 5, I pointed to the increasing internationalization of television. Not only is it the case that ownership is becoming internationalized, as media empires are built up which cross national frontiers, but so is content. Partly for economic reasons – chiefly the cost of producing television – many countries which have newly started up television broadcasting are forced to import programmes from other countries. The United States, in particular, is a major exporter of television programming. At the same time, I have been arguing in the previous section of this chapter that different sections of the audience have different tastes and respond differently to what they watch. With this degree of audience fragmentation it becomes difficult to see how a truly international audience is possible when national identities are so very distinct. In many ways, the answer to this problem is similar to that discussed in the section on the social structure of the audience. Television is a mass medium in the sense that it is provided in a non-segmented way. On the other hand, audiences are segmented in the sense that different audience groups appropriate television in different ways. Therefore, on the one hand, television is global while, on the other, it is local.

A number of anthropological studies indicate the globalization of the television experience. For example, Sreberny-Mohammadi (1991) argues that:

> What is often omitted from discussions on effects, are the deeper shifts in cultural orientations and patterns of sociability, in modes of perception and information-processing, that the advent of media create everywhere, albeit in different forms relative to the pre-existing local culture; that is to say it is the very 'fact of television', as Cavell (1982) calls it, in our social lives, not so much its content, that is most often overlooked. (p. 129)

The arrival of television in traditional societies, previously without it, has altered patterns of sociability and the use of time and has introduced conflicts within families between men and women and between young and old. At the same time such societies are able, over time, to integrate the new technology into their customary practices to some extent. Communal sociability, for example, may actually be enhanced by the existence of a television set. Television, in other words, plays its part (and it is only a part) in the renegotiation between traditional, national or local identities and the more widespread, even global, identities represented by television.

Nor is the *content* of television programmes at all irrelevant to this process. I have already pointed to the significant amount of imported television, mostly American, that most national television systems, especially in the third world, have to show. Some particular programmes do seem to attain an almost global popularity. *Dallas*, for example, was shown in over ninety countries and became a craze in many. In the Netherlands, for instance, over half of the population watched the programme at the height of its success in the spring of 1982 (Ang, 1985). The reaction to this popularity on the part of politicians, intellectuals and other opinion formers in many countries was very hostile. They saw *Dallas* as merely the latest, and most intrusive, symbol of the domination of American popular culture. Despite this hostility, the interest shown by audiences of very different cultural orientations across the world does indicate the need to explain the appeal of the programme. Liebes and Katz (1993) propose three reasons for the world-wide success of *Dallas*:

> (1) the universality, or primordiality, of some of its themes and formulae, which makes programs psychologically accessible; (2) the polyvalent or open potential of many of the stories, and thus their value as projective mechanisms and as material for negotiation and play in the families of man; and (3) the sheer availability of American programs in a marketplace where national producers – however zealous – cannot fill more than a fraction of the hours they feel they must provide. (p. 5)

Dallas has a general psychological appeal, trading on themes which are more or less humanly universal. For Ang (1985), whose study is based on letters that viewers wrote to her about *Dallas*, the appeal lies in 'the construction of a *psychological* reality and is not related to its (illusory) fit to an externally perceptible (social) reality' (p. 47). Viewers do not care if their social circumstances do not match those depicted in *Dallas*. What moves them is the feelings that are manifested in the relationships between the characters, feelings which are, perhaps, universal to the human condition.

However, the fact that *Dallas* appeals so widely to viewers across the world does not mean to say that it appeals in the same way, that audience reactions and interpretations are all identical. Indeed, there is every reason to believe that audiences of different nationality and ethnicity will have very different responses, as I will show in more detail in the next chapter. At its extremes, this variability of response is shown in countries in which *Dallas* was not a success. In Japan, for example, the programme was a dismal failure.

To the extent that there is an international audience for a programme like *Dallas*, therefore, it is one whose unity is as much illusory as real. In any case, as many commentators have pointed out, no subsequent television programme has managed to repeat the success of *Dallas*. Furthermore, there is considerable demand for local programming which trades on local cultural differences, whether national, ethnic or regional (Tunstall and Palmer, 1991). This is particularly obvious in regions within nation states which have strong minority identities of their own. Griffiths (1993), for example, carried out a study of the reception of a Welsh-language soap opera amongst school children in Wales. The children identified closely with the distinctive Welsh culture and language represented in the programme. One particular episode showed the tensions aroused when an outsider from England tried to buy a house in the community. The story line predominantly showed the negative effects of this 'invasion' and the viewers strongly supported this interpretation, citing their own experiences of the harmful consequences of English families moving into Welsh villages.

Fans

Fan groups do not seem so prominent in television as they are in film or rock music. To the extent to which there are television fan groups they also seem to take a different form from those based around other forms of media. In general, there is less concentration on being a fan of a star or individual performer, and this may be related to the way in which television creates personalities rather than stars (see chapter 5 for a discussion of this issue). Indeed, it is notable that people become fans of television *series* such as *Coronation Street, Dr Who* or *Star Trek*. It is the world that is created by such series that primarily attracts the dedicated interest of the fan, rather than individual characters or actors.

Two recent studies (Bacon-Smith, 1992; Jenkins, 1992) give ethnographic accounts of American television fan groups, Bacon-Smith concentrating on women fans. People can form fan groups around a variety of television shows including *Star Trek, Blake's 7, The Professionals, Starsky and Hutch* and *Dr Who*. Curiously, many American fan groups choose British series as objects of fandom because they are better written and do not present their characters in such black and white terms. The interest in the television series occupies a substantial part of the fan's time. Fans will meet with others to view the series concerned, to attend meetings and full-scale conventions, and, above all, to engage actively with the medium in a variety of ways.

Fans are organized in different ways, formally and informally. They may meet fairly frequently in small local groups in each other's houses (in 'circles'). Rather more formally, local clubs may be formed which are dedicated to a particular show. More formally still, conventions are held regularly all over the country and abroad, which may attract from 50 to 10,000 fans. At the same time there are a large number of fanzines, to which the fans contribute, which again vary in their degree of organization from several photocopied sheets to larger, more professionally produced publications. With all these activities, however, there is a great deal of variation in the behaviour of individual fans. As Bacon-Smith says:

> The media fan community has no established hierarchy or profit-making economy. While the group as a whole looks to no authority figures, some fans assume leadership roles in some aspects of the community's activities. These individuals are often core members of core circles. Not all

fans participate in the community with the same intensity. Some may collect fanzines, even write occasionally without engaging in communal
interactions at all. Others may participate peripherally in media fanzines,
while locating their home community in one of the many interlocking
fandoms such as gaming or literary science fiction. Still others look to the
community for 'family' relationships. (p. 41)

For Jenkins, fandom offers at least five types of activity. First, it
involves a particular mode of reception. Fans watch their favourite
programmes with a mixture of emotional engagement and critical
distance. They pay close attention, playing and replaying episodes
again and again. Second, fans deploy a particular set of critical and
interpretative practices:

Part of the process of becoming a fan involves learning the community's
preferred reading practices. Fan criticism is playful, speculative, subjec-
tive. Fans are concerned with the particularity of textual detail and with
the need for internal consistency across the programme episodes. They
create strong parallels between their own lives and the events of the
series. Fan critics work to resolve gaps, to explore excess details and
undeveloped potentials. (p. 278)

Third, fandom constitutes a basis for consumer activism. Fans organize themselves to lobby television stations, to object to scheduling
decisions, and to criticize the content of particular programmes.
Fourth, fans engage in forms of cultural production. Fan writers,
artists, musicians and video makers create work that is derived
from commercial popular culture but becomes non-commercial
popular culture in its own right. Fifth, and last, fandom functions as
an alternative social community. Fans in Jenkins's study would
often contrast the alienation and superficiality of their ordinary day-
to-day lives with the intimacy and communal sharing of the fan
group.

For Bacon-Smith, probably the two most important activities
involved in fandom are viewing the 'source material' – the original
programmes that inspired the fandom – and creative activity that is
derived from that source material. New fans have to be initiated into
the particular way of viewing and interpreting the source material
adopted by the community. This may well take the form of a 'total
immersion weekend' in which as much as twenty hours of videotape
may be seen, accompanied by a running commentary from an experi-
enced fan. Thereafter, the fan has to interpret what she or he sees in

terms of a relationship between 'microflow' and 'macroflow'. The microflow concerns the details of the plot, the setting and the actions of the characters in any one episode. The macroflow concerns the broader readings of character and plot that will extend across all episodes of the series in question. The new fan will be helped by the fan community to interpret the microflow by reference to the macroflow, which at first will be difficult to get at. In order to do this the new fan will be shown episodes regarded by established fans as crucial for the macroflow but which may well be out of order in the series. Gradually she or he will build up a large-scale map which will help her or him to make sense of a whole series. The next step will be to extend the macroflow to the literature created by the fan community to enlarge the source material.

The fan groups studied by Bacon-Smith and Jenkins were not passive viewers of television material. Using the characters in the programmes of which they were fans, they wrote stories, plays and poetry, composed songs, drew portraits, made costumes, created photographs from video, designed jewellery, pottery or needlework, published books or fanzines, devised indexes and catalogues, and wrote essays of criticism. The stories could be of several different forms. One type, for example, involves a woman as a heroine who saves the *Enterprise* but dies in the attempt. Another type is built around the supposition that Captain Kirk and Mr Spock have a sexual relationship. Almost any type of story is possible. Alternate universe stories, for instance, put characters from one programme in a quite different universe. In one, Ray Doyle from *The Professionals* becomes an elf. Fans can show extraordinary ingenuity in developing story lines out of the original programmes. Jenkins, for example, notes no fewer than ten ways in which a television show can be rewritten, including recontextualization, which involves writing short vignettes in which gaps in the characters' history are filled in, extending the time-line of the plots forwards or backwards, changing the genre of the story to a quite different one, and reversing the morality of the original characters so that heroes become villains and vice versa. Many of the resulting stories are collective products in which a whole fan community develops the plot over time, interweaving the story itself with illustration, poems and song. Story trees arise in which one story builds on another using the same characters.

The most important point stressed by both Bacon-Smith and

Jenkins is that fans are very far from being passive consumers of television programmes. Quite the contrary: they are extremely active in transforming what they watch. This point is developed extensively in the next chapter.

7
Watching Audiences

Television and the Domestic Setting

Television is a domestic medium. It is watched at home. Ignored at home. Discussed at home. Watched in private and with members of family or friends. But it is part of our domestic culture in other ways too, providing in its programming and its schedules models and structures of domestic life, or at least of certain versions of domestic life. It is also a means for our integration into a consumer culture through which our domesticity is both constructed and displayed. (Silverstone, 1994, p. 24)

Most television is watched at home. Furthermore, as I showed in the last chapter, a very large proportion of the leisure time taken in the home is spent watching television. Television is also watched in families. Despite some fundamental changes in household structure, one consequence of which is a rise in the number of single-person households, television is watched by members of families together, so the family should be the unit of analysis, not the individual (Goodman, 1983). As Lindloff and Traudt (1983) point out, television is a form of *mediated communication*, mediated, that is, by the family. In sum, television is domestic and familial. One way of putting these points is to refer to the *privatization* of television, of leisure and of social life in general.

It is often argued that modern societies are becoming more privatized. This is usually taken to mean that people turn their energies, loyalties, time and commitment towards the private activities of the family, and perhaps the self, and away from public activities such as the church, the wider community, and the rights and duties of citizenship (Sennett, 1977; Habermas, 1989). Leisure activities are also increasingly privatized. Of course, it is possible that television does not simply follow a trend to domestic privatization but is one of its causes. As Lull (1990) says:

> A major trend in the western world apparent in the 1980s is that more and more families prefer to stay at home for their evening entertainment . . . Other reasons cited for the stay-at-home trend are the high cost of entertainment, a fear of violence, a lack of community involvement generally, and the easy availability of cable television and video. The phenomenon may signal a trend toward more conservative, traditional family lifestyles in the United States, Europe, and Great Britain, where 'home centredness' is a contemporary social development. We cannot say that television has caused this phenomenon, but it has given families a substantial added reason to stay home. Television interacts with other factors – social, economic, and cultural – to create the stay-at-home trend. (pp. 157–8)

These obvious facts concerning the domesticity of television provide one of the keys for an understanding of the role of television in society. Several of the issues that have been discussed in this book already are clearly intimately bound up with this domesticity. For example, the mode of address and the conversational style of television discussed in chapter 2 has to do with the informal, domestic setting in which television is received and in which conversation of this kind is a normal mode of social interaction. Again, as I showed in chapter 5, the way in which television executives schedule programmes is based on assumptions about the way in which people live their domestic lives. Further, the content of television programmes reflects a domestic orientation. A good deal of television is simply about family life. Situation comedies and soap operas bring fictional families to the screen, while quiz shows, talk shows and documentaries of various kinds frequently display real families.

Television has, relatively quickly in Western societies, become integrated into the routines of everyday life. Silverstone (1994) has formulated an account of the place of television in modern social life that gives this everyday quality of the medium a central place. He argues that our sense of security is maintained by the familiar routines of daily life, by our commonsense understandings and practical knowledge. An important part of this consists of rituals and symbols of which we may be largely unaware: 'the symbols of daily life: the everyday sights and sounds of natural language and familiar culture; the publicly broadcast media text on billboards, in newspapers, on television; the highly charged and intense private and public rituals in domestic or national rites of passage or international celebrations' (Silverstone, 1994, p. 19). In this symbolic and ritualistic construction of everyday life, television has a crucial part to play, as an object in the room providing a focus for conversation, as a medium locating us in local, national and global relationships, and as an entertainer and informer.

One of the major ways in which everyday life is organized is by *time*. A sense of security is given by the routines that occur at more or less fixed times – going to bed, getting up, meal-times. Television has a major part to play in this fixing of events in time. Hobson (1982), for example, shows how her respondents integrated the now defunct soap opera *Crossroads* into their domestic lives. Viewers of the programme frequently referred to their viewing as a 'habit'. They did not mean anything negative in their use of this word but only that 'the regular scheduling of programmes which are transmitted at the same time means that those programmes become part of a certain "time band" in people's lives' (p. 115). A routine or habit develops in which *Crossroads* is integrated with tea-time or children's bed-time. The domestic and the televisual revolve around each other. So programming schedules are determined by the domestic pattern of life. The reverse is also true; household rhythms are organized around television programmes which can regulate meal-times, bed-times and occasions for going out. Bryce (1987) distinguishes two types of household that organize their time in different ways. In the first (the monochronic), there is great emphasis on planning the household's activities, which have to be carried out in a linear sequence. Children are encouraged to do only one thing at a time and to finish whatever it is that they are engaged in. Being on time is a major virtue and these households abound with clocks and calendars. The second, polychronic type of family, by contrast, places much less emphasis on planning and has great difficulty in keeping appointments. A large number of activities are undertaken at the same time and much less importance is attached to finishing any one of them. Such houses contain very few clocks and watches. Bryce notes that television plays quite a different role in monochronic and polychronic households. In the former, television watching is organized around other activities. It is planned and scheduled, but, while the television set is on, the family is expected to give it all their attention and not to do anything else. Polychronic households, however, organize their household activities around the television, which acts as a kind of clock. They have little planning of viewing and often only give sporadic or intermittent attention to what is on the set.

All that I have said so far implies that it is possible to see television not as destructive of the quality of family life, but as *used* by families in certain ways for their own purposes. Lull (1990) identifies two primary types of social use of television in the home by families (see also Wolf et al., 1982). He is careful to stress 'social' use because so much audience research tends to concentrate on the use of television by individuals, divorced from their social contexts. He distinguishes structural from relational uses of television. In turn these types have sub-types, 'structural' being divided into environmental and regulative while 'relational' is divided into communication facilitation, affiliation/avoidance, social learning, and competence/dominance (see table 7.1).

Television is employed as a background of continuous noise against which other activities – domestic work or family conversation – can take place. It provides, in other words, an *environmental resource* for a family to draw upon as it needs. It can function too as a *behavioural regulator*. I have already referred to the way that television structures daily life in families, many of whose activities are organized around programmes. Parents may also use television to structure the lives of their children more directly, as when, for

Table 7.1   The social uses of television

Structural

Environmental: background noise; companionship; entertainment.

Regulative: punctuation of time and activity; talk patterns.

Relational

Communication facilitation: experience illustration; common ground; conversational entrance; anxiety reduction; agenda for talk; value clarification.

Affiliation/avoidance: physical, verbal contact/neglect; family solidarity; family relaxant; conflict reduction; relationship maintenance.

Social learning: decision-making; behaviour modelling; problem-solving; value transmission; legitimization; information dissemination; substitute schooling.

Competence/dominance: role enactment; role reinforcement; substitute role portrayal; intellectual validation; authority exercise; gatekeeping; argument facilitation.

Source: Lull (1990), p. 36

example, they only allow access to the set when homework has been completed.

As far as the relational uses of television are concerned, the medium first acts as a facilitator of communication. People will refer to television programmes in their everyday conversation and use characters and events to illustrate what they want to say. Soap opera is often used in this way, as I will show later on in this chapter. Buckingham (1987) illustrates this point, and also the earlier point about the sense of security given by the domestic use of television, in his study of youthful viewers of *EastEnders*. One 17-year-old felt that television enabled him to talk to his parents about problems like drugs by presenting characters who were involved in drug use. As this interviewee said:

> The other thing that it does, is that you sit there, and normally you're with your parents, and you're sitting down watching it, and you just talk . . . The conversation arises from that, and so you're talking to your parents about it, and so it probably makes you feel a bit comfortable, like if you need the backing from your parents, and the security there. (p. 163)

Lull also argues that it can be used *instead* of conversation to cover up embarrassing pauses or simply because there is nothing to talk about. Or the set can be a stimulus to conversation while it is actually on, for family members or visitors.

More generally still, television may promote either affiliation or avoidance in families. Communal watching of programmes provides opportunities for displays of family warmth and affection. Studies which have directly observed families watching television have observed that parents and children touch each other and are more physically affectionate than they are at other times. It can also be a source of domestic unity, as families can laugh together or be harrowed together. At the same time, watching television can allow avoidance of social interaction as a watcher buries himself or herself in a programme. People who are angry or just tired can use television to repel the attentions of others in the family. Television can create a social space which relieves tension in much the same way as reading a newspaper or book (see Radway, 1987).

To some extent, the description of the use of television in domestic life is based on the assumption that, for some of the time at least, families gather round the set together and watch, and talk about, programmes as a family unit. Such an assumption might seem to be put at risk by the growth in the numbers of sets in households.

About half of the households in Britain have more than one television set. One might well think that this would only make sense if the household was trying to maximize choice and family members frequently watched different programmes on different sets. In practice, however, this happens only to a limited extent (Barwise and Ehrenburg, 1988). Second or third sets are hardly ever used to extend the choice of programmes. For most of the time only one set is on. When more than one set is on, for about half of the time they are tuned to the same channel. In these circumstances, people are permitted to move about the house and to continue to watch the programme. Hobson (1982) illustrates this point in her study of *Crossroads*. Many of her respondents would have two sets on at the same time, one in the kitchen, while preparing meals. They were able to move backwards and forwards between the two sets, as the needs of their family, or the demands of the programme, dictated.

So far I have talked of the domestic uses of television as if families were harmonious unities. Clearly this is not always the case. There are conflicts, negotiations and compromises in families as there are in any other social setting. In chapter 6, I described the complex processes of negotiation about what to watch that typically take place within families and which explain the discrepancy between what people say they want or like to watch and what they in fact end up watching. The process of negotiation – or lack of it – most studied in television research is that taking place between men and women in the household. Lull (1990), for example, shows that men control what is watched by the whole household. In a study based on observing how decisions on what to view were made, Lull found that men were more than twice as likely to decide to switch the set on or off, or to change channels, than their female partners. Children were next most likely to exercise control of this kind. In 90 per cent of the decisions, the man of the household made his choice without any discussion with others who might be watching. On the relatively small number of occasions on which women did exercise control, they were more likely to discuss it first (though not a great deal more likely).

Such control by the man is enhanced by the presence of a remote control device, which means that he does not even have to leave his armchair. Morley (1986) found that the remote control was an almost symbolic possession of the man, an indication of his power to determine the family's viewing. Many of the women in Morley's sample indicated considerable irritation at the behaviour of the men, who would obsessively flick through channels while the women were watching something they liked. Gray (1992) came to similar conclusions. As one of her respondents reported:

Yes, now this is interesting; when we sit down to watch the video with some specific programme in mind that we know is on the video, James tends to have the remote control, and I spit with rage at his flicking from thing to thing instead of locating on what it was we wanted to watch. (p. 174)

Gray notes that it is not just control over programme decisions and of the remote control that is at issue, but also control over the video-recorder. Women are very unconfident in setting the recorder and operating the timer, although similar pieces of household equipment of equal complexity, the cooker for instance, do not pose any difficulty. This effectively gives power to the men (and male children) who are able to set the device. The result is that women record much less for themselves, due partly to their unconfidence with the equipment and partly to their feeling that they do not have the time to watch a recording because of their domestic commitments.

Television Talk

Although 'television conversations' may often be about the comings and goings of fictional characters or 'personalities', they provide ways of talking about a great many features of the world: sex, sin, retribution and death. Indeed, as we said earlier, in some cases it seems that television drama has only properly occurred, been thoroughly realized, when the plots and the moral messages they contain have been discussed and interpreted and re-dramatized in the company of friends or mere acquaintances. (Taylor and Mullan, 1986, pp. 205–6)

As I have implied already, one of the critical qualities of television seems to be its capacity to provoke conversation, to encourage talk. Indeed, television often seems to be *about* talk. As a medium it really consists of visually illustrated talk. In this respect it should be compared with film, which is much more visual, and in which the visual images are more crucial in conveying meaning and in giving the audience pleasure. This, indeed, may be one reason why television is so much more a writer's, and less a director's, medium than cinema (see chapter 5). Television is intended to be received in a domestic context, which, as I have already said, is characterized by conversational interchanges. Television mirrors and interacts with the conversational lives of its audience. This feature is clearly related to what I have described in chapter 2 as television's *mode of address*. Television has a particularly direct way of addressing its audience, as if a conversation were taking place between the people appearing on the set and those watching it.

Quite a few television genres, of course, are essentially organized around conversation, including talk shows, soap opera and situation comedy. For others, news and documentary for instance, talk appears to be the major ingredient. Still others, including police shows, give more prominence to visual images. However, there is also evidence that people frequently do not attend to the visual images on television, whatever kind of programme is on, but instead treat television as a talk medium. For example, Hobson (1982) shows that watchers of *Crossroads* are only half watching the programme, as they are frequently engaged in domestic work at the same time. They are, however, *listening*, and may give their full attention to the set only when something interesting comes up. Here is one of Hobson's interviewees describing how she watches the show (DH standing for Hobson and D for the interviewee):

> DH: In general, then, do you watch it regularly?
> D: Yes – I miss the odd one or two, I don't always, actually – well, I don't sit and watch it. I'm usually pithering about, but I listen to it. I know what's going on. I think I prefer to listen rather than watch.
> DH: So you rarely actually go in there and watch it?
> D: No, I never watch it in there. Just an odd time if somebody looks as if they've got something interesting on, I go in to see what colour it is. Or if there was something like a wedding I suppose, a sort of occasion, when it would be a bit out of the ordinary, then I'd probably go and see what they were all wearing and . . . but normally I'd just pither about in here. (p. 56)

In the household, television talk takes place in a variety of settings – in the sitting room, around the kitchen table, in bedrooms – and with a variety of participants. Such talk also takes place in non-domestic settings – at work, school, on the bus. At present, there is no research which has investigated the extent of television talk in different settings or the effect that the settings have on the nature of the talk (see Buckingham, 1993b). It is not unlikely, however, that settings have different rules (discursive rules) about television talk and that people will talk differently, say, at work about what they have watched from the way that they talk to members of their family over a meal (but for a contrary opinion, see Hobson, 1989). People's interpretations, views and opinions about any particular television programme, in other words, are not fixed, but vary depending on the context in which they talk.

We do, however, know a little about the way in which different social groups differ in their use of television as a conversational opportunity. It appears, for example, that men talk less about television than women. As Morley (1986) points out, although women watch television less intensively then men, they talk about it more. As one of his respondents says:

> I go round my mate's and she'll say, 'Did you watch *Coronation Street* last night? What about so and so?' And we'll sit there discussing it. I think most women and young girls do. We always sit down and it's 'Do you think she's right last night, what she's done?' Or, 'I wouldn't have done that', or 'Wasn't she a cow to him? Do you reckon he'll get . . . I wonder what he's going to do?' Then we sort of fantasize between us, then when I see her the next day she'll say, 'You were right' or 'See, I told you so.' (p. 156)

Men, on the other hand, generally in Morley's sample, will only admit to talking about sport. It is not clear whether this is because they really do not talk about television programmes or because they are reluctant to admit that they do – and it may well be both. Certainly men do display considerable contempt for much television, particularly 'women's programmes'. In many ethnographic studies men will not admit to watching fictional television, soap opera for instance, although the survey evidence shows that they do actually do so. Men may in other words be *pretending* not to like soap opera, a characteristic which might well lead to their not admitting that they talk about it. Box 5 reproduces part of an interview which appears to confirm this point.

In the discussion so far, it is clear that both watching television, and talking about it, are social acts in which there is a collaborative process of understanding and interpretation of programmes. Liebes and Katz (1993) refer to this process as *mutual aid*. Theirs is a study of the ways in which audiences decode *Dallas*. They chose their interviewees from six different communities. Four of these came from Israel – Arab citizens, Russian immigrants, Moroccan Jews of long standing, and residents of a kibbutz born in Israel. To these

Box 5 Do men pretend?

In the following extract from Buckingham (1987), a number of young people are discussing their viewing habits. DB indicates the interviewer.

FIONA	Men don't really like soap opera.
STEPHEN	My dad watches it, but he pretends he don't like it. He goes 'Oh that's a load of rubbish, they can't even act'. So why does he watch it then?
DB	Why do you think he pretends?
NATASHA	So he can be more macho!
STEPHEN	Like *Dynasty*. My mum loves *Dynasty*, and my brother. I call him a pouff.
FIONA	*Dynasty* is good!
NATASHA	I wouldn't call nobody a pouff . .
DB	But you watch it as well.
STEPHEN	Yeah, but I pretend I don't like it. That's what me and my dad do, when it comes on we start whistling and singing the tune.
DB	So what is it about *Dynasty* that boys and men aren't supposed to like?
STEPHEN	In *Dynasty*, it's all kissing everywhere, isn't it?

Source: Buckingham (1987), pp. 197–8

were added people from the west coast of the United States (for whom the programme was originally intended) and people from Japan (where the programme failed). Interviews were conducted in groups because this best imitates the way that people actually talk about television in real life. The groups were chosen to represent the communities, being based on one couple and their near neighbours and friends. As a result, there were 66 groups and 400 participants taking part in the study. Once assembled in their groups, the interviewees were shown the current episode of *Dallas*, which was followed by a tape-recorded discussion initiated by an interviewer.

Liebes and Katz argue that there are four ways in which audience members help each other in relating to the programme. Thus, there is mutual aid in legitimation, orientation, interpretation and evaluation. At an elementary level, audience members may find it difficult to justify watching a programme, even if they want to, because it may be regarded by others as trivial or even immoral. Others may give them support in deciding to watch, may *legitimate* the decision to watch. This is often the case for soap opera, which is for many women a 'guilty pleasure' in need of legitimation from other women (or daughters).

Secondly, audience members may require help in *orientation*, in understanding what is going on in the plot or the characterization. Liebes and Katz, in that they were examining the viewing of *Dallas* in some countries whose language and culture were far removed from those of the United States, came across many viewers who needed the assistance of others in identifying characters or following intricate plot lines. The same process, if to a lesser extent, would also occur in American families. All families cooperate in supplying information which will help every member to make sense of television programmes.

More important than the technical mutual aid involved in orientation is assistance in *interpretation*, in offering help 'to fellow group members who need an explanation or who find interest in why something has happened or why a character has behaved in a certain way' (p. 85). In providing interpretative guidance for *Dallas*, audience members drew on their own experience of life and knowledge of the series and related it to the programme.

Lastly, people helped each other in *evaluating* the programme along a number of dimensions – moral, aesthetic and ideological. Individual audience members in Liebes and Katz's groups would form an opinion of the moral behaviour of characters, either for or against. But it was also the case that groups as a whole would form an opinion not only of the individual characters but also of the programme as a whole, or even of Americans as represented by the programme. These large-scale judgements would be created by setting *Dallas* against the moral culture of the group. For example, one Arab group concluded that *Dallas* exhibited the vices of American materialism together with a collapse of family values and virtues such as respect and patience. Aesthetic judgements about the production values or characterization are also made by mutual aid.

Television talk, and the mutual aid that it makes possible, is not, of course, a smooth, conflict-free process in which everybody agrees with everybody else. Quite the contrary: in most homes there can be fierce argument about orientation, interpretation or evaluation. Liebes and Katz distinguish discussion, which has no disagreement, from debate, which may have quite a lot. Table 7.2 shows how the forms of mutual help are distributed statistically between discussion and debate. It is clear that interpretation is subject to a good deal more dispute than either orientation or evaluation.

Table 7.2   The rhetorical context of mutual aid (in percentages)

Type of mutual aid	Discussion	Debate
Orientation	34	17
Interpretation	47	74
Evaluation	17	10
Total units of interaction	(517)	(433)

Source: Liebes and Katz (1993), p. 91

The suggestion that television talk is social, that watching and talking about television is a collaborative act, strengthens the claims of those who argue that group interview methods are the most appropriate ones for studying television audiences. Group discussion, it would appear, mimics the way that people deal with television in their everyday lives, not as an individual matter, but as a collective enterprise. Liebes and Katz are unequivocal on this point. They are quite certain that the transcripts of their discussion groups are records 'of the way these people normally talk to one another, even if it is unlikely that they talk in such a sustained way about a television programme' (p. 34). The discussions seemed natural and unforced and the participants frequently referred to previous naturally occurring conversations on the same topic. Buckingham (1987), similarly, has no doubt that his discussion groups of young people who watched *EastEnders* were simply continuing conversations that they had with each other every day. The presence of the interviewer, and the relatively formal structure of the group interview, may have made the conversation more serious and abstract, but the enthusiasm of the young people about the subject convinced Buckingham that the discussions were not forced.

At the same time, there must remain some doubt as to how close group discussions of this kind come to conversations in natural settings. Part of the difficulty is that we do not have any quantitative indication of how *much* people talk about television. As I have indicated, there is some reason to believe that some people, particularly men, talk about television relatively little. Perhaps the most significant difficulty, however, is the apparent assumption that group discussion mimics *the* natural setting. Actually, as I have already pointed out, there is a *variety* of natural settings in which television talk occurs. In these settings it may vary greatly in its structure and themes, and this sort of variation is not necessarily picked up in constructed group discussion. In sum, what is needed is more study of the occurrence of television talk in natural settings. Investigation of this kind can only really be carried out by observation, and I will be discussing one or two such studies later in this chapter.

Regimes of Watching and the New Audience

People can watch the television in a number of different ways. For example, they can watch with varying degrees of attention. On p. 174 I discussed the way that a *Crossroads* viewer listened to, rather than watched, the show. She looked at the screen only when something caught her attention. Hobson (1982) points out in her study of *Crossroads* that, as television watching is part of everyday life for her viewers, it is not a separate activity conducted in a darkened room, in comfortable surroundings, and with maximum concentration. A number of other writers have noted the way that women in the household do not attend to the set all the time. Modleski (1984) calls this *distracted viewing*. Women watch television in a distracted state because this is the one that fits best with their domestic work. Similarly, Morley's (1986) study of television use in the family, based on interviews with a number of households, points to the way that women's domestic work occupies them while they are watching – or not watching – the television (see also Gray, 1992).

Morley notes that current social conventions still define the home as a place of leisure, relaxation and enjoyment, away from the rigours of employment, for the man of the household, while, for women, the home is a place of work, domestic work, even if she is also engaged in paid work outside the home. For many women, this means that domestic work has to be fitted in when the household is gathered round the television set. As a result, a man's characteristic mode of viewing is attentive, a woman's inattentive. This difference does not arise out of the different biological constitutions of men and women, or out of any 'natural' inability of women to concentrate, but is a socially determined difference related to the different obligations and expectations placed on the two genders in the organization of the household.

For Morley one of his major findings is the consistency of this difference between men and women.

Essentially the men state a clear preference for viewing attentively, in silence, without interruption 'in order not to miss anything'. Moreover, they display puzzlement at the way their wives and daughters watch television. This the women themselves describe as a fundamentally social activity, involving ongoing conversation, and usually the performance of at least one other domestic activity (ironing etc.) at the same time. Indeed, many of the women feel that to just watch television without doing anything else at the same time would be an indefensible waste of time, given their sense of domestic obligations. To watch in this way is something they rarely do, except occasionally, when alone or with other women friends, when they have managed to construct an 'occasion' on which to watch their favourite programme, video, or film. The women note that their husbands are always 'on at them' to shut up. The men can't really understand how their wives can follow the programmes if they are doing something else at the same time. (p. 150)

A number of commentators stress that it is the domestic obligations of women that are exclusively responsible for this difference in attentiveness. It certainly is true that there is evidence that women would like to view attentively and do so when they are alone and their family is out of the way. However, an alternative explanation is implied in the quotation from Morley above – for women, television watching is a more social experience. For men the relationship with the television set is an individual one. For women, on the other hand, it is social or collective, both at the time of watching and afterwards in television-related talk, in which women engage much more than men. Intriguingly, the social quality of women's engagement with television is mirrored in the social quality of the text of 'women's television', especially soap opera (Abercrombie and Longhurst, 1991).

So far, I have discussed the issue of attentiveness as if it were entirely a gendered question. It is not. It is actually normal not to pay attention to the television set. The point has been simply demonstrated by the device of filming the audience while they are watching television. In an early experiment of this kind, Bechtel et al. (1972) found, by comparing diaries filled in by viewers with the filmed record, that people significantly overestimated the amount of television that they watched. Part of the reason for this was that people spend a good deal of time not actually watching the set while it is on. Table 7.3 shows how Bechtel et al. classified modes of television viewing.

The data shows that all these modes of watching go on in families and are fused together.'Globally the data point to an inseparable mixture of watching and not-watching as a general style of television viewing behaviour' (p. 298). Furthermore an extremely wide range

Table 7.3 Categories of involvement in television viewing

Code	Behaviour
Attending screen	
1	Participating, actively responding to the TV set or to others regarding content from the set
2	Passively watching (doing nothing else)
3	Simultaneous activity (eating, knitting, etc.) while looking at the screen
Not attending screen	
4	Positioned to watch TV but reading, talking or attending to something other than television
5	In the viewing area of the TV but positioned away from the set in a way that would require turning to see it
6	Not in the room and unable to see the set or degree of impact of TV content

Source: Bechtel et al. (1972), p. 279

of other behaviours is associated with both watching and non-watching, including answering back to the television set, eating, scratching (someone else and self), sorting the wash, dressing and undressing, doing homework, playing games, and answering the telephone. The authors conclude that:

> The findings point to the fact that television viewing is a complex and various form of behaviour intricately interwoven with many other kinds of behaviour. It will not be a simple matter to sort out how the way pro-grammes are viewed finally impinges on sense receptors, nor to interpret how the interfering behaviours filter out the television stimulus. (p. 299)

Another set of experiments conducted by Collett (Collett and Lamb, 1985) involved the mounting of a video-camera and a micro-phone inside television sets and filming people watching the televi-sion. Collett found an enormous variety of ways of watching. Some viewers were slumped in front of the set while others were paying rapt attention, concentrating on everything going on. Still others were paying no attention at all and played the flute, wrote letters, engaged in animated conversation completely unrelated to what was on the set, did handstands, vacuumed the carpet – and left the room. There have been attempts to measure the degree of inatten-tion in audiences (Barwise and Ehrenberg, 1988). During commercial breaks about 20 per cent of people apparently 'watching the programme' are in fact out of the room, 10 per cent are not viewing, 30 per cent are viewing but also doing something else, and only 40 per cent are viewing only. While actual programmes are on, the proportion of people who are not attentively viewing is lower, but is still 40 per cent of the total.

Conclusions like these – that, for much of the time that the television set is on, people are doing practically anything except watch it – will be well known to almost everybody who thinks about their television habits. It is implied in the arguments reviewed earlier in this chapter concerning the domestic nature of television. It is precisely because television is so closely integrated in everyday, domestic life that it is so widely ignored. Such a finding also makes measurement of actual hours of viewing a somewhat complex issue, as I indicated in the last chapter.

Hartley refers to these different modes of watching the television as *regimes of watching* (Hartley, 1984, quoted in Fiske, 1987, p. 73). More generally, Abercrombie (1992) argues that people appropriate *all* cultural objects in different ways. It is not just for television that there are different regimes of watching: there are parallel modes of appropriation for books, films and music. Abercrombie distinguishes two modes of appropriation – literary mode and video mode – at least one of which prescribes the correct way to relate to cultural objects. The literary mode – so called because it is modelled on reading a book – insists that, when engaging with a cultural object, whatever it is, people should give it their whole attention and not be distracted by any other activity. It is not possible, or proper, to read several books at once, for example. Culture cannot function as background or wallpaper. Again, the correct sequence of activities must be observed. The cultural object must be gone through in the right order; there must be no dodging about and starting with the end or looking at favourite bits over and over again. Further, there has to be an analytical relationship to the text. The text is not to be taken for granted; it is there to be evaluated.

The outcome of the literary mode of cultural appropriation is, first, seriousness and, secondly, order. Cultural appropriation is a serious matter dedicated to work; in this sense the literary mode is in no sense playful, although that is not to say that it is not pleasurable, an important difference. In video mode, on the other hand, so called because the use of the videorecorder is the archetypal form, one does not treat the cultural object as if it were a book. Audiences do not necessarily use the 'correct' sequence – they hop backwards and forwards, enjoy the best bits again and again without any context; they do not obey the narrative rules. They are not interested in evaluation or analysis as necessary features of the experience. They often do not give full attention to it, doing several things at the same time, or give attention to several cultural objects at once.

In our society, these two modes are very differently evaluated. The literary mode is generally highly valued, while the video mode is treated as inferior. One might say that the literary mode is that favoured by high culture while the video mode is that employed in popular culture. As I have already said, this notion of video and literary modes will apply to any cultural form. Thus a film, a book or a piece of music can, at least theoretically, be appropriated in either mode. As far as television is concerned, video mode is very similar to the distracted or inattentive mode of viewing that I have been describing. This explains the contempt with which men frequently greet women's viewing of soap opera. It is not only the content of soaps that is derided, but also the distracted way in which they are watched. Men's watching, on the other hand, is much more in literary mode, which tends to attract greater social approval.

Television audiences, then, do not watch with the same degree of attention all the time. There are indications, though, that this is a relatively new phenomenon. As audiences have got used to the new medium, they have got used to drifting in and out of engagement with it. This can be seen as the acquisition of a skill, and Mace (Lawrence and Mace, 1991; Mace, 1992) emphasizes this by comparing the skills of television watching with those of literacy. When television began to reach large numbers of people in the 1950s, the medium was rather overwhelming. People did not know how to use it, how to integrate it into their everyday lives. As a result, they fell back on other models of appropriation, drawn from the theatre or cinema, media which demand greater attention. Gradually, however, the skill of television use developed, a skill which not only allows very different modes of watching but was buttressed by greater knowledge of how television is produced, how it achieves its effects.

Root (1986) draws a contrast between a new audience, with new ways of watching television, and an old one, which had a tendency to concentrate fiercely on the set. She argues, from evidence from diaries kept by members of the Mass Observation movement, that during the 1950s it was much more common to sit in absolute silence while the television was on, in the dark, with the curtains drawn. A woman recalling the earlier days of television said to an interviewer: 'When television first came out you'd go to call on somebody and they'd say "hush, we're watching so and so". Nobody does that nowadays' (p. 27).

The idea that the contemporary television audience is qualitatively different from that of forty years ago is not based entirely on these different regimes of watching. Ang (1991), for example, points to the large number of technological changes which have greatly increased potential viewer choice of what and when to watch. As I have already pointed out, more than half of households have more than one television set, which allows family members to watch what they want without having to make compromises with others. Remote control devices, now almost universal, allow rapid and frequent changes of channel – or zapping as it is better known. Not a great deal is known about the extent of zapping. However, Ang mentions one study which found that some 20 per cent of households could be classified as heavy zappers, changing channels more than once every two minutes. The widespread ownership of videorecorders permits viewers to disregard television schedules and watch what they want when they want. Viewers can also use their videorecorders to manipulate the image they receive in ways that are not possible with simple broadcast television. They can replay scenes of which they are particularly fond, use the fast-forward (zipping) to bypass unwanted material (usually used for advertisements), and replay in slow motion for detailed consideration. At the same time, there has been a proliferation of sources of programming. In both Britain and the United States, network broadcasting has been supplemented by cable and satellite broadcasting, the former more common in the United States and the latter in Britain (see chapter 4 for further discussion of these technologies). The effect of cable and satellite is, of course, to increase the number of channels that are available to viewers. As a result, viewers have an ever-greater capacity to 'graze' – to move restlessly between a large number of channels.

It is tempting to see technological changes, and changing audience dispositions and skills, as creating a qualitatively new type of television audience. Such an audience would operate exclusively in video mode, be fond of zipping, zapping and grazing, be unable to concentrate for long on anything, be inattentive, capricious, erratic, unpredictable and, in Ang's word, intractable. One might go further and see this as a description of a postmodern audience interested in non-narrative, non-realist forms (see chapter 2 for further discussion of this point).

This would be, however, to go too far. There almost certainly have been changes in the behaviour of audiences over the past forty years or so. As I have already said, these are chiefly due to the incorporation of television into domestic life and the acquisition of 'television skills', which have permitted greater variation in how people watch television, different regimes of watching. However, it is much less clear that the *technological* changes have substantially changed viewer behaviour. As I pointed out earlier in this chapter, in households that have more than one television set, for the bulk of the time, only one set is on. There is no serious evidence that zapping and grazing are particularly common, although every viewer may well perform these unnatural acts from time to time, and people do not, on the whole, make use of the range of programming by looking at it all. Lastly, videorecorders turn out to be a much underused resource (Levy and Gunter, 1988). They are mostly used for 'time-shifting', that is, recording programmes for later viewing. However, for most households, material watched on video makes up perhaps 10 per cent of total viewing. For most households, therefore, watching broadcast television at the time it is broadcast is still the preferred option. The varied facilities of videorecorders are also not used very much. Freeze-frame and slow motion are used by sports enthusiasts to some extent and fast-forward is employed (by half of households) to avoid commercials. However, as is the case with many other pieces of domestic equipment, half of the facilities are never used.

Referential and Critical Framings

So far in this chapter I have been discussing how people watch television. I turn now in this section to a closer examination of one aspect of what they get out of watching.

When people talk about what they have seen on television, they frequently relate events or characters to their own lives. For example, in discussions of soap opera, viewers will interpret the behaviour of one of the characters by noting his or her similarities to someone they know. Such a strategy enables prediction of what will happen next or some reflection on the plausibility of the character's actions. The reverse may also happen, in that people may interpret events in their own lives by reference to the way that a television character behaves. Such uses of television may be termed *referential*

– television refers to everyday life. There are other ways of relating to television. In particular, audiences may be *critical*. This does not mean that they criticize programmes, rather that they apply critical methods to them. It does mean that they may discuss the acting or sets or suggest that characters are not behaving consistently.

Referential Framings

The idea that, when people talk about television, they systematically relate it to their everyday lives informs a large number of empirical studies of television audiences. Box 6 reproduces extracts from interviews with audience members from three studies that illustrate this point.

In all the extracts in box 6, the interviewees are using their experiences of daily life to interpret television programmes. The conversations represent a more or less seamless unity between references to experience and references to the characters in the soap; people bounce effortlessly backwards and forwards between their own world and the world of the soap opera. As Willis (1990) puts it:

> the young women who watch soaps are constantly judging them and reworking the material they provide, finding echoes in their own lives and spaces which allow them to ask what would happen 'if'. TV watching is, at least in part, about facilitating a dialectic between representation and reality as a general contribution to symbolic work and creativity. The audience is not an empty room waiting to be furnished in someone else's taste. (p. 36)

If audiences use their experience to illuminate their television watching and talk, they also do the reverse and use situations or insights from television in their everyday lives. Adults may make comparisons between a real-life event and one that has occurred on television in order to manage their relationships. Children may use television programmes to investigate and discuss the secrets of the adult world (Buckingham, 1987). Within certain communities, television watching may be used to manage tensions of various kinds. Gillespie (1993) carried out a study of the viewing of soap opera in a Punjabi community in Southall in London. Young people within this community used their watching of *Neighbours* to understand the relationship of their community to the surrounding white society:

Box 6 Referential interpretations of television

On *Crossroads*:

DH   What do you think about this part with her and this American lawyer?

S   Oh she is just going to make a hash of things, isn't she.

DH   If she marries him it will be just another disastrous marriage.

J   But then again, she's doing it for her own means.

S   She's doing it 'cos she wants her child back. She's not doing it for him, is she.

DH   And do you think that's realistic, that she would do that?

J   Ooh yes. Personally, I think you would do it yourself.

S   Ooh yes, you would, you know. You imagine having your child taken off you. I think she sees him too often for her status, like, but naturally you would want to go and see him, even at the other side of the world, as often as you possibly could. But if you'd got a chance to get him back you'd take that chance, no matter what, if you was a true mother, like.

J   Especially her, 'cos she doesn't think nothing of marriage, does she, so it's second nature for her to try and use it. It'll be her third marriage now.

Source: Hobson (1982), pp.133–4

On *EastEnders*:

CALISTA: She's got to take the other people around her into consideration. I mean, it's her baby, it is her body, it is her life, but these other people, she's living with them, and they're the ones who've got to bear the brunt of whatever is happening. She's going to have this baby, and she's too young to have a baby, anyway.

DONNA: She's under age now, isn't she? She's still under parent guard.

SHEILA: I think it was wrong that she didn't tell her parents who the father is. Any parent is going to find out. Any parent is going to drag it out of them. I mean your parents know you better than anyone does. I think that the father should have the right to know. I mean it would bring out more in *EastEnders* wouldn't it?

CALISTA: I suppose that they're saving it really, to use later on. And if their ratings go down, then they're going to use that to pick up their ratings.

SANDRA: I read somewhere that they're going to name the baby Victoria and then everyone's going to start saying 'Aha! Victoria! It must be Den!' (Laughter).

DONNA: That's what it said, it's going to get some tongues wagging.

SANDRA: But all the time, she keeps dropping hints. Like when she heard about Jan coming down to the pub, she sat down and started crying. I mean, things like that, you would pick up these little pieces and start putting it all together. And I reckon Lofty should know who the father is. He should demand to know.

CALISTA: Think about it though: why did Den give him that engagement ring? All these things! If it was me, I'd start thinking 'Why is he giving me this ring?'

Source: Buckingham (1987), pp. 170–1

On *EastEnders* – JC is the interviewer:

MARGARET: Yeah, like drugs as well . . . Like Mary, she's a one . . . she's a single parent. But she's a prostitute, she's taking drugs now, which will be interesting to see. And Wixy, he's gonna catch AIDS the way he's carrying on.

RACHEL: Why?

SANDRA: . . . he has a girl every single night, and I mean, he, he's just disgusting, he's so slack.

JC: Do you think that it's typical that a single mother that's on the dole becomes a . . .

SANDRA: If she's really desperate.

RACHEL: It depends. She can be on the dole, have a child, but still live at home.

MARGARET: Depends on how she's been brought up. If she had a lot of freedom.

RACHEL: Because I know somebody who's a one-parent family and she, she ain't nothin' like that, nothing at all.

SANDRA: It depends. If you ain't got no family or anything, and you live in a really bad flat, then they might decide to be a prostitute. For that only purpose.

Source: Willis (1990), p. 35

While young people regularly emphasize the *differences* between the soap world and their own cultural experience, in another sense they stress strong *parallels* between the soap world and the social world of Southall . . . In certain respects, the soap opera embodies many of the characteristics of local life: the central importance of the family; a density of kin in a small, geographically bounded area; a high degree of face-to-face contact; a knowable community; and a distinctive sense of local identity . . . While young people's own families and those in their social networks provide their primary frame of reference about family life, soap families not only extend but offer alternative sets of families as reference groups by which young people can compare and contrast, judge and evaluate, and, in certain cases, attempt to critique and transform aspects of their own family life. (p. 32)

These occasions of the use of television can also be playful. For example, Palmer (1986) conducted a study of a group of children who used the series *Prisoner: Cell Block H* as a basis for games in the playground. As a matter of routine, they would re-enact or invent episodes of the programme, sometimes involving a teacher in the playing of the role of prison officer. Fiske (1987) points out that *Prisoner: Cell Block H* provides the children with a ready-made way of understanding and playing through their experience of school, for, in certain respects, schools and prisons are similar. Thus, it gives a means of understanding the actions of authority of different types and characters. Both kinds of institution are characterized by rules which the inmates often seek to break. Various kinds of oppositional culture spring up in both schools and prisons. Both sets of institutions will contain conformists as well as rebels.

Television references are also used more seriously in everyday work lives. Pacanowsky and Anderson (1982), for example, show how police officers routinely employed such references when carrying out their duties. This happened in three ways. First, nicknames drawn from police shows on television were used to provide a commentary on their individual characteristics. Usually these were used ironically, a television character's name being used to suggest the opposite of the officer's real character. Second, by using the language of television cops, particularly in the way that criminals or members of the public are described, policemen dramatized their work, drafting the excitement of television into their everyday work life. Third, policemen contrasted their own daily routine with the way that a cop's life is dramatized on television. This is a way of showing what police work is really like to each other and to the public at large; that is, it is uneventful, the distinction between good and bad is not easily made, and real police do not take unnecessary risks.

Liebes and Katz's (1993) study of the appeal of *Dallas* to an international audience refines and develops the notion of referential readings – or framings, as these researches prefer to call them. They found that the referential comments that occurred in their interviews could be reduced to four types: motivations for action, kinship relations and norms, moral dilemmas, having mainly to do with the price of success, and business relations. Amongst all the ethnic groups in different countries bar one, motivation was the reference most often made; reference to motivation in the story led to discussion of motivation in real life and vice versa. References to family relationships were the next most frequent subject.

Most references are *real*. That is, they are serious and realistic. A minority, however, are playful or ludic and involve 'the trying on of characters, i.e., group members imagining how wonderful or awful it would be to be like them' (Liebes and Katz, 1993, p. 103). The following passage from an interview illustrates such playfulness:

> BEVERLEY: I think we have to be a scuzzy person to be able to act like that to begin with. I mean, if I had a million dollars (he's talking about fifty million dollars for just a place to store his damn oil), if I had fifty million dollars I would give it all to my friends, all my kids; I wouldn't connive and cheat to get more. (p. 104)

As table 7.4 shows, ethnic and national groups differ in the extent to which they favour real or ludic 'keyings'. Americans and Israelis from a kibbutz were most likely to use playful or ludic keyings.

To make the classifications even more complex, Liebes and Katz further divide referencing statements by the kind of referent and whether or not the statement involves a moral judgement. In turn, kinds of referent are classified into self and family, ethnic group and nation, and abstract categories like businessmen or women. The interviewed groups differed in the kinds of referent used. Russians were the most abstract, Arabs were the only group making substantial use of ethnic or national classifications, while Americans and kibbutz Israelis stressed the personal and familial. There were also differences between the groups in their use of interpretations of

Table 7.4 Real and ludic keyings in referential statements, by ethnicity (in percentages)

	Americans	Moroccans	Arabs	Russians	Kibbutz
Real keyings	79	87	87	92	75
Play keyings	21	13	13	8	25
Number of referential statements	(213)	(236)	(147)	(145)	(135)

Source: Liebes and Katz (1993), p. 105

Dallas which involve a moral judgement. The Arabs were the only group to make extensive use of this evaluational orientation.

Referential framings are, of course, possible for factual programmes. Dahlgren (1985) introduces a similar concept – associational reception – in an analysis of how audiences read television news broadcasts.

> Associational reception involves the viewer's pre-existing stocks of knowledge and frames of reference. Zones of relevance and schemes of typification are set in motion. Semantic and visual associations are activated; symbols and images play upon viewers' pre-existing thesaurus of factual knowledge as well as affective dispositions, prompting reinforcement and/or modification. (p. 245)

Viewers will attempt to relate what they see on news broadcasts to their own experience. I return to this issue later in the chapter.

Critical Framings

In Liebes and Katz's study, critical framings are less common than referential ones. In general, people talk about television by relating it to their own experience rather than by commenting on the acting or the production values or, perhaps, the ideologically manipulative intentions of the producer. Liebes and Katz distinguish three major types of critical framing: the semantic, the syntactic and the pragmatic.

In *semantic* framing, viewers are exercising their ability to perceive a theme, message or issue in a fictional narrative. There are three levels of semantic framing, the first of which is closest to referential framing. In the study, viewers detected a *theme* that they thought ran through *Dallas*, that the programme reflected the degeneracy of capitalism or the fact that the rich are unhappy, for example. Rather more distant from the referential is the perception of a *message*. In using this form of critical framing audiences are saying not only that the themes of the programme are intended by the producers, but also that they are put there with the intention to manipulate. *Dallas* was a message sent by the producers with the intention to deceive. A still higher level of semantic framing is the *archetypal*, in which viewers detected in *Dallas* some general theme that spanned a whole collection of stories or programmes. For example, a Japanese viewer noted the archetypical quality of a father bestowing his blessing on that son who will deliver a first heir, as occurs in a number of Japanese stories.

Syntactic criticism consists in the ability to discuss programmes as *constructions* in terms of their genres, conventions or narrative schemes, their character types or production conditions. Viewers would concentrate on the repetitiveness of the stories, or the characteristics of the soap opera genre, or, in more sophisticated mode still, on the reasons why *Dallas* was not a typical soap opera. Alternatively, audiences were sensitive to the qualities of characters who had been placed in the story to achieve particular dramatic effects. Some groups of viewers were especially attuned to the organizational and business constraints which may have determined how the story line progressed.

Viewers, when they deploy *pragmatic* criticism, are expressing an awareness of their own involvement in the characters or narrative. For example, driven by genre conventions, audience members will spend much time trying to work out what will happen next, inventing solutions to the problems left by the previous week's episode. Many of the remarks made by the younger audience members in box 6 above are of this pragmatic kind in that they try to imagine how characters or events are likely to develop.

Liebes and Katz note that the national and ethnic groups differ widely in their deployment of the different varieties of critical framings. Russians, for example, were disproportionately prone to adopt the ideological aspect of semantic framing, seeing *Dallas* as a series of messages. Americans, on the other hand, were more likely than other groups to take up syntactic framings of all kinds, perhaps because they were more familiar with television in general and *Dallas* in particular.

Unlike referential framings, critical framings have not received much attention in the literature, and they deserve more. A number of writers point to the capacities of television audiences to see television programmes as constructions, or in Liebes and Katz's terms, to apply syntactic interpretations. For example, Leal and Oliven (1988) asked Brazilian television viewers to retell the plot of a soap opera that they had just seen. They discovered a number of differences between social class groups in the manner of the retellings. For the working-class informants, the soap opera tale assumed the importance of reality and it was discussed as if it were real. For the upper-class group, on the other hand, the soap opera was merely a story which could be well or poorly done. Similarly the working-class viewers always referred to the characters by their names in the story even when they knew the names of the actors. Upper-class viewers, to the contrary, used the actors' names and added critical comments on their performance while all the time taking an ironic and detached view of the programme. Upper-class respondents, in other words, were definitely aware of the soap opera's construction. In an entirely different genre, Livingstone and Lunt (1994) argue that the people that they interviewed who were viewers of talk shows were also aware of the way that the programmes were constructed and of the way that the production processes might bias the programme. In their interviews there were comments about the limitations of finance, of scheduling and of the daytime audience. There was also considerable understanding of the genre and its constraints – the necessity for a debate with two sides, participants who are lively and articulate, and a generally fast-moving and entertaining style.

A number of writers have also argued that, from a comparatively young age, television audiences have some notion of how the programmes they watch are created and that there is some process of construction behind the fiction (Buckingham, 1993a). As a result, their conversation is peppered with comments about how well the actors and actresses play their roles, criticisms of the writing, and speculations about who is about to leave the serial because there has been a dispute between actor and management. All of this critical attitude is informed by the way that neighbourhood gossip and, particularly, tabloid journalism focus on the doing of television personalities. As Buckingham (1987) notes:

> The extent to which the children I interviewed were prepared to question the plausibility of events in the programme was quite remarkable. Yet this questioning was informed, not merely by comparisons with their own experience, but also by an understanding of the *production process* of television. Although they clearly enjoyed playing the game of make-believe, they were also, as Dorothy Hobson argues, well aware that it was only a game. Yet the pleasures gained through this willing suspension of disbelief were, if anything, enriched by the pleasures gained from questioning and, in many instances, ridiculing the artifice. What was perhaps most remarkable was the children's flexibility of response, their ability to shift between these two perspectives with little sense of contradiction. (p. 180)

Although I have separated various types of response, of framing, and although it is true that different groups within the audience typically adopt different types, it is nevertheless important to stress that any audience will switch – or commute – between them in talking about television. As I have already indicated at various points in the discussion, audiences are very mobile and, to this extent, the boundaries between types of framing are fairly fuzzy. This commuting is aptly illustrated in the second extract in box 6 above. All the speakers move, as Buckingham says, from a vantage point inside the text to one standing outside it and back again. Calista's opening moral judgements use an essentially critical framing, treating the behaviour of the characters from inside the story. Donna continues this treatment, but Sheila moves towards a more referential framing in talking about parents in general and then moves back again to her concluding remark, which is about how *EastEnders* might work. This critical framing is taken up by Calista, who talks about the manipulation of ratings, and continued by Sandra and Donna, who use their (alleged) knowledge of what is going to happen next. Sandra and Calista's concluding remarks return partly to a referential frame in referring to what they would do or think in the characters' place.

The discussion about commuting between different framings raises two further issues which have been touched on earlier in this book. There is first the question of 'reality' and the extent to which viewers literally live in the world of television. It is often said that some soap opera viewers cannot tell fact from fiction. Some viewers, for instance, apply for jobs at the corner shop or at the Rover's Return in *Coronation Street*. Again, there have been cases of actors who play unpopular characters on television being abused, or even attacked, in the street. Less extremely, perhaps, people frequently appear to talk as if the characters in favourite programmes are real, a characteristic that can attract the derision of those less involved in the programme concerned. This apparent merging of fiction and reality is not unrelated to the claim that television is a supremely postmodern form which appeals to a new, postmodern audience, for whom television defines reality (see chapter 2 for discussion of this claim). Actually, the evidence of the way in which audiences frame television programmes indicates that people manage their commuting from the reality of television to the reality of everyday life very easily. If anything, as we have seen, audiences judge the televisual reality by the reality of everyday life. Television watching is not escapism either, a flight from a dreary unsatisfying reality to a fantasy world. This may be an element of the appeal, but it is outweighed by the pleasure of relating the events and characters on television to everyday life.

The second issue is that of realism, discussed in chapter 2. The evidence from audience framings is that realism, often in the technical sense, is in itself a lively topic for viewers. That many British soaps are realist is an important source of the viewing pleasure.

Here is a *Crossroads* watcher describing why she watched the programme:

J   Well they are sort of close to Birmingham people. You can make the connection between *Crossroads* and your life. I'm not saying our lives are like *Crossroads*, but it's nearer than *Coronation Street* and it's, I don't know – it's sort of not common, but unassuming, I think . . . I think Diane's good 'cos she's sort of an all-rounder, if you know what I mean. She gets a lot of different situations and you can see how she copes with them and the problems.

DH But do you think that the situations they get into and how they cope with them is why people might like it?

J   Yes, because they are down to earth situations, not like *Dallas*. I mean, deals of fifty million falling through and all that . . . people watch *Dallas*, I think because it's over the top, and people watch *Crossroads* because it's down to earth and things that are sort of in between and in the middle aren't interesting because they are neither here nor there. (Hobson, 1982, pp. 119–20).

Ang (1985) provides a similar argument for the viewers of *Dallas*. The realism of the serial and the capacity of the actors to convey genuine and believable emotion are important parts of the viewers' pleasure. Critical viewers, on the other hand, tended to describe the characters as improbable.

The effect of 'genuineness' is then the most important thing these viewers expect. Only when they experience the fiction of the serial as 'genuine' can they feel involved in it. They have to be able to believe that the characters constructed in the text are 'real people' whom they can find pleasant or unpleasant, with whom they can feel affinity or otherwise, and so on. It could be said that such involvement is a necessary condition for the pleasure of *Dallas*. (p. 34)

It is this sense of involvement that I turn to now.

Distance and Involvement

It is often assumed that television will have a greater effect on people the more involved they are in what is going on on the screen. If they are bound up with the action or with the characters, it seems probable that they are more likely to accept values and attitudes that appear in the programme. Conversely, if viewers are able to maintain a distance from the programme, it might seem reasonable to suppose that they are more insulated from any ideological content that it might have and are able to take an oppositional stance.

The question arises, therefore, as to how these features of distance and involvement are related to the critical and referential framings that I have discussed. This turns out to be a much more complex issue than at first appears, and I start an investigation of it by looking at how Liebes and Katz relate their categories of critical and referential to two emotional states, which they call *hot* and *cold*.

Liebes and Katz coded statements about *Dallas* as 'hot' if they manifested considerable emotional loading. 'Cold' statements, by contrast, were cognitive rather than emotional. In general, they found that most referential statements were hot and most critical statements were cold. This association did not hold under all circumstances, however. Some forms of critical framing were hot, as in the case of ideological readings. The Russian groups, for example, became very emotional in framing critically by ascribing ideological intent to *Dallas* and criticizing the programme for its portrayal of capitalist values. Similarly, referential framings could be cool. For instance, Americans were relatively unemotional when employing ludic keyings of referential framings. Indeed, of all the ethnic and national groups studied, the Americans were the coolest, perhaps showing that those social groups most used to television – the most 'media skilled' – were also the least emotionally involved. A diagrammatic representation of these relationships is given in table 7.5.

Referential modes of relating to television tend therefore to be more emotionally involving and critical modes more emotionally distancing. However, involvement and distancing are not only emotional questions. Liebes and Katz point out that critical and referential framings can be equally productive of pleasure for the audience. Furthermore, there can be just as much investment of thought and energy in critical responses as in referential. The upshot of these points is that one cannot precisely equate distance from the text

Table 7.5 The relationship between hot and cold and referential and critical framings

	Referential	Critical
Hot	Moral	Ideological
Cool	Ludic	Aesthetic

Source: Liebes and Katz (1993), p. 128

with the capacity to provide critical framings, and involvement with
the text with referential framings. The most that one is entitled to
say is that a critical stance is *more likely* to give distance from the
television text and hence enable an audience member to evaluate
the text rather than simply be absorbed by it.

One way in which some writers have conceptualized distance and
involvement is by means of the idea of identification. The proposition would be that the more an audience is *identified* with a television personality the more *involved* it is with the programme.
concerned. Horton and Wohl (1956) refer to this process as parasocial interaction, so called because the relationship between audience and personality is like a face-to-face relationship but is not
actually one. Television manages to create this illusion because of
its peculiarly direct mode of address, discussed at the beginning of
this chapter. For Desaulniers (1985) this relationship between identification and involvement is nicely illustrated by the television series
M*A*S*H:

> On 28 February 1983 the CBS network presented the final transmission
> – after eleven years of weekly broadcasting and the production of over
> 250 original programmes – in the series *M*A*S*H*. Two hundred mil-
> lion American and Canadian TV viewers looked on as the military hospi-
> tal was disbanded and the group broken up. After the transmission, some
> thousands of people got together in more or less spontaneous *M*A*S*H*
> parties. Most of the partygoers had dressed up as the character to whom
> they felt closest and with whom they had identified for all these years. All
> at once an anonymous crowd discovered traits in common, and realised
> that its members shared an imaginary symbolic life made up of the
> humour, the psychology and the philosophy so characteristic of the
> series. Here, in the winter of 1983, a cultural community had sprung up
> from nowhere – a tribute to the creators of *M*A*S*H*, but above all an
> intense expression of the phenomenon of communication and identifica-
> tion. (p. 112)

Distance and involvement do not by themselves, of course, tell
one very much about the degree to which audiences oppose or agree
with what they perceive the text to be saying. How, for example, do
the categories that I have been illustrating in this section map on to
Morley's decoding strategies, described in chapter 6? Morley, it will
be remembered, classified the reactions of various groups of viewers
of a documentary into dominant, negotiated and oppositional. If a
section of the audience responds in dominant mode, they are using
the values, attitudes and beliefs that are dominant in society. If they

use oppositional modes, they are, as the term implies, employing a way of thinking that contradicts the dominant mode. Other groups within the audience using the negotiated mode are neither oppositional nor dominant, but have a meaning system that can live with dominant values without necessarily accepting them.

Again, perhaps unfortunately, the relationship between these modes of response, on the one hand, and the processes of distance and involvement or critical and referential framings, on the other, is not at all straightforward. Liebes and Katz's view, for example, seems to be that either critical or referential framings can be oppositional. This is particularly the case for hot responses in either critical or referential mode which are not simply oppositional; they are confrontational. For example, 'within the referential, confrontational statements are those in which the viewer feels called upon to defend group norms, to treat the program as real, to relate to it seriously, and to evaluate it in terms of the norms . . . for example *Dallas* is challenged by the culture of the Moroccan group as representative of American anomie' (p. 109). Cooler readings can also be oppositional but, rather than expressing moral outrage, they indicate a refusal to take the programme seriously, rather in the manner of Morley's black students who saw the *Nationwide* programme as simply irrelevant.

The proposition that either critical or referential framings can produce oppositional readings in Morley's sense is further illustrated in a study by Philo (1990). This study is unusual in this context because it involved the way that news items are decoded. As Corner (1991c) points out, contemporary audience studies have almost entirely moved away from news, current affairs and documentary to drama of various kinds. Philo investigated the responses of groups of television viewers to the British coal miners' strike of 1984–5. His method is also unusual in two respects. First, he conducted the study one year after the strike itself. Second, he tapped responses by asking the groups to write their own news programme about the strike, using a set of photographs supplied by Philo of various events during it. The strike excited great passion on both sides and it is therefore a reasonable assumption that some viewers would take up oppositional positions to the television presentation, while others would be in dominant or negotiated mode. There was very widespread agreement on the part of Philo's interviewees that television news at the time presented the strike in terms of the violence on the picket line. Violence constituted the agenda of television news. However, a substantial proportion of the viewers opposed this agenda, largely because they did not think that violence was the issue and the strike was not particularly violent. A substantial proportion also believed that, to the extent the strike was violent, this was not the fault of the miners, but rather was caused by the police or outside agitators.

What, then, is the relationship of Philo's findings to critical and referential framings? (I should point out that these are not Philo's terms and some of what he says may be lost by representing his findings by means of these concepts.) First, Philo found that the more direct contact with any of the events surrounding the strike that viewers had, the more likely they were to reject the agenda set by the news. Interestingly, as indicated in my earlier discussion of Philo's book, such a tendency was unrelated to any other views held by the interviewees, or by their social background. For example, a solicitor who did not sympathize with the miners' case nevertheless rejected the notion that the strike was violent, because he had driven past the picket line and had seen what was going on directly. So viewers who were able to refer events as depicted on television to their actual experience were more likely to distrust the accuracy of the news. In this sense, then, referential framings provide the space for oppositional interpretations. Second, and apparently counterintuitively, Philo also found that an awareness of how television programmes were constructed did not necessarily lead to an oppositional reading. Critical framings, in other words, had an uncertain relation to opposition (see also Corner, et al. 1990).

The foregoing discussion illustrates that there is a great deal more research to be done on the relationship between referential and critical framings, distance and involvement, and acceptance and opposition. Such research is of crucial importance, since it would provide the link between the micro-studies of small groups of television viewers and the large-scale surveys of attitude change alleged to result from television. It would unite the older effects and uses and gratifications research with the newer decoding tradition. It would, in other words, help us to understand better the complex mechanism by which television achieves its effects on viewers (see Livingstone, 1991; Livingstone and Lunt, 1994).

The Active Audience

In one sense, much of the discussion in the last two chapters has been about the active audience. That is, the central underlying

question is: how active is the audience in relation to the television text? In answer to this question one may identify two extreme positions at either end of a spectrum. On the one hand, the text is seen as monolithic, containing a well-marked preferred meaning making it difficult for alternative meanings to emerge (see chapter 2 for further discussion of this idea). The audience is passive, the prisoner of the text, and is bound, therefore, to be very heavily influenced by the preferred meaning. Such a view – the *dominant text* view – of the relationship between television text and audience is implicit in the image of the couch potato discussed at the beginning of chapter 6. More academically, it has also informed many Marxist accounts of the role of television and society. These see television as an agent of the domination of capitalist society through the ideological character of the text (see chapter 2) and the passive nature of the audience. In watching television, people are persuaded to accept a view of society, and of their place in it, that confirms their subordination.

The contrary view of the relationship between television text and audience might be called the *dominant audience* view. This tends to see the text not as monolithic, with a strong preferred meaning, but rather as polysemic, containing a number of possible meanings and therefore allowing a range of audience interpretations. In turn, the audience is not passive in front of this more loosely organized text, but is active, discussing and analysing it. Such activity, such awareness of the text, is more likely to lead to oppositional readings, though, as the discussion in this chapter has indicated, the mechanisms of such readings are bound to be very complex. In the dominant audience view, the audience dominates the text and is free to make of it what it wants. Taking the audience as a whole, therefore, any television programme will receive a very wide variety of interpretation.

It should be stressed that these are two extreme views and no theorist of television has completely endorsed either one of them. They do, however, represent the ends of a continuum and, over the past forty or fifty years, television research has see-sawed between them, sometimes emphasizing the activity of the audience and sometimes the powers of the text. As Morley (1989) has said: 'The history of audience studies during the post-war period can be seen as a series of oscillations between perspectives which have stressed the power of the text (or message) over its audiences and perspectives which have stressed the barriers "protecting" the audience from the potential effects of the message' (p. 16).

Many of the recent contributions to the debate about television audiences reviewed in chapter 6 and this chapter have seen themselves as contributing more to the dominant audience end of the spectrum than the dominant text end. A particularly forceful position is taken by Fiske (1989). In Fiske's view, audiences are free to make of television, and popular culture generally, what they will, within two major sets of constraints. The first of these is the text itself, while the second is the set of social forces that impinge on audience members and form the attitudes, opinions and beliefs that mould the interpretations that they make of television programmes. What makes Fiske's view distinctive, and closer to the dominant audience end of the spectrum than any other, is his belief that the constraints are set fairly widely, giving more power to the audience:

> People can and do make their own culture, albeit within conditions that are not of their own choosing. How much power is available within this terrain, and how fixedly its boundaries are determined are matters of considerable debate, in which I align myself with those who propose that ideological and hegemonic theories of popular culture have overestimated the power of the determinations and underestimated that of the viewer. (p. 57)

And for television specifically:

> What television delivers is not programs but a semiotic experience. This experience is characterized by its openness and polysemy. Television is not quite a do-it-yourself meaning kit but neither is it a box of ready-made meanings for sale. Although it works within cultural determinations, it also offers freedoms and the power to evade, modify, or challenge these limitations and controls. All texts are polysemic, but polysemy is absolutely central to television's textuality. (p. 59)

Although Fiske's may be a particularly extreme view, an emphasis on the active audience is more or less the norm in recent television research. Most of the work discussed in chapter 6 and this chapter, for example, in that it stresses the diversity of interpretation, the importance of the way that programmes are processed in television talk, the skills of the audience in criticizing programmes and the persistent referencing of television to everyday life, embraces a model of the active audience. One of the books cited in those chapters will serve as illustration. So Buckingham (1987) argues that his view of the audience for *EastEnders* as active decoders of the programme flies in the face of many commonsense understandings of the power of television:

> I shall argue that viewers actively seek to construct their relationship with the programme on their own terms – terms which are often very different from those which appear to be on offer. The meaning of *EastEnders* is not something which is wholly contained within the text, and which is there to be discovered by viewers. On the contrary, it is determined through a process of negotiation between the text and the viewer, in which viewers retain a considerable degree of autonomy to construct their own meanings and pleasures. (p. 154)

These perspectives of the active audience were formed in reaction to earlier emphases on the power of the text. One consequence of this is a stress on the capacity of audiences to form 'resistive' readings of television texts. Audiences do not just have the capacity to provide varying interpretations of the texts confronting them, they also actively resist the preferred meaning that those texts contain. Brown (1994), for example, argues from her study of the way that women talk about soap opera that they use the programmes to express their own dissident attitudes to the power exercised by men. So, even if the preferred reading of most soap opera is fundamentally patriarchal, women can still subvert this reading by laughing together about the behaviour of men or by talking together about the way that soap characters are acting in the way they do because of the powerlessness of women. Brown distinguishes two kinds of pleasure that women take in resistance and that she believes are represented in the soap opera talk that her respondents engaged in. *Active* pleasure for women in soap opera groups 'affirms their connection to a women's culture that operates in subtle opposition to dominant culture. It is this culture of the home and of women's concerns, recognized but devalued in patriarchal terms, that provides a notion of identity that values women's traditional expertise' (p. 173). *Reactive* pleasure, on the other hand, is one in which a subordinated group recognizes its oppression and reacts to that oppression. Reactive pleasure, 'while not rejecting the connection women often feel toward women's cultural networks and concerns, also recognizes that these concerns often arise out of women's inability to completely control their own lives. Thus they are able to recognize and feel at an emotional level the price of oppression' (p. 173).

Theorists adopting the active audience position have, however, not had the debate all their own way. Three major points are made against them. First, it is claimed that texts have *some* constraining power and the active audience approach has simply overemphasized the capacity of audiences to make their own meanings. For example, Curran (1990) argues that television texts are not infinitely open; even if they contain a plurality of meanings, there is definitely one preferred reading and that is bound to limit what audiences can do with the text. Philo's study of television viewers' responses to the miners' strike of 1984–5, mentioned earlier in this chapter, illustrates this point. Philo shows that there was a correspondence between the major themes of television reporting and what viewers remembered one year later. As Curran comments: 'Perhaps partly due to the cumulative impact of constantly reiterated images and themes, TV meanings were not drowned out by the discourses that audiences brought to bear' (p. 152).

A second difficulty with the active audience perspective concerns its claims about the capacity of the audience to resist the preferred reading in the text or at least to subvert it. As Cobley (1994) points out, activism does not of itself give power or even the capacity to resist. Audiences can be active and give their own meanings to television texts without any implication that the preferred meaning of the text is being subverted. Seaman (1992) goes further. As he says:

In my view it is not always clear what makes a cultural practice 'resistant' towards a particular ideological construction, say, for example, towards a sexist stereotype; still more difficult is the judgement of whether or not the practice contributes to transforming the oppressive relationship that the particular ideology functions to maintain. (p. 301)

Furthermore, even if the preferred reading is subverted by a particular section of the audience, other sections of the audience may well have their prejudices confirmed by that preferred reading. 'Whether or not, for example, particular women interpret a particular text in a "subversive" manner tells us nothing of how particular men interpret the text' (p. 301).

A third and last counter-argument to the active audience position is of a rather different kind. This concentrates not so much on the influence or power of the text as on its aesthetic and moral qualities. The difficulty is that, in emphasizing the powers of the audience, the text is forgotten. In celebrating the activity of the audience, the artistic or moral poverty of the text may be concealed, and there is the real danger of a kind of populism in which television programmes must be good just because the audience is active in relation to them. People may watch a programme, but that does not mean to say that it is good; it just may be the only one available. As Brunsdon (1989) argues:

What we find, very frequently, in audience data is that the audience is making the best of a bad job. The problem of working always with what people are, of necessity, watching, is that we don't really ever address that something else – what people like to watch . . . The recognition of the creativity of the audience, must, I think, be mobilized back into relation to the television text, and the demands that are made on program makers for a diverse and plural programming which is adequate to the needs, desires and pleasures of these audiences. (p. 126)

To a very great extent the debate over the active audience is rather artificial. No one will argue for the absolute autonomy of the audience from the text and no one will argue for the absolute power of the text over the audience. Rather the debate is properly about the balance of text, audience and social context, and that is entirely a matter of empirical investigation. Within this debate the essential question concerns the mechanisms by which members of the audience turn a television programme into something recognizable by them – and some of these have been described in this chapter.

8

Postscript: Text, Producer, Audience

In chapter 1, I argued that any full analysis of the relationship of television and society must pay attention to the three aspects of text, producer and audience. The chapters that follow looked in more detail at each of these three aspects in turn. Like any method of dividing up the topic, this one has its drawbacks. Chief amongst these is the tendency to isolate analysis of text, producer and audience from each other. Most of the larger questions concerning the social role of television can, in fact, only be satisfactorily tackled by considering the *interrelationship* of text, producer and audience. At the end of the previous chapter, for example, I argued that it is difficult to conceive of audience response as independent of the television text. To conclude this book, I will briefly revisit two examples drawn from earlier chapters to illustrate this point.

First, it is widely claimed that contemporary society and culture is postmodernist. In chapter 2, I reviewed a number of senses in which such a claim might be true and speculated on the extent to which television might be influenced by postmodernist cultural forms. In some senses television fits the definition of postmodernism and, indeed, might be counted as *the* postmodernist form. In its flow, its apparently meaningless conjunction of different topics, its self-referentiality, its celebration of surface appearance, and the way that it defines – or becomes – reality, it is postmodernist. On the other hand, the majority of television texts, and the most popular, in their use of strong narratives and realist aesthetics, conform to more traditional rules of structure and content. To concentrate on the level of the text alone, however, makes this debate a little inconclusive since it becomes a matter of rival definitions of postmodernism. By introducing issues of producer and audience it can be given more substance. So, some understanding of what aesthetic or cultural preconceptions motivate producers, and what image of their audience they operate with, will give an idea of how television texts acquire the form they do, postmodernist or not. There is further the question of the degree to which the political economy of television production influences the kinds of text that are produced. In Jameson's (1991) view, for example, postmodernism is the cultural logic of late capitalism. Extending such a view might imply that the kinds of change taking place in the structure of the television industry, particularly its subcontracting, noted in chapter 4, are more likely to produce postmodernist texts.

More important still is the question of audience. Even if one could give some substance to the notion that television texts are postmodern, and that production systems correspond in some way to these new texts, is there such a thing as a postmodern audience there to appreciate them? Again, the evidence that one can derive from chapters 6 and 7 is contradictory and may reflect the fact that there is as yet no good theoretical account of what the postmodern audience would look like. On the one hand, audience preferences remain with traditional genres, soap opera and action-adventure, for example. Furthermore, it is clear that, in their television talk, audiences maintain an active, critical engagement with programmes. On the other hand, the inattentive regimes of watching, and any tendency to zipping and zapping, could well indicate a postmodern audience sensibility that runs parallel with texts that have an interest only in surfaces.

My second example concerns the concept of ideology. An analysis of television as ideological might well start with a reading of the texts of television. That reading establishes the dominant themes, codes or discourses in the text (see the discussion in chapter 2); that is, it establishes whether, and in what ways, the text is ideological. However, this merely starts off a series of questions, for the analyst will want to know *why* the text carries a particular discourse and what the audience will *do* with the text. Therefore, a complete account of television as ideology has to start from the text but should move on from there to consider production and audience. As Hall (1980) points out, it is not simply a matter of looking at the three aspects independently; it is actually the way that they fit together that is of chief interest in considering the relationship between cultural form and ideology. Therefore, a detailed consideration of the organization of the television industry would show how owners do or do not constrain the programmes that producers make so that unpopular views are not transmitted and only dominant discourses get an airing (see chapter 4). Similarly, the organization of production teams, and the occupational culture of television personnel, may well produce a particular way of looking at the world which will have ideological effects on the programmes that they produce (see chapter 5). Even if one could show that both texts and producers were ideologically predisposed, it still might be the case that audiences decoded texts against the grain. The evidence reviewed in chapters 6 and 7 shows that audiences are fairly intractable from this point of view. There are very great variations in the ways that audiences interpret television programmes and, more important, the skills that audiences have developed allow them to subject what they watch to critical analysis.

Finally, it is important to note that the interrelationship of text, producer and audience is not merely a matter of academic interest but also a question of wider moral and political concern. The institutions of the mass media – the press, radio and television – have always been thought to be important because they are, at least potentially, organs of information, debate and, in the last analysis, influence. They are, therefore, important components of an informed democracy. This role of the mass media has often been described in terms of the concept of the *public sphere*. This is a concept borrowed from the work of Habermas (1989), for whom the public sphere is a realm between the state on the one hand and private interests on the other, and in which citizens can freely debate issues of public interest. As Curran (1991) puts it, from Habermas's contribution:

> can be extrapolated a model of a public sphere as a neutral zone where access to relevant information affecting the public good is widely available, where discussion is free of domination by the state and where all those participating in public debate do so on an equal basis. Within this public sphere, people collectively determine through the processes of rational argument the way in which they want to see society develop, and this shapes in turn the conduct of government policy. The media facilitates this process by providing an arena of public debate, and by reconstituting private citizens as a public body in the form of public opinion. (p. 83)

Television is clearly *potentially* part of this public sphere. Virtually everybody owns a television set and people look at it a great deal of the time. Information given by the television is widely trusted. The way in which the television service has been set up in Britain owes a great deal to notions of public service, as I showed in chapter 4 (see also Garnham, 1990; Scannell, 1990). These, and others, are reasons why one might argue that television contributes effectively to a healthy public sphere, but any final determination of the role of television in this respect can only be made by looking at the interrelationships of text, producer and audience. There has first, therefore, to be discussion of the nature of the text. Is television trivial or demanding? Does it inform or conceal? Is it biased or impartial? In turn, these aspects of the text have to be related to the means by which they are produced. Is there a journalistic professionalism which keeps television neutral to some extent? Do owners interfere? Does the fact that television systems are often commercially based interfere with its public service role? Is there excessive intervention by the state? Perhaps above all, however, we have to see how audience members are involved. Is the viewing experience fragmented? Can viewers respond critically? Do audience members engage at all with the medium?

From the argument and evidence offered in this book, the answers to these questions are ambiguous and the present and future roles of television as an instrument of democracy are uncertain. Much of this uncertainty arises from the fact that television, like the media generally, is in a process of transition. One may detect a pessimistic and an optimistic view of this transition, the pessimists tending to emphasize issues of production and text, while the optimists will stress the capacities of the audience more.

The pessimists will argue that the deregulation of television will necessarily destroy its potential public sphere role. The intrusion of commercial values means that television producers will aim at maximizing audiences. The notion that television should be informed by some conception of public service will wither as owners and producers seek profit above all other considerations. Programmes will no longer seek to inform or educate and will necessarily descend into triviality. These inclinations will be reinforced by changes in ownership, which will become more and more concentrated not only in the television industry itself, but also across the various branches of the media. The present tendency for television to reflect the values of the status quo may be further promoted by concentration of ownership. In turn, the audience will be moulded by these changes. Greater fragmentation of the viewing experience is the likely consequence of the proliferation of channels and programming, making any kind of collective public debate difficult. A likely response is a postmodernist inattention and lack of involvement, which will mean that the audience is unable to engage seriously with public issues.

The optimists, scarcely surprisingly, view many of these changes more positively. For them, deregulation and the introduction of market principles into the television industry can have beneficial consequences. Monolithic and bureaucratic organizations like the BBC can stifle creative talent and tend to reinforce the values of the status quo. The introduction of competition and the reorganization of television production with a much greater degree of subcontracting can introduce greater diversity of approach and variety of moral and political viewpoints into programming. A larger number of channels, sources of programming, will offer greater choice to the viewing public. A less regulated television industry is less subject to the government interference that has plagued the BBC throughout its history.

While many in the optimist camp, particularly those who are involved in owning television companies, are enthusiasts for the absolute minimum of government regulation, there are others who look to government to mitigate some of the worst effects noted by the pessimists. This latter group would, therefore, argue that a degree of regulation could control the concentration of ownership and continue to insist on some measure of public service in programming. In their eyes, it is possible to have the best of both worlds – the freedom, creativity and diversity of greater deregulation *and* the continuance of the public service tradition, without the overwheening power of media moguls.

In many ways, however, the optimist case rests rather more on a consideration of the audience; optimists will argue that the pessimists underestimate the capacities and powers of the viewer. So optimists suggest that, whatever programmes are provided, an increasingly skilled audience is critical and aware. From such a viewpoint, television audiences can be seen as *citizens* participating, if at some distance, in a public debate, judging the arguments presented, applying standards of rational and fair argument and coming to their own conclusions. For many optimists, then, audiences have the power to save us from producers.

Bibliography

Abercrombie, N. (1992), 'Pavarotti in the park', University of Lancaster, Inaugural Lecture Series.

Abercrombie, N. and Longhurst, B. (1991), 'Individualism, collectivism, and gender in popular culture', Salford Papers in Sociology, University of Salford.

Abercrombie, N., Lash, S. and Longhurst, B. (1992), 'Popular representation: recasting realism', in J. Friedman and S. Lash (eds), *Modernity and Identity*, Oxford, Blackwell.

Adorno, T. (1991), *The Culture Industry: Selected Essays on Mass Culture*, ed. J.M. Bernstein, London, Routledge.

Adorno, T. and Horkheimer, M. (1979), *Dialectic of the Enlightenment*, London, Verso.

Allen, R. (1987), '*The Guiding Light*: soap opera as economic product and cultural document', in Newcomb (1987).

Allen, R. (ed.) (1992), *Channels of Discourse, Reassembled*, 2nd ed, London, Routledge.

Alvarado, M. and Buscombe, E. (1978), *Hazell: The Making of a TV Series*, London, British Film Institute.

Alvarado, M. and Stewart, J. (1985), *Made for Television: Euston Films Limited*, London, British Film Institute.

Ang, I. (1985), *Watching Dallas: Soap Opera and the Melodramatic Imagination*, London, Methuen.

Ang, I. (1991), *Desperately Seeking the Audience*, London, Routledge.

Bacon-Smith, C. (1992), *Enterprising Women*, Philadelphia, University of Pennsylvania Press.

Barker, M. (1988), 'News bias and the miners' strike: the debate continues . . .', *Media, Culture and Society*, vol. 10, no. 4.

Barthes, R. (1975), *S/Z*, London, Cape.

Barwise, P. and Ehrenberg, A. (1988), *Television and its Audience*, London, Sage.

Baudrillard, J. (1983), *Simulations*, New York, Semiotext(e).

Bechtel, R.B., Achelpohl, C. and Akers, R. (1972), 'Correlates between observed behaviour and questionnaire responses on television viewing', in E. Rubinstein, G. Comstock and J. Murray (eds), *Television and Social Behaviour. Vol. 4, Television in Day-to-day Life: Patterns of Use*, Washington, DC, United States Government Printing Office.

Bennett, T., Mercer, C. and Woollacott, J. (eds) (1986), *Popular Culture and Social Relations*, Milton Keynes and Philadelphia, Open University Press.

Bennett, T., Boyd-Bowman, S., Mercer, C. and Woollacott, J. (eds) (1981), *Popular Television and Film*, London, British Film Institute/Open University.

Blumler, J. (1991), 'The new television marketplace: imperatives, implications, issues', in Curran and Gurevitch (1991).

Braham, P. (1982), 'How the media report race', in Gurevitch et al. (1982).

Brown, M.E. (1994), *Soap Opera and Women's Talk*, London, Sage.

Brunsdon, C. (1983), 'Crossroads: notes on soap opera', in Kaplan (1983).

Brunsdon, C. (1984), 'Writing about soap opera', in Masterman (1984).

Brunsdon, C. (1989), 'Text and audience', in Seiter et al. (1989).

Bryce, J. (1987), 'Family time and television use', in T. R. Lindlof (ed.), *Natural Audiences*, Norwood, Ablex, 1987.

Buckingham, D. (1987), *Public Secrets: EastEnders and its Audience*, London, British Film Institute.

Buckingham, D. (1993a), *Children Talking Television*, London, Falmer Press.

Buckingham, D. (ed.) (1993b), *Reading Audiences*, Manchester, Manchester University Press.

Burns, T. (1977), *The BBC: Public Institution and Private World*, London, Macmillan.

Cantor, M.G. (1987), 'Audience control', in Newcomb (1987).

Cantor, M.G. and Pingree, S. (1983), *The Soap Opera*, London, Sage.

Cavell, S. (1982), 'The fact of television', *Daedalus*, vol. III, no. 4, pp. 75–96.

Christopherson, S. and Storper, M. (1986), 'The city as studio; the world as back lot: the impact of vertical disintegration on the location of the motion picture industry', *Environment and Planning D: Society and Space*, vol. 4, pp. 305–20.

Clarke, A. (1992), ' "You're nicked": television police series and the fictional representation of law and order', in Strinati and Wagg (1992).

Clarke, A. and Clarke, J. (1982), ' "Highlights and action replays" – ideology, sport and the media', in J. Hargreaves (ed.), *Sport, Culture and Ideology*, London, Routledge.

Cobley, P. (1994), 'Throwing out the baby: populism and active audience theory', *Media, Culture and Society*, vol. 16, no. 4, pp. 677–88.

Cohen, S. (1980), *Folk Devils and Moral Panics*, Oxford, Martin Robertson.

Cohen, S. and Young, J. (eds) (1973), *The Manufacture of News*, London, Constable.

Collett, P. and Lamb, R. (1985), 'Watching people watching television', unpublished report to the IBA.

Collins, R. (1990), *Television: Policy and Culture*, London, Unwin Hyman.

Collins, R., Garnham, N. and Locksley, G. (1988), *The Economics of Television: The UK Case*, London, Sage.

Collins, R., Curran, J., Garnham, N., Scannell, P., Schlesinger, P. and Sparks, C. (eds) (1986), *Media, Culture and Society: A Critical Reader*, London, Sage.

Connell, I. and Curti, L. (1985), 'Popular broadcasting in Italy and Britain: some issues and problems', in Drummond and Paterson (1985).

Corner, J. (ed.) (1986), *Documentary and the Mass Media*, London, Edward Arnold.

Corner, J. (ed.) (1991a), *Popular Television in Britain: Studies in Cultural History*, London, British Film Institute.

Corner, J. (1991b), 'General introduction', in Corner (1991).

Corner, J. (1991c), 'Meaning, genre and context: the problematics of "public knowledge" in the new audience studies', in Curran and Gurevitch (1991).

Corner, J., Richardson, K. and Fenton, N. (1990), *Nuclear reactions: Form and Response in Public Issue Television*, London, John Libbey.

Cottle, S. (1995), 'Producer driven television', *Media, Culture and Society*, vol. 17, no. 1, pp. 159–66.

Cultural Trends (1992), no. 13, London, Policy Studies Institute.

Cumberbatch, G., McGregor, R. and Brown J. (1987), 'Arresting knowledge: a response to the debate about TV and the miners' strike', *Media, Culture and Society*, vol. 10, no. 1.

Cumberbatch, G., McGregor, R. and Brown, J. with Morrison, D. (1986), *Television and the Miners' Strike*, London, Broadcasting Research Unit.

Curran, J. (1990), 'The new revisionism in mass communication', *European Journal of Communication*, vol. 4, part 2/3, pp. 135–64.

Curran, J. (1991), 'Mass media and democracy: a reappraisal', in Curran and Gurevitch (1991).

Curran, J. and Gurevitch, M. (eds) (1991), *Mass Media and Society*, London, Methuen.

Curran, J., Gurevitch, M. and Woollacott, J. (eds) (1977), *Mass Communication and Society*, London, Edward Arnold.

Dahlgren, P. (1985), 'The modes of reception: for a hermeneutics of TV news', in Drummond and Paterson (1985).

Dahlgren, P. and Sparks, C. (eds) (1983), *Communication and Citizenship: Journalism and the Public Sphere in the New Media Age*, London, Routledge.

Davis, H. and Walton, P. (eds) (1983), *Language, Image, Media*, London, Blackwell.

Desaulniers, J.-P. (1985), 'Television and nationalism: from culture to communication', in Drummond and Paterson (1985).

Drummond, P. and Paterson, R. (eds) (1985) *Television in Transition*, London, British Film Institute.

Drummond, P. and Paterson, R. (eds) (1986), *Television and its Audience*, London, British Film Institute.

Drummond, P., Paterson, R. and Willis, J. (eds) (1993), *National Identity and Europe*, London, British Film Institute.

Dunnett, P.J.S. (1990), *The World Television Industry*, London, Routledge.

Dyer, R. (1979), *Stars*, London, British Film Institute.

Dyer, R., Geraghty, C., Jordan, M., Lovell, T., Paterson, R. and Stewart, T. (1981), *Coronation Street*, London, British Film Institute.

Eagleton, T. (1991), *Ideology: An Introduction*, London, Verso.

Eco, U. (1966), 'Narrative structure in Fleming', in E. del Buono and U. Eco (eds), *The Bond Affair*, London, MacDonald.

Eco, U. (1984), 'A guide to the neo-television of the 1980s', *Framework*, vol. 25, pp. 18–27.

Eldridge, J.T. (1993), 'News, power, and truth', in Glasgow University Media Group (1993).

Ellis, J. (1982), *Visible Fictions*, London, Routledge and Kegan Paul.

Espinosa, P. (1982), 'The audience in the text: ethnographic observations of a Hollywood story conference', *Media, Culture and Society*, vol. 4, no. 1, pp. 77–86.

Ewan, S. (1988), *All Consuming Images*, New York, Basic Books.

Fairclough, N. (1994), *Media Discourse*, London, Edward Arnold.

Fairclough, N. (1995), *Critical Discourse Analysis*, Harlow, Longman.

Featherstone, M. (1991), *Consumer Culture and Postmodernism*, London, Sage.

Feuer, J. (1983), 'The concept of live television: ontology v. ideology', in Kaplan (1983).

Feuer, J. (1986), 'Narrative form in American network television', in MacCabe (1986).

Feuer, J. (1992), 'Genre study and television', in Allen (1992).

Fiske, J. (1987), *Television Culture*, London, Methuen.

Fiske, J. (1989), 'Moments of television: neither the text nor the audience', in Seiter et al. (1989).

Fiske, J. (1991), 'Postmodernism and television', in Curran and Gurevitch (1991).

Fiske, J. and Hartley, J. (1978), *Reading Television*, London, Methuen.

Flitterman, S. (1983), 'The real soap operas: TV commercials', in Kaplan (1983).

Flitterman-Lewis, S. (1992), 'Psychoanalysis, film, and television', in Allen (1992).

Galtung, J. and Ruge, M. (1973), 'Structuring and selecting news', in Cohen and Young (1973).

Gans, H. (1980), *Deciding What's News*, London, Constable.

Garnham, N. (1990), *Capitalism and Communication: Global Culture and the Economics of Information*, London, Sage.

Geraghty, C. (1981), 'The continuous serial – a definition', in Dyer et al. (1981).

Geraghty, C. (1991), *Women and Soap Opera*, Cambridge, Polity Press.

Gershuny, J. and Jones, S. (1987), 'The changing work/leisure balance in

Britain, 1961–1984', in J. Horne, D. Jary and A. Tomlinson (eds), *Sport, Leisure and Social Relations*, London, Routledge.

Giddens, A. (1990), *The Consequences of Modernity*, Cambridge, Polity Press.

Gillespie, M. (1993), 'Soap viewing, gossip and rumour amongst Punjabi youth in Southall', in Drummond et al. (1993).

Gitlin, T. (1982), *The Whole World is Watching: Mass Media in the Making and Unmaking of the New Left*, Berkeley, CA, University of California Press.

Gitlin, T. (1983), *Inside Prime Time*, New York, Pantheon.

Glaessner, V. (1990), 'Gendered fictions', in Goodwin and Whannel (1990).

Glasgow University Media Group (1976), *Bad News*, London, Routledge and Kegan Paul.

Glasgow University Media Group (1980), *More Bad News*, London, Routledge and Kegan Paul.

Glasgow University Media Group (1982), *Really Bad News*, London, Writers and Readers Publishing Co-operative Society.

Glasgow University Media Group (1985), *War and Peace News*, Milton Keynes, Open University Press.

Glasgow University Media Group (1993), *Getting the Message*, London, Routledge.

Golding, P. and Murdock, G. (1991), 'Culture, communications and political economy', in Curran and Gurevitch (1991).

Goodhardt, G.J., Ehrenberg, A.S.C. and Collins, M.A. (1987), *The Television Audience: Patterns of Viewing*, London, Gower.

Goodman, I.F. (1983), 'Television's role in family interaction: a family systems perspective', *Journal of Social Issues*, vol. 4, no. 2, pp. 405–24.

Goodwin, A. (1990), 'TV news: striking the right balance?', in Goodwin and Whannel (1990).

Goodwin, A. (1993), *Dancing in the Distraction Factory*, London, Routledge.

Goodwin, A. and Whannel, G. (eds) (1990), *Understanding Television*, London, Routledge.

Gray, A. (1992), *Video Playtime: The Gendering of a Leisure Technology*, London, Routledge.

Griffiths, A. (1993), 'The construction of national and cultural identity in a Welsh language soap opera', in Drummond et al. (1993).

Grossberg, L. (1987), 'The in-difference of television', *Journal of Communication Inquiry*, vol. 10, no. 2, pp. 28–42.

Gumpert, G. and Cathcart, R. (eds) (1982), *Inter/Media: Interpersonal Communication in a Media World*, New York, Oxford University Press.

Gunter, B. and McAleer, J.L. (1990), *Children and Television: The One-Eyed Monster?*, London, Routledge.

Gunter, B., Sancho-Aldridge, J. and Winstone, P. (1994), *Television: The Public's View 1993*, London, John Libbey.

Gurevitch, M. (1991), 'The globalization of electronic journalism', in Curran and Gurevitch (1991).

Gurevitch, M., Bennett, T., Curran, J. and Woollacott, J. (eds) (1982), *Culture, Society and Media*, London, Methuen.

Habermas, J. (1989), *The Structural Transformation of the Public Sphere*, Cambridge, Polity Press.

Hall, S. (1973), 'A world at one with itself', in Cohen and Young (1973).

Hall, S. (1980), 'Encoding/decoding', in Hall et al. (1980).

Hall, S. (1982), 'The rediscovery of Ideology: the return of the repressed in media studies', in Gurevitch et al. (1982).

Hall, S., Hobson, D., Lowe, A. and Willis, P. (eds) (1980), *Culture, Media, Language*, London, Hutchinson.

Hallin, D.C. (1994), *We Keep America on Top of the World*, London, Routledge.

Harrison, M. (1985), *TV News: Whose Bias?*, London, Policy Journals.

Hartely, J. (1984), 'Regimes of pleasure', *Eye*, no. 2.

Hartley, J. (1987), 'Invisible fictions: television audiences, paedocracy, pleasure', *Textual Practice*, vol. 1, no. 2, pp. 121–38.

Hartmann, P. and Husband, C. (1974), *Racism and Mass Media*, London, Davis Poynter.

Hobson, D. (1980) 'Housewives and the mass media', in Hall et al. (1980).

Hobson, D. (1982), *Crossroads: The Drama of a Soap Opera*, London, Methuen.

Hobson, D. (1989), 'Soap operas at work', in Seiter et al. (1989).

Hodge, R. and Tripp, D. (1986), *Children and Television*, Cambridge, Polity Press.

Horton, D. and Wohl, R.R. (1956), 'Mass communication and parasocial interaction', *Psychiatry*, vol. 19, pp. 215–29.

Hoskins, C. and Mirus, R. (1988), 'Reasons for the US dominance of the international trade in television programmes', *Media, Culture and Society*, vol. 10, no. 4.

Hurd, G. (1981), 'The television presentation of the police', in Bennett et al. (1981).

Intintoli, M. (1984), *Taking Soaps Seriously*, New York, Praeger.

Jameson, F. (1991), *Postmodernism: or the Cultural Logic of Late Capitalism*, London, Verso.

Jenkins, S. (1992), *Textual Poachers*, London, Routledge.

Jhally, S. and Lewis, J. (1992), *Enlightened Racism*, Boulder, CO, Westview Press.

Jordan, M. (1981), 'Realism and convention', in Dyer et al. (1981).

Kaplan, E.A. (ed.) (1983), *Regarding Television*, Los Angeles, American Film Institute/University Publications of America.

Kaplan, E.A. (1987), *Rock Around the Clock*, London, Methuen.

Katz, E. and Lazarsfeld, P. (1955), *Personal Influence*, New York, Free Press.

Katz, E., Blumler, J. and Gurevitch, M. (1974), 'Utilization of mass communication by the individual', in J.G. Blumler and E. Katz, *The Uses of Mass Communications*, London, Faber.

Kellner, D. (1987), 'TV, ideology, and emancipatory popular culture', in Newcomb (1987).

Kent, R. (ed.) (1994), *Measuring Media Audiences*, London, Routledge.

Kozloff, S. (1992), 'Narrative theory and television', in Allen (1992).

Larrain, J. (1979), *The Concept of Ideology*, London, Hutchinson.

Lawrence, J. and Mace, J. (1991), *Television Talk and Writing*, Cambridge, National Extension College.

Leal, O.F. and Oliven, R.G. (1988), 'Class interpretations of a soap opera narrative: the case of the Brazilian novella "Summer Sun" ', *Theory, Culture and Society*, vol. 5, no. 1, pp. 81–99.

Lévi-Strauss, C. (1968), *Structural Anthropology*, Harmondsworth, Penguin.

Levy, M. and Gunter, B. (1988), *Home Video and the Changing Nature of the Television Audience*, London, John Libbey and IBA.

Lewis, J. (1986), 'Decoding television news', in Drummond and Paterson (1986).

Lewis, J. (1990), 'Are you receiving me?', in Goodwin and Whannel (1990).

Lewis, J. (1991), *The Ideological Octopus*, London, Routledge.

Liebes, T. and Katz. E. (1993), *The Export of Meaning*, Oxford, Oxford University Press.

Lindloff, T. and Traudt, P. (1983), 'Mediated communication in families: new theoretical approaches', in M. Mander (ed.), *Communications in Transition*, New York, Praeger.

Livingstone, S.M. (1990), *Making Sense of Television: The Psychology of Audience Interpretation*, Oxford, Pergamon.

Livingstone, S.M. (1991), 'Audience reception: the role of the viewer in retelling romantic drama', in Curran and Gurevitch (1991).

Livingstone, S.M. and Lunt, P. (1994), *Talk on Television*, London, Routledge.

Longhurst, B. (1987), 'Realism, naturalism and television soap opera', *Theory, Culture and Society*, vol. 4, no. 4, pp. 633–49.

Lovell, T. (1980), *Pictures of Reality*, London, British Film Institute.

Lovell, T. (1981), 'Ideology and Coronation Street', in Dyer et al. (1981).

Lull, J. (1990), *Inside Family Viewing*, London, Routledge.

Lusted, D. (1991), 'The glut of personality', in C. Gledhill (ed.), *Stardom: Industry of Desire*, London, Routledge.

McArthur, C. (1981), 'Days of hope', in Bennett et al. (1981).

MacCabe, C. (1981a), 'Realism in the cinema', in Bennett et al. (1981).

MacCabe, C. (1981b), 'Days of hope: a response to Colin McArthur', in Bennett et al. (1981).

MacCabe, C. (ed.) (1986), *High Theory/Low Culture*, Manchester, Manchester University Press.

McCombs, M.E. and Shaw, D. (1972), 'The agenda-setting function of the mass media', *Public Opinion Quarterly*, vol. 36, pp. 176–87.

McQuail, D. (1987), *Mass Communication Theory*, London, Sage.

Mace, J. (1992), 'Television and metaphors of literacy', *Studies in the Education of Adults*, vol. 24, no. 2, pp. 162–75.

Masterman, L. (ed.) (1984), *Television Mythologies: Stars, Shows and Signs*, London, Comedia/MK Media Press.

Mattelart, A., Delcourt, X. and Mattelart, M. (1984), *International Image Markets*, London, Comedia.

Medhurst, A. (1991), 'Every wart and pustule: Gilbert Harding and television stardom', in Corner (1991a).

Miles, A. (1988), *Home Informatics*, London, Pinter.

Miller, T. (1993), 'National policy and the traded image', in Drummond et al. (1993).

Millington, B. and Nelson, R. (1986), *Boys From the Blackstuff: The Making of a TV Drama*, London, Comedia.

Mitchell, J. (1982), 'Television: an outsider's view', in F. Pike (ed.), *Ah Mischief: The Writer and Television*, London, Faber.

Modleski, T. (1984), *Loving with a Vengeance: Mass Produced Fantasies for Women*, London, Methuen.

Modleski, T. (ed.) (1986), *Studies in Entertainment: Critical Approaches to Mass Culture*, Bloomington and Indianapolis, Indiana University Press.

Morley, D. (1980), *The Nationwide Audience: Structure and Decoding*, London, British Film Institute.

Morley, D. (1986), *Family Television*, London, Comedia.

Morley, D. (1989), 'Changing paradigms in audience studies', in Seiter et al. (1989).

Morley, D. (1992), *Television Audiences and Cultural Studies*, London, Routledge.

Murdock, G. (1980), 'Authorship and organization', *Screen Education*, no. 35, pp. 19–34.

Murdock, G. (1990), 'Redrawing the map of the communication industries: concentration and ownership in the era of privatization', in M. Ferguson (ed.), *Public Communication, the New Imperatives: Future Directions for Media Research*, London, Sage.

Negrine, R. and Papathanassopoulos, S. (1990), *The Internationalization of Television*, London, Pinter.

Newcomb, H. (ed.) (1987), *Television: The Critical View*, New York, Oxford University Press.

Newcomb, H. and Alley, R. (1983), *The Producer's Medium: Conversations with America's Leading Producers*, New York, Oxford University Press.

O'Shaughnessy, M. (1990), 'Box pop: popular television and hegemony', in Goodwin and Whannel (1990).

Pacanowsky, M. and Anderson, J.A. (1982), 'Cop talk and media use', *Journal of Broadcasting*, vol. 26, pt 4, pp. 741–54.

Palmer, P. (1986), *The Lively Audience: A Study of Children Around the TV Set*, Sydney, Allen and Unwin.

Paterson, R. (1990), 'A suitable schedule for the family', in Goodwin and Whannel (1990).

Philo, G. (1988), 'Television and the miners' strike – a note on method', *Media, Culture and Society*, vol. 10, no. 4.

Philo, G. (1990), *Seeing and Believing*, London, Routledge.

Philo, G. (1993), 'From Buerk to Band Aid: the media and the 1984 Ethiopian famine', in Glasgow University Media Group (1993).

Postman, N. (1986), *Amusing Ourselves to Death*, London, Methuen.

Propp, V. (1968), *The Morphology of the Folk Tale*, Austin, TX, University of Texas Press.

Radway, J. (1987), *Reading the Romance: Women, Patriarchy and Popular Literature*, London, Verso.

Rajagopal, A. (1993), 'The rise of national programming: the case of Indian television', *Media, Culture and Society*, vol. 15, no. 1, pp. 91–112.

Root, J. (1986), *Open the Box*, London, Comedia.

Ryall, T. (1970), 'The notion of genre', *Screen*, vol. 11, no. 2.

Ryall, T. (1975), 'Teaching through genre', *Screen Education*, no. 17.

Scannell, P. (1990), 'Public service broadcasting: the history of a concept', in Goodwin and Whannell (1990).

Scannell, P. (ed.) (1991), *Broadcast Talk*, London, Sage.

Schlesinger, P. (1978), *Putting 'Reality' Together. BBC News*, London, Constable.

Schudson, M. (1991), 'The sociology of news production revisited', in Curran and Gurevitch (1991).

Schumpeter, J.A. (1942), *Capitalism, Socialism and Democracy*, New York, Harper.

Seaman, W.R. (1992), 'Active audience theory: pointless populism', *Media, Culture and Society*, vol. 14, no. 2, pp. 301–11.

Seiter, E., Borchers, H., Kreutzner, G. and Warth, E.-M. (eds) (1989), *Remote Control: Television, Audiences, and Cultural Power*, London, Routledge.

Sennett, R. (1977), *The Fall of Public Man*, London, Faber.

Sharot, T. (1994), 'Measuring television audiences in the UK', in Kent (1994).

Silverstone, R. (1981), *The Message of Television: Myth and Narrative in Contemporary Culture*, London, Heinemann.

Silverstone, R. (1994), *Television and Everyday Life*, London, Routledge.

Skovmand, M. and Schroder, K.C. (eds) (1992), *Media Cultures*, London, Routledge.

Sparks, R. (1992), *Television and the Drama of Crime*, Buckingham, Open University Press.

Sreberny-Mohammadi, A. (1991), 'The global and the local in international communications', in Curran and Gurevitch (1991).

Stacey, J. (1994), *Stargazing: Hollywood Cinema and Female Spectatorship*, London, Routledge.

Strinati, D. and Wagg, S. (eds) (1992), *Come on Down: Popular Media Culture in Post-war Britain*, London, Routledge.

Taylor, L. and Mullan, B. (1986), *Uninvited Guests*, London, Chatto and Windus.

Thompson, J. (1984), *Studies in the Theory of Ideology*, Cambridge, Polity Press.

Thompson, J. (1990), *Ideology and Modern Culture*, Cambridge, Polity Press.

Thompson, K. (1986), *Beliefs and Ideology*, London, Tavistock.

Todorov, T. (1977), *The Poetics of Prose*, Oxford, Blackwell.

Tolson, A. (1991), 'Televised chat and the synthetic personality', in Scannell (1991).

Tomlinson, J. (1991), *Cultural Imperialism*, London, Pinter.

Tracey, M. (1977), 'Yesterday's men: a case study in political communication', in Curran et al. (1977).

Tracey, M. and Morrison, D. (1979), *Whitehouse*, London, Macmillan.

Tulloch, J. (1990a), *Television Drama*, London, Routledge.

Tulloch, J. (1990b), 'Television and black Britons', in Goodwin and Whannel (1990).

Tulloch, J. and Alvarado, M. (1983), *Dr Who: The Unfolding Text*, London, Macmillan.

Tunstall, J. (1993), *Television Producers*, London, Routledge.

Tunstall, J. and Palmer, M. (1991), *Media Moguls*, London, Routledge.

Wallis, R. and Baran, S. (1990), *The Known World of Broadcast News*, London, Routledge.

Whannel, G. (1992), *Fields in Vision*, London, Routledge.

Williams, G. (1994), *Britain's Media: How They are Related*, London, Campaign for Press and Broadcasting Freedom.

Williams, R. (1974), *Television: Technology and Cultural Form*, London, Fontana.

Willis, P. (1990), *Common Culture*, Buckingham, Open University Press.

Winston, B. (1993), 'The CBS Evening News, 7 April 1949: creating an ineffable television form', in Glasgow University Media Group (1993).

Wolf, M., Mayer, T. and White, C. (1982), 'A rules based study of TV's role in the construction of social reality', *Journal of Broadcasting*, vol. 26, no. 4, pp. 813–29.

Wright, W. (1975), *Six Guns and Society*, Berkeley, CA, and Los Angeles, University of California Press.

Index

222 Index